The Political Economy of the Sherman Act

THE
POLITICAL
ECONOMY
OF THE
SHERMAN ACT

The First One Hundred Years

Edited by
E. THOMAS SULLIVAN
DEAN AND PROFESSOR OF LAW
UNIVERSITY OF ARIZONA

New York   Oxford
OXFORD UNIVERSITY PRESS
1991

Oxford University Press

Oxford   New York   Toronto
Delhi   Bombay   Calcutta   Madras   Karachi
Petaling Jaya   Singapore   Hong Kong   Tokyo
Nairobi   Dar es Salaam   Cape Town
Melbourne   Auckland
and associated companies in
Berlin   Ibadan

Library of Congress Cataloging-in-Publication Data
The Political economy of the Sherman Act :
the first one hundred years /
[edited by] E. Thomas Sullivan.
p. cm. Includes bibliographical references and index.
ISBN 0-19-506642-1
1. Antitrust law—United States—History.
I. Sullivan, E. Thomas (Edward Thomas)
KF1649.P65 1991 343.73′0721—dc20 [347.303721]
90-36227

9 8 7 6 5 4 3 2 1

Printed in the United States of America
on acid-free paper

To Susan
My partner in life

Preface

On the occasion of the one hundredth anniversary of the Sherman Antitrust Act, it seems appropriate to take stock and review the history of the act. This book is an examination of the legislative intent of the Act and the political economy that informed the legislation. It also reviews and analyzes the contemporary debates concerning the goals and values that underlie the Sherman Act.

The first principle of antitrust is that our economic system should operate through market forces and that American markets should be competitive. As a body of law, antitrust attempts to regulate the relationship between buyers and sellers in individual markets when there is a breakdown of the natural market forces. When the market deviates from this competitive ideal, antitrust intervention is an accepted norm. But care must be exercised in the case of intervention so that the costs of government enforcement do not exceed the costs of the market imperfection. The study of antitrust, then, is also the study of the role of government in regulating markets, and the balance that must be struck between the idea of limited government and the protection of free, open, and competitive markets.

To say that antitrust is designed to maintain and promote competition is only the starting point. The Sherman Act did not explicitly define the term "competition"; the debate on that issue continues today. That issue, to be sure, is central to the entirety of antitrust law and policy. We know that antitrust has a procompetitive foundation, but the history of antitrust demonstrates that the idea of competition has had various meanings in the last one hundred years. Economic and political ideologies have shaped that meaning over time. This volume is an attempt to capture the meaning of the antitrust movement. It focuses on the relationship between the political economy and the legislative history of the act, and the current debates. If antitrust is to have a future in the twenty-first century, we must learn from the course of its history in the twentieth century.

A current reexamination of antitrust is relevant also because of the increased international nature of markets. Few students of antitrust doubt that we live in a globalized economy. The changing face of our markets reveals that the globalization of the economy dictates that we rethink market definitions and how the American viewpoint of competition affects both domestic and international business.

A case in point is the European Economic Community (EEC), which plans to create by 1992 a single market. The magnitude of this undertaking is enormous. It may require the adoption of hundreds of pieces of legislation to remove intracommunity barriers to trade. And with the fall of Eastern Europe and the move toward market economies throughout all Europe, we can expect the EEC's competition policy to be even broader than originally planned.

This portends even greater importance for U.S. competition policy. It is likely that the global competition movement will find as highly relevant the American experience with competition and open markets. As other countries turn to an examination of our competition policy we, too, can reflect on our own market definitions and how they shape our conclusions about market power, economies of scale, and barriers to entry. But all students of antitrust and competition policy must consider, in the final analysis, that the influence of culture and human experience may dictate the preferred definition of competition. Hence, the American definitions of competition, as explored in this volume, may not be transferable to other countries and cultures. Thus as we compare various models of competition from that of a "process of rivalry" to "allocative efficiency," we suggest that the American experience with competition has changed over time and continues to change in light of the dynamics of the market, political ideologies, and, now, international developments.

The stakes are high in this debate. In the United States we believe that society is better off if markets behave competitively. Whether competition is defined broadly or narrowly as a regulatory limitation on business has important economic consequences here and abroad. When governments regulate markets and intervene in the marketplace to correct market failures, winners and losers emerge. Consumers win when markets are competitive through the interaction of sellers and buyers in the dynamic process of exchange. When competitive markets break down through collusion or the exercise of monopoly power, consumers lose through higher prices and fewer goods. As this volume suggests, we are all affected, individually and society as a whole, by the model of competition that our government selects. Ultimately, that decision is shaped by political, economic, and cultural ideologies.

A number of dedicated individuals assisted in this project and deserve recognition. A special thank you goes to Jane Bettlach, Bobbi Miller, Ellen Beerdsen, and Barbara Clelland and their staffs for their patience and indispensable secretarial skills. The research assistance of Wendell Sherk, Washington University law class of 1989, Steve Tully, University of Arizona law class of 1991, and Robert Brown, University of Arizona law class of 1992, is gratefully acknowledged.

For permission to reprint the articles included in this book, a special thanks is extended to the authors and publishers. The essays, which were published earlier in substantially longer form, are, I believe, some of the most thoughtful and provocative articles written on antitrust policy. They represent some of the very best research and analysis that have been contributed to this genre. In addition, these essays cover a broad range of antitrust philosophy. Together they strike a balanced, diversified approach in presenting a wide spectrum of ideas regarding the goals and values of antitrust policy.

Tucson   E. T. S.
June 1990

Acknowledgments

Robert H. Bork
Professor of Law
Yale Law School
"Legislative Intent and the Policy of the Sherman Act"
9 Journal of Law and Economics 7 (1966)

John J. Flynn
Hugh B. Brown Professor of Law
University of Utah
"Legal Reasoning, Antitrust Policy and Social 'Science' of
    Economics"
62 Antitrust Bulletin 713 (1988)

Eleanor M. Fox
Professor of Law
New York University
"The Modernization of Antitrust: A New Equilibrium"
66 Cornell L. Rev. 1140 (1981)

Richard Hofstadter
The Late DeWitt Clinton Professor of American History
Columbia University
"What Happened to the Antitrust Movement," in The
    Paranoid Style in American Politics and Other
    Essays (1965)

Herbert Hovenkamp

Professor of Law
University of Iowa
"The Sherman Act and the Classical Theory of
    Competition"
74 Iowa L. Rev. (1989)

Louis Kaplow

Professor of Law
Harvard University
"Antitrust, Law and Economics, and the Courts"
50 Law & Contemp. Probs. 181 (1987)

Carl Kaysen

Professor of Economics
Harvard University
Antitrust Policy: An Economic and Legal Analysis (1959)

Robert H. Lande

Attorney
Federal Trade Commission
"Wealth Transfers as the Original and Primary Concern of
    Antitrust: The Efficiency Interpretation Challenged"
34 Hastings L.J. 67 (1982)

David L. Meyer

Special Assistant to the Assistant Attorney General
Antitrust Division, U.S. Department of Justice
"An Antitrust Enforcement Policy to Maximize the
    Economic Wealth of All Consumers"
62 Antitrust Bulletin 677 (1988)

David Millon

Assistant Professor of Law
Washington & Lee University
"The Sherman Act and the Balance of Power"
61 S. Cal. L. Rev. 1219 (1988)

Rudolph J. Peritz

Assistant Professor of Law
New York Law School
"The 'Rule of Reason' in Antitrust Law: Property Logic in
    Restraint of Competition"
40 Hastings L.J. 285 (1989)

Richard A. Posner

Lee & Brena Freeman Professor of Law
University of Chicago
"The Chicago School of Antitrust Analysis"
127 U. Pa. L. Rev. 925 (1979)

Charles F. Rule

Assistant Attorney General
Antitrust Division, U.S. Department of Justice
"An Antitrust Enforcement Policy to Maximize the
    Economic Wealth of All Consumers"
62 Antitrust Bulletin 677 (1988)

George Stigler

Charles R. Walgreen Distinguished Service
Professor Emeritus
University of Chicago
"The Origin of the Sherman Act"
14 Journal of Legal Studies 1 (1985)

Donald F. Turner

Professor of Law
Harvard University
Antitrust Policy: An Economic and Legal Analysis (1959)

Contents

PART II   POSTMODERN ANTITRUST, 161

Part I

THE FOUNDATIONS OF ANTITRUST

On July 2, 1890, the Sherman Act became law. As we celebrate the one hundredth anniversary of the act, we should pause and reflect on the role that the Sherman Act has played in the twentieth century and the role it may serve in the next century. In this volume we ask whether the course of antitrust over the last century has been faithful to its legislative roots. We inquire whether its genesis was informed by political or economic theories, or both. We probe what the central theme of "competition" has been since Senator Sherman introduced the legislation. Furthermore, we consider who wins and loses when the law is applied in individual cases.

In order to understand antitrust policy today, one must have an understanding of the rich textual background that informs the law. The political economy of the law serves as our benchmark. American antitrust law is not only "law" but also a sociopolitical statement about our society and what role, if any, government should play as a market regulator. In general, the idea of limited government has been central to the development of the American legal system. The same can be said regarding the Sherman Act in particular.

The act, itself, was an attempt to resolve certain perceived economic and political problems. The culture of American society favored a market economy. As a matter of congressional enactment, the Sherman Act mandated that markets—the interaction of buyers and sellers allocating products and resources—should be competitive. But the Sherman Act used only general language to accomplish this objective. Although it made certain common law practices against public policy and enforceable as public crimes, it did not make clear how the courts should define "competition" nor, within that context, how interventionist the government should be in encouraging competition. This volume addresses these issues as well.

Part I focuses on the relationship between the political economy and legislative history of the Sherman Act. It sets the stage for us to consider in Part II from where antitrust has come and whether certain changes in the law are necessary to fulfill the legislation's ambitions. The essays in this section attempt to explicate the goals of the Sherman Act through a clearer understanding of the environment and culture in which the Fifty-first Congress passed the Sherman Act.

What becomes clear in this study is that antitrust, at its origin and in its development, is about public policy and ideology. It is about a market economy and limited government. At its core, antitrust attempts to harmonize and synthesize a body of law designed to correct market imperfections. It invites government intervention when market failures or externalities occur, but it does so only through ad hoc interdiction and without the remedy of a pervasive industrial policy or a systemic regulatory scheme.

The history of antitrust, as revealed in this volume, shows contradictions and inconsistencies in the goals of the Sherman Act. It raises the question whether there is an irreconcilable dichotomy between antitrust and an economic system run by market forces. Or, whether antitrust policy can be rationalized within the context of the political economy of the time. The theme that emerges is that antitrust has changed course throughout history to accommodate certain economic and political ideologies.

As a movement, antitrust is cyclical. Theories of competition change as our understanding of contemporary markets changes. In turn, ideologies are applied to those changes. Antitrust has not been static, as a body of law, because it is addressed to markets that are dynamic and diverse. Whether politics has influenced our economic understanding of antitrust or whether economics has influenced our political understanding and consequently shaped the development of antitrust is the subject of the discourse that follows.

In "What Happened to the Antitrust Movement," Professor Richard Hofstadter advances the premise that antitrust as a movement is almost uniquely American. In part this is due to the degree of monopolization and, because Americans were alone, except for Canada, in accepting economic competition as fundamental. "The idea of competition [became] a means of social regulation." From the beginning, Hofstadter recalls, the economy was based on diffused, mobile, and entrepreneurial competitors. This system was believed to be natural and God ordained. Americans had a deeply rooted fear of institutions that had the potential for monopolistic power. Whether economic or political, power had to be decentralized.

Hofstadter observes that the shift from the traditional entrepreneurial economy to centralized, concentrated production was a change of dramatic proportions. He recognizes that the progressive philosophers of the time were prophetic in claiming that the American emphasis on small-scale business and decentralization would ill serve the country's need to compete in world markets—an early comment that speaks to international developments today. People within a generation watched as a whole way of life passed away and a new one emerged. Yet Hofstadter notes that the way of thinking, of understanding economics could not change so quickly; people still understood large to be dangerous. They could see small businesses disappearing. The fear of the future was reflected in the demand for some federal action on the "trust problem." Social pressures mounted for regulation.

The Sherman Act may have been passed as a "sop" to these popular sentiments, Hofstadter opines. On the other hand, he concedes that most legislators believed in competition as "the cornerstone of the whole democratic way of life." The statute was written in broad terms like a constitution, as a guide for future conduct.

The goals of antitrust, Hofstadter finds, were multifarious; they were economic, political, moral, and social. Hofstadter concludes that the economic goals were the most confused and that antitrust was really a political rather than economic enterprise. This was the preexpert era. Economists had not testified on the legislation. Furthermore, the economic schools were divided on the meaning of competition and the danger or value of combinations. Given the uncertainty among economists at the time, Hofstadter does not condemn Congress for choosing to enact broad statements of principles rather than sharply taking sides in the debate. He does believe, though, that "some members of Congress" embraced the classical model of competition and its view that economic efficiency would be maximized by competition.

The monopolies and trusts were considered a political as well as an economic problem. The fear of a single power center, whether economic or political, was profoundly frightening. Democratic government itself was threatened when power was centralized. Indeed, a combination of trusts could be more powerful than the government and the governed.

The social and moral objectives were, in effect, aimed at vindicating the American charter. Self-reliance was at the core of the American fabric. Competition facilitated individualism and discipline. The Protestant ethic was strong. Small property holders and entrepreneurs were the cornerstone of the forces of good. An almost secular religion emerged that made the preservation of small business fundamental to the American psyche.

The foundations of antitrust grew, then, from the tenor of this antibig business fervor and from the cultural context. Hofstadter observes that the "political impulse behind the Sherman Act was clearer and more articulate than the economic theory." The antitrust legislation that followed the debates was, at its core, more a political statement than an economic guideline.

Professor George Stigler opens his discussion with a restatement of the well accepted claim, shared by Hofstadter, that the Sherman Act was the result of a populist movement. Deflation, the depressed agricultural economy, and the fear of monopolies and trusts were concerns of the agrarian movement in the late nineteenth century. The result, according to many scholars, was the emergence of a wave of antitrust legislation. But Professor Stigler, applying an economist's rational behavior model, finds this consensus of scholarship to be unpersuasive. According to him, the theory that the agrarian movement of the late nineteenth century was responsible for antimonopoly political activity does not seem to be based on rational behavior. He argues that farmers were an unlikely group to level the charge against monopolies and, likewise, that the railroads were unlikely villains.

Farmers, in contrast to other sectors of society, were less vulnerable to monopolistic exploitation, he opines. Given the fact that farmers were not significant purchasers of goods and products other than land and credit, the agrarian distress explanation for the Sherman Act fails. Farmers were, however, purchasers of the service of transportation. Thus their real target must have been railroads. But this thesis, too, fails Stigler's model.

Even the most drastic cuts in railroad profit margins "would have made an almost negligible addition to farm incomes," Stigler contends. Moreover, railroads served to stabilize farm incomes by regularizing the transportation service available. Accordingly, the cost of transportation for farmers should have been reduced. Income to the farm sector should have been larger and more stable with the existence of railroads. "For the farmers to combat the railroads ... was in fact perverse behavior" and contrary to the wealth maximization expectation of economists.

Another reason distressed agriculture probably did not lie

at the heart of the antitrust movement, according to Stigler, is that antitrust policy became stronger after 1890, when the agricultural industry had recovered and their separate political movement (The Granger Movement) had died.

Stigler turns next to the self-interest hypotheses. He notes that efficient firms and the "average business" would not be "losers" under an antitrust regime. Obvious losers would be present and future monopolies—firms in highly concentrated industries. Those would be the firms with self-interest to oppose enactment of the Sherman Act. The beneficiaries would be small business. Both groups, then, had self-interest in the defeat or passage of the Sherman Act. Stigler finds these group interests to be highly and inversely related.

In looking at state antitrust laws before the passage of the Sherman Act, Stigler also finds a self-interest hypothesis at work. Larger businesses opposed the act and smaller ones supported the legislation. States with a larger than average share of potential monopolists tended toward antitrust legislation. In addition, he finds that a state's congressional delegation was more likely to vote for passage "the lower the fraction of the state's nonagricultural labor force in 'monopolizable' industries." But this latter finding was not based on statistically significant data.

In sum, Stigler finds support for the passage of the Sherman Act in the self-interest hypothesis. Small business believed it was in its interest to support legislation and regulation; monopolies, or potential monoplies opposed it. In turn, these findings validate the economists' rational behavior model; they also reject antitrust convention that farmers, Grangers, and the agrarian movement were responsible for enactment of the Sherman Act.

Stigler's insights into the origin of the Sherman Act are interesting but, as the story unfolds in this volume, incomplete. His essay rests on the narrow market model of wealth maximization: a transaction in the market or petition for government action only occurs when one's own self-interest is advanced. Self-interest is defined in terms of profit motivation. Accordingly, "irrational behavior" is narrowly defined. Political activity is viewed as irrational if not centered on self-interest. The economic model of self-aggrandizement gives rise to Stigler's public choice theory of the origins of the Sherman Act. In turn, the early legislature history of the Sherman Act is rebuked and replaced with an economic reinterpretation.

In striking contrast to Hofstadter's political and cultural interpretation of the Sherman Act, Robert Bork finds the legislative intent of the Sherman Act quite different. He discovers one value or goal underlying the Sherman Act. Wealth maximization is the only coherent theme he finds in the legislative history. He forcefully argues, in his provocative work, that the Fifty-first Congress that passed the Sherman Act had but two questions in mind when it sought to condemn certain business conduct: Does the challenged transaction increase wealth through efficiency, or does it decrease it through output restrictions?

Bork comments that Congress targeted three basic phenomena when it debated the Sherman Act: cartels, monopolistic mergers, and predatory practices. Each target, he finds, is consistent with his model of allocative efficiency or consumer welfare. He rejects the philosophy, embraced by Judge Learned Hand, that industrial power and consolidations are inherently undesirable, regardless of their economic results. Economic results in the particular transaction under challenge matter to Bork. They are the determining factor under any Sherman Act determination. Congress, he notes, was interested in the net economic consequences of the antitrust conduct, not whether great aggregations of capital resulted.

The populist movement behind the Sherman Act, described by Hofstadter and Stigler, is not part of Bork's history. Although some members of Congress may have been motivated by other issues, such as the protection of small business, he argues that the predominant concern was wealth maximization. He further advances the unconventional idea that legislators voting in favor of the Sherman Act may have voted for the enactment based on a range of values that they knew would not be "reflected in the criteria that the law requires the courts to use." In short, he reads these populist statements out of the legislative history through his notion that Congress did not intend the courts "to take such [stated] concerns into account under the statute."

Among the supporters of the legislation, Bork finds no expressed values in conflict with his wealth maximization theory. Indeed, those few favoring conflicting values did so in expressing opposition to the statute, he asserts. But, here, Bork is mostly drawing his support from negative inferences. He bases his theory that no "conflicting" values were expressed on his initial interpretation of what values were expressed in the first place. It is at this point that he discounts or overlooks substantial evidence unearthed by other scholars. An example is illustrative of Bork's interpretations of the legislative history.

Many scholars and judges have cited the condemnation attributed to Senator Sherman of "great aggregations of capital" as an example of the populist, individual-oriented attitude underlying the Sherman Act. In other words, great aggregations of capital should be dissolved "because of the helplessness of the individual before them." Bork argues, however, that although Senator Sherman used political analogies, he was really speaking of economic harms and not political power or the oppressive effects of trusts. His argument is succinct: Monopoly power can lead to price setting above marginal costs; this, in turn, can be supported through output restrictions that interfere with allocative efficiency and the consumer welfare. Only when these conditions exist, he concludes, should antitrust courts intervene.

Although Bork's logic is forceful and remains today the definitive interpretation accepted by advocates of antitrust deregulation as described in Part II, its accuracy is seriously questioned by other prominent scholars of antitrust. To be sure, their viewpoint is on the ascendancy in this era of postmodern antitrust as illustrated by the thought-provoking essay by Robert Lande. When we compare Bork's arguments with antitrust convention, we see that his thesis is at war with the work of many other scholars. Bork draws a distinction between what motivated Congress to pass the Sherman Act and how he thinks Congress wanted the act interpreted. The battle for the soul of antitrust continues.

Professor Robert Lande's essay is a direct refutation of Bork's thesis and scholarship. Lande argues that, while Congress passed the antitrust laws to further the economic objectives of curbing high prices caused by market power and restricted output, these objectives centered more on distributive concerns than efficiency goals. He views the legislative history of the Sherman Act as an expression of concern over preventing unfair transfers of wealth from consumers to firms with monopoly power. The distributive goals of antitrust, Lande contends, were directed toward protecting consumer surplus from the market grip of monopolists. "Congress did not pass the antitrust laws to secure the 'fair' overall distribution of wealth in our economy or even to help the poor. Congress merely wanted to prevent one transfer of wealth that it considered inequitable, and to promote the distributions of wealth that competitive markets would bring." High prices were condemned because of the wealth transfer from the consumer to the producer, not because such pricing caused allocative inefficiency.

Lande describes three effects caused by monopolies: allocative inefficiency, wealth transfers, and productive inefficiency. All economists condemn allocative inefficiency—monopoly pricing above marginal costs accompanied by output restrictions—but Lande argues that the redistributive effects of market power exceed by a significant amount the allocative inefficiency. Allocative inefficiency allows the mo-

nopolist to capture a larger portion of consumer surplus than
a competitive market would permit, resulting in an "unfair"
transfer of wealth. It is this redistributive effect—the impact
of monopolies on the consumer—that Congress sought to
curb. Congress, in short, clearly expressed a proconsumer
bias, Lande argues, to ensure that the benefit of a competitive market and consumer surplus would ensue to the benefit
of consumers.

Unlike Bork's thesis that Congress was concerned only
with allocative efficiency, Lande maintains that the legislative history of the Sherman Act demonstrates that the aim
was to prevent distributive inequities. Congress knew that
correcting the wealth transfer effects of monopoly power
might have a negative impact on efficiency. By condemning
monopoly power, Congress knew that the Sherman Act
would not necessarily maximize society's economic efficiency. But Congress was willing to balance this cost, Lande
opines, against the benefits to consumers of retaining their
surplus.

Furthermore, Lande finds evidence that Congress believed
"that trusts and monopolies possess excessive social and political power, and reduce entrepreneurial liberty and opportunity." Bork, on the other hand, maintains that Congress
was only concerned with allocative inefficiency and not with
who benefits or loses from the wealth transfers due to the
inefficiency. Bork *assumes* that allocative efficiency descends
eventually to the benefit of consumers. Lande, however,
asserts that this does not necessarily follow, and even if the
monopolist is efficient there is no evidence that cost savings
and increased profits will be passed on to the consumer.
Instead, the monopolist, having no competition, will retain
its supraprofit and increase the producer surplus at the expense of the consumer surplus. The battle lines are drawn
at this point. Each identifies what the Fifty-first Congress
saw as the first principles of antitrust.

Lande's thesis is strengthened by the fact that the technical theory of monopoly pricing and allocative efficiency, articulated by Bork, had not yet been developed at the time the Sherman Act was debated, although certainly it is true that the legislators were concerned with rising prices and restricted output. These concerns, Lande asserts, were relevant to distributive injustices and fears of wealth extraction. Senator Sherman spoke to this point. "It is sometimes said of these combinations that they reduce prices to the consumer by better methods of production but all experience shows that this saving of cost goes to the pockets of the producer." And, although the trusts were known at that time to be extremely efficient, they were, in fact, the target of the legislature. Efficiency, then, in an economically technical sense as Bork uses it could not have been at the heart of the act.

Finally, Lande observes, as Hofstadter has, that Congress also was motivated by a desire to curb the social and political power of large business and to assist small businesses. Alarm over accumulations of power pervaded the congressional debate. This concern, Lande argues, was consistent with Congress's desire to maintain competitive prices, consumer surplus, and distributive equality. Congress wanted "to restructure the economy in ways insuring a 'fair' process for economic, social and political decisionmaking." "An economic system providing free opportunities for entry and enough producers to ensure vigorous competition" was the general framework that Congress sought.

Professor David Millon, like Hofstadter before him, views the Sherman Act as a political document—one designed to advance individual liberty at the expense of political and economic power. He offers the view that monopoly power and the efficacy of competition helped shape the political and economic theory underlying the Sherman Act. The great trusts were viewed in the traditional context of the connection between individual liberty and economic organization. Trusts threatened personal liberty in two ways, he notes.

First, they had the economic power to exclude individuals from opportunities for material success and, second, immense wealth can corrupt the legislative process and affect government decisionmaking. Accordingly, liberty depended on decentralized economic power.

Efficiency could not justify the evils inherent in concentration. A "balance of economic power in American society" was, in the main, the ideology that shaped the Sherman Act. "Presentation and promotion of competitive opportunity would ensure a balance of economic power, and thus protect society from monopoly and its incidental social and political evils."

Like Lande, Millon rejects the Borkian interpretation that the legislation was directed at promoting efficiencies. Instead, the Sherman Act's design was "to control political power [of trusts] through decentralization of economic power." There is some evidence also that the act was intended as a small business protection device, although Millon argues that it was not the protection of small business per se but rather the protection of atomization. Small business would still have to compete to stay alive, but it should not be dominated by the trusts. Domination by and dependence on the large trusts were the legislative targets. He argues that the economic imbalance created by the trusts and corporate concentration of power proved to be the impetus for a law that would redistribute the balance of power both in the market and in the political arena. The Sherman Act, therefore, was an attempt to return to the classical approach of defining competition with market opportunities available to all rivals through dispersion of economic power.

The debate continues with Professor Rudolph Peritz's observation that the Sherman Act was a compromise forged by interests advancing property rights in an era dominated by natural law and classical economics. According to Peritz, assuring competitive markets was never the sole concern of the Sherman Act. Instead, the legislation centered on balancing the tension between competition and property rights. Literalists of the Sherman Act argued for the maintenance of pure competition, while rule-of-reason proponents sought to vindicate property rights, including freedom of contract. Hence, the rule-of-reason approach to antitrust regulation did not begin its life as a procompetitive theory, he asserts.

This interpretation by Peritz is, by his own admission, strikingly different from the orthodox view held by many antitrust scholars. His essay focuses on "industrial liberty," the theme that he finds as the foundation of the Sherman Act. His benchmark is the political economy that informed Senator Sherman and his colleagues. They feared "combinations of capital" that would wield market power and result in monopoly pricing. Liberty in this context means a state of affairs where one would be free from the great combinations of capital so that competition could prevail. The public interest could only be protected when competition was vigorous and the market free from monopoly power. Industrial liberty also meant that the public "as competitors" should be freed from the market power of the trusts. In short, it fostered a system of roughly equal, rivalrous, and presumably small marketplace participants.

Peritz explains that industrial liberty also implicated political liberty. Rough competitive equality is not simply a necessary prerequisite to a healthier competition. It also is fundamental to a democratic society where equality and freedom of choice and opportunity are core principles. Trusts, of course, were antithetical to the concept of industrial liberty, but so, too, was the improper use of power by the government.

Government was to ensure industrial liberty, according to Peritz, by protecting "the natural process of competition from market power of unnatural competition." This could be achieved by government action dissolving private agreements in restraint of competition. On the other hand, industrial liberty also meant "freedom to enter into contracts to further one's own interests." In other words, this theory of liberty, at bottom, meant freedom from either government or market power. Obviously, however, the right to have all voluntary contracts enforced and the right to be free from market power—even that created by private contracts—were conflicting goals. One was the right to do with and dispose of one's own property as desired, the other sought to free the naturally competitive market.

Although the twin goals of industrial liberty created divergent tensions, they shared a single remedy: fair price. The property view argued that the seller had the right to a "fair profit." Rate wars and unrestrained competition destroyed competitors and prevented a seller from asking a fair price for its products. Fair price was a social good the government should enforce as it does when it protects property from theft or extortion.

Conversely, the competition theory argued that a fair price was the logical result of a competitive market. Peritz observes that the tension, here, seems inherent. "Fair" as that term was used in the debates could result from a combination—the price allowing some profit to the seller—or from competition—a low price to the consumer. Competition and combination, thus, were viewed as two great forces in contention with each other. The policy of industrial liberty was the theme that united these otherwise conflicting theories. Both were at the heart of the American ethos in the late nineteenth century and, in turn, the Sherman Act debates.

Two currents of thought informed the industrial liberty approach. Natural law and classical economics were popular at the time. For many, competition and combination seemed like natural forces, albeit conflicting tendencies. Natural law and its rationality could explain the tendency to combine, but "classical legal and economic doctrines . . . espoused the inevitability of competition." Classical economics allowed state intervention against combination so long as it conformed to property law formulations that all persons are entitled to sell or dispose of their property or the fruits thereof. If coercion or involuntary conduct formed the basis of the exchange, even classicists would condemn the restraint.

Peritz concludes, in stark contrast to Bork, that the political economy of the Sherman Act, with its sociopolitical foundations, does not reveal that allocative efficiency alone is a proxy for the "competition policy" adopted under the Sherman Act. Industrial liberty, as a policy formulation, was not so one dimensional. It represented the confluence of property law and classical economics. The Sherman Act debates were in turn a discourse on the idea of competition and its effects on liberty and property rights.

The classical theory of competition discussed in Peritz's article is the focus of a careful, detailed analysis in Professor Herbert Hovenkamp's essay. His paper completes Part I of this volume, which sets forth the early foundations of antitrust. Hovenkamp's article explicates in detail the economic underpinnings and the common law origins of early antitrust jurisprudence. He treats us to a historical understanding of the political economy of the Sherman Act.

Hovenkamp's thesis is that the Sherman Act has always been subject to economic ideologies. To be sure, this is true of the common law as well, particularly with regard to monopolies and restraints of trade. The only issue in drafting the act was what economic model would be employed, classicism or neoclassicism. The fact that an economic approach would be utilized was never in doubt.

Hovenkamp notes that classical political economists and lawyers of the period were often the same people. The great legal and economic values were the same: "individualism, liberty of contract, abhorrence of forced wealth transfers." Although the literature of political economy was not cited in many cases, the theories were similar. Both economists and lawyers had faith in "competition."

The common law, Hovenkamp observes, was distinctly

private, but it expressed one public policy goal: the avoidance of trade restraints. This accommodated the "economic" policy goal of providing the benefits of competition to the public and the freedom to compete to the individual.

The classical competition theory was a function of individual self-interest, self-determination, entrepreneurial opportunities, and limitations on state power to interfere or to give special privileges. It was a theory that incorporated both buyers and sellers; each competed for scarce resources. Competition was, in one phrase, the process of rivalry. The development of a supplier-based theory of competition, with concerns of price fixing and market structure, only came later.

In the classical model, coercion and involuntary transactions were condemned; voluntary combinations were accepted. Cartels, interestingly, were not considered shocking because no one's freedom was being denied. It was not until the advent of neoclassical theory that we considered that a market could be changed so as to make it coercive by removing opportunity for rivalry. Indeed, price fixing was not necessarily considered illegitimate. Buyers had a choice; they could simply stop buying. The contract might not be enforceable, but it was not actionable by third parties either. It was only at the beginning of the 1890s, Hovenkamp notes, that neoclassical price theory overtook the language employed in section one of the Sherman Act regarding restraint of trade.

Numerous dissents by Justice Holmes demonstrate that in his view—the classical view—the Sherman Act had nothing to do with competition as that term is used today. Holmes argued, according to Hovenkamp, that exclusionary practices, not price fixing, were condemned at common law, and that public policy was violated only when combinations prevented competitors from competing for business.

The classical view espoused by Holmes was "that the Sherman Act, like the common law, must be concerned with artificial restrictions placed on the individual's freedom to act." Voluntary exchanges such as mergers or cartels were not the target of the common law and thus not addressed in the Sherman Act, according to Holmes. These concerns came later, during the era of neoclassicism, when the argument was advanced that cartelization of enough producers could impair competition. Before the antitrust movement, there was no effective law against price fixing. The Sherman Act reflected the shift in thinking by making trade restraints illegal rather than simply unenforceable. But it was the rise of neoclassicism that affected how we viewed the common law and how the Sherman Act would later be interpreted. Important classical concepts such as liberty of contract and freedom from coercion took on new meaning. As Hovenkamp aptly demonstrates, one can not understand the origins and development of the Sherman Act without first understanding the ideology and political economy of the common law that helped shaped it. Importantly, both the common law and the Sherman Act have been driven by certain ideologies. Each gives meaning to our current interpretations.

A review of these essays makes clear that the goals of the Sherman Act, as the textual record demonstrates, are multidimensional. No one theme or objective emerges as decisively predominant. No single paradigm drove the farmers' intent other than the idea that competition is complementary to democracy. As a result, the Sherman Act is an organic document, a complex statute formed through compromise, having a character that has evolved and developed through a confluence of political, economic, and ideological debates. That interpretations of the Sherman Act have not been "frozen in time" or mired in ideology as the country has grown and matured is the continuing strength of the document.

What Happened to the Antitrust Movement?

RICHARD HOFSTADTER

The antitrust movement and its legislation are characteristically American. Perhaps this is attributable to the particularly flagrant form that monopoly took in America during the early years of its development. It may also be said that, except for the Canadians, no other people has taken the principle of economic competition so earnestly as to try to underwrite it by statute, until recently when some European countries began to show interest in the American approach to the subject. The idea of competition as a means of social regulation—as an economic, political, and moral force—has grown stronger roots in the United States than elsewhere, partly because it has had little to compete with in the way of aristocratic, militaristic, or labor-socialist theories. Founded to some degree in the common-law tradition, whose injunctions against restraint of trade proved an inadequate basis for the protection of competition, the antimonopoly tradition also rested intellectually upon classical economic theory and upon the pluralism of American democratic thought.

But in America competition was more than a theory: it was a way of life and a creed. From its colonial beginnings through most of the nineteenth century, ours was overwhelmingly a nation of

Reprinted from *The Paranoid Style in American Politics* and *Other Essays* (1965). New York: Alfred A. Knopf.

farmers and small-town entrepreneurs—ambitious, mobile, optimistic, speculative, anti-authoritarian, egalitarian, and competitive. As time went on, Americans came to take it for granted that property would be widely diffused, that economic and political power would be decentralized. The fury with which they could be mobilized against any institution that even appeared to violate these expectations by posing a threat of monopoly was manifest in the irrational assault on the Bank of the United States during Jackson's presidency. Their most respected thinkers habitually assured them that their social order was God-ordained or natural, and they probably thought it would last forever.

Then, with extraordinary rapidity as historical time is reckoned, that order was overwhelmed by the giant corporation. In the last three decades of the nineteenth century a wholly new economy came into being. An American born in 1828, the year of Jackson's election, came of age in a society in which the old small-enterprise economy, however dynamic and expansive, had kept its fundamental pattern more or less intact. But in his mature years he would have seen that economy fast becoming obsolete, and if he lived as late as 1904, he would have seen industry concentrated to a degree inconceivable not only to his fathers but even to him during most of his adult life. This economic transformation happened so fast that the mind could not easily absorb it. An entire people could hardly be expected to cease overnight to dream the dreams of the small entrepreneur. In 1900 the problem of big business and the threat of monopoly were still so new that it was hard to get one's bearings. Bigness had come with such a rush that its momentum seemed irresistible. No one knew when or how it could be stopped.

It is hardly surprising that the men of the first antitrust generation made some frightening projections into the future. In 1890, and even in 1914, bigness had not yet been domesticated either as a force in the economic world or as a factor in the American imagination. A nation that had gone so fast from competitive small enterprise to corporate giantism might readily go with equal speed from corporate giantism to a system of monopolistic tyranny. Hence, discussions of big business in the last decades of the nineteenth and the opening decade of the twentieth century are full of dark prognostications, most of them plausible enough at the time, however little they have been realized.

Since it had been widely assumed that competition, being "natural," would be largely self-perpetuating, the classical theory had not reckoned with the possible necessity of underwriting competition by statute. But by the 1880's the old confidence in the self-sustaining character of competition was dead, and there seemed no adequate protection for competition in existing law. As soon as it became clear that the common-law tradition against restraints of trade had ceased to have any force and that state laws on the subject were altogether inadequate to the purpose, the demand for federal action arose. George Gunton thought in 1888 that "the public mind has begun to assume a state of apprehension almost amounting to alarm," and that the social atmosphere was "surcharged with an indefinite but almost inexpressible fear of trusts."[1] Senator Sherman warned his colleagues that "the popular mind is agitated with problems that may disturb the social order," singling out inequities of wealth and the formation of combinations of capital so great that they threatened to produce "a trust for every production and a master to fix the price for every necessity of life." Congress must heed the appeal of the voters, he said, "or be ready for the socialist, the communist, and the nihilist. Society is now disturbed by forces never felt before."[2] Historians, like contemporaries, have differed as to how imperative the demand for federal action was. In a careful survey of articulate opinion on the "trust" problem in 1890, Hans B. Thorelli concludes that public demand, though perhaps less than an irresistible tide, was too strong to be ignored by the politicians.

Was the Congress of 1890 cynically offering a sop to public sentiment? The plutocratic character of that Congress lends some credence to this view, as does the observation of Senator Orville Platt, at one point in the debate, that the conduct of the Senate during the previous days was "not in the line of honest preparation of a bill to prohibit and punish trusts" but was merely an effort "to get some bill headed 'A bill to punish trusts' with which to go to the country."[3] These circumstances of its origins have helped to confirm many historians in their suspicion that antitrust was, from beginning to end, only a charade.

But there is also reason to believe, on the contrary, that most congressmen thought of the competitive order in business as being the cornerstone of the whole democratic way of life and that they considered themselves to be making the first tentative step in formulating a policy for the control of trusts, which, if it could be put on sound constitutional footing, might serve as the basis for corrective litigation and perhaps subsequent statutory changes. Admittedly, they were breaking new ground. Senator Hoar said that Congress was entering a wholly new field of legislation and that "the opinions of Senators themselves, of able and learned and experienced lawmakers, were exceedingly crude in this matter."[4]

It is true, of course, that Congress emerged with a statute written in the most general terms, which for many years was emasculated by judicial decisions and administrative lethargy. But it is very likely that, with its broadly worded prohibition of conspiracies in restraint of trade and of efforts to monopolize, Congress was attempting to lay down a general declaration of policy that would serve as a guide to future action in much the same flexible way as the Constitution itself had served the country after 1787. Many congressmen doubtless believed that the self-enforcing features of the law would be far more effective than they actually became— that is, that the triple-damage suits authorized for victims of restraints of trade would cause businessmen themselves to carry on a good deal of the policing of the economy. Perhaps the problem confronting Congress can be reconstructed with greater sympathy if we try to imagine whether a drastically different and significantly more effective law would have been passed by a wholly populistic and militantly anti-big-business Congress, and whether such a law could have been expected to receive a more successful implementation than the Sherman Act in the hands of the subsequent administrative officers and judges.

One may say with reasonable assurance that the confusion of Congress over the economic significance of antitrust mirrored a more general confusion in American society. The goals of antitrust were of three kinds. The first were economic; the classical model of competition confirmed the belief that the maximum of economic efficiency would be produced by competition, and at least some members of Congress must have been under the spell of this intellectually elegant model, insofar as they were able to formulate their economic intentions in abstract terms. The second class of goals was political; the antitrust principle was intended to block private accumulations of power and protect democratic government. The third was social and moral; the competitive process was believed to be a kind of disciplinary machinery for the development of character, and the competitiveness of the people—the fundamental stimulus to national morale—was believed to need protection.

Among the three, the economic goal was the most cluttered with uncertainties, so much so that it seems to be no exaggeration to regard antitrust as being essentially a political rather than an economic enterprise.[5] A fundamental difficulty in economic thought, troubling from the very start, arose over the relative claims of combination and competition. The Sherman Act was framed and debated in the pre-expert era, when economists as a professional group were not directly consulted by the legislators. But even if they had been, they would have given mixed and uncertain advice. The profession was split. A few years earlier the American Economic Association had been founded by men in revolt against the classical tradition and laissez-faire doctrines, although, of course, many economists of the older school were still ensconced in universities and colleges. Economists were familiar with the argument that the competitive order, far from being fixed in a permanent, beneficent, self-sustaining equilibrium, might have a strong tendency toward self-liquidation through the disappearance of weaker competitors. One of the early historicists, E. Benjamin Andrews, argued in 1893 that laissez-faire was no more than a systematized expression of anarchy, and the following year warned:

> Bills have been brought before half the legislatures of the Union to free competition by making trade syndicates absolutely illegal. To my mind there is no question that such legislation will be vain. The age of competition as we have known it is gone forever. As well try to waken the dead.[6]

The more influential voice of Richard Ely was also raised in protest against the ideal of pure competition. He was among those who insisted that size should not be equated with monopoly, and long before Thurman Arnold he held that antitrust legislation was not only futile but actually encouraging to monopoly, because it caused business leaders to replace "soft" combinations by "hard" combinations in the form of mergers.[7]

No consensus was to be had on the proper line of governmental action on trust or on the kind of law Congress should pass. Nearly all economists believed that attempts simply to prohibit combinations by law would be futile. There was a growing disposition to consider that both competition and combination needed some measure of control and that neither could be eliminated by law. In this sense, as William Letwin has pointed out, the counsel that was available from the economist, however much attended to or ignored, shared the ambiguity that the legislators themselves could feel as lawyers:

> The economists thought that both competition and combination should play their parts in the economy. The lawyers saw that the common law permitted combination in some instances and prohibited it in others. Congressmen seized on this hidden agreement, and set out to construct a statute which by the use of common-law principles would eliminate excesses but allow "healthy" competition and combination to flourish side by side.[8]

If one gives due regard to the uncertainties of the matter and to the improbability that any attempt at a quick solution would be effective, one may arrive at a more charitable judgment of the Congress of 1890. Its members were probably trying to lay down general guidelines by means of which their successors might evolve a policy that would give society the advantages of both competition and combination. As Senator Sherman said, "All that we, as lawmakers, can do is to declare general principles."[9] These principles could hardly have been enunciated in more sweeping language than that used in the Sherman Act. Presumably, many congressmen hoped that the courts would find a way of striking at the notoriously unfair methods of competition that had already been used to build such companies as Standard Oil and the National Cash Register Company, without barring useful consolidations or even such restrictive agreements as were intended to eliminate intolerably rigorous competition.

This original uncertainty about the economic rationale for antitrust continued to haunt well-intentioned Progressives in the years before the First World War. The vagueness and inconsistency so often expressed by intelligent and relatively candid political leaders during this era must be taken as a reflection not on the caliber of the leadership but rather on the intrinsic difficulty of the problem.

Theodore Roosevelt represents, on this count, a maximum of shrewdness combined with a minimum of anxiety. With the exception of railroad regulation, Roosevelt was not profoundly interested in the economic issues that agitated the American public during his presidency; indeed, he was quite candid in confessing his reluctance to tackle them head on. When in difficulties, as in 1907, he was disposed to trust to the judgment and the political and financial leadership of the conservatives in the Senate or the economic powers in Wall Street. However, he saw the trust problem as something that must be dealt with on the political level; public concern about it was too urgent to be ignored. He understood how important it was to assure the public that the government of the United States had the will and the power to assert its authority over large corporations. Accordingly, his antitrust prosecutions, although few, were in some cases appropriately spectacular. When he assessed the significance of the Northern Securities case, he did not say that it would open the way to a general assault on bigness, but rather that it was important for showing that "the most powerful men in this country were held to accountability before the law." His fundamental solution for the problem—that bigness must be accepted as a part of the modern industrial and social order, and that its behavior should be subjected to administrative control under full publicity—comes somewhat closer than the views of most of his political contemporaries to anticipating the future course of antitrust procedure.

Roosevelt was accompanied, or perhaps followed, by a school of liberal publicists—among them Charles R. Van Hise, Herbert Croly, and Walter Lippmann—who accepted his conviction that the Sherman Act philosophy was the product of what he called a "sincere rural Toryism" long since outgrown. Lippmann, in one of the most penetrating attacks on the antitrust philosophy, characterized it as the philosophy of "a nation of villagers." This school of Progressives saw the Western world as entering upon a new era of organization and specialization for which the old competitive philosophy was hopelessly retrograde. Some of them, notably Croly and Van Hise, also saw small-scale business as inadequate to the task of competing in the world's markets, which they believed to be a necessity of the American situation. In retrospect, they appear more sophisticated and prophetic than those who put great stock in the Sherman Act as a force for actual dissolution. They foresaw the decline of antitrust as a movement, and in some instances recognized that if the Sherman Act persisted it would be as a basis for occasional *ad hoc* regulatory suits rather than as an instrument for dismantling the corporate economy.

Woodrow Wilson spoke more feelingly for the "rural Toryism" and the village democracy which seem to have been at the center of popular antitrust feeling; but by the same token he illustrates more clearly than Roosevelt their intellectual difficulties. Speaking in the campaign of 1912, which afforded a full-dress display of the differences between the two schools of thought on trusts, he asserted that he too was not against size as such. He was all for bigness as an inevitable and natural growth, whenever it was the outcome of superior efficiency. But he was against "the trusts," which had grown out of illicit competition. He was never very successful, however, in explaining why a business that had become large through legitimate methods might not become just as menacing to competition as one that had grown large through illicit competition. His statement "I am for big business and I am against the trusts" seems hardly more than an unsatisfactory attempt to evade the argument that there is a self-liquidating threat inherent in competition.[10]

The political and social arguments against monopoly were pressed with greater clarity than the economic argument and with hardly less fervor. Antitrust must be understood as the political judgment of a nation whose leaders had always shown a keen awareness of the economic foundations of politics. In this respect, the Sherman Act was simply another manifestation of an enduring American suspicion of concentrated power. From the pre-Revolutionary tracts through the Declaration of Independence and *The Federalist* to the writings of the states' rights advocates, and beyond the Civil War into the era of the antimonopoly writers and the Populists, there had been a perennial quest for a way of dividing, diffusing, and checking power and preventing its exercise by a single interest or by a consolidated group of interests at a single center. Hence, the political impulse behind the Sherman

Act was clearer and more articulate than the economic theory. Men who used the vaguest language when they talked about "the trusts" and monopolies, who had not thought through the distinction between size itself and monopolistic practices, who had found no way of showing how much competition was necessary for efficiency, who could not in every case say what competitive acts they thought were fair or unfair, or who could not state a rational program that reconciled their acceptance of size with their desire for competition, were reasonably clear about what it was that they were trying to avoid: they wanted to keep concentrated private power from destroying democratic government.

One of the glories of the competitive model had been that it purported to solve the question of market power by denying that such power had any particular location. The decisions of the market were beautifully impersonal, since they were only the averagings of the decisions of thousands of individuals, none of whom enjoyed any decisive power. The market mechanism suggested that power was not really exercised by anyone. With the perfect impersonality of Adam Smith's "invisible hand," the market made decisions that ought not be vested in the hands of any particular man or body of men. Hence, the market mechanism met the desire for the diffusion of power and seemed to be the perfect economic counterpart of American democratic pluralism.

Where power *must* be exercised, it was agreed that it should be located in governmental and not in private hands. But the state governments were inadequate; in sheer mass, business enterprises already overshadowed them. Charles William Eliot pointed out as early as 1888 that the large corporations, considered as units of economic organization, had already begun to tower over the states. A Boston railroad company, for example, employed 18,000 persons and had gross receipts of about $40,000,000 a year, whereas the Commonwealth of Massachusetts employed only 6,000 and had receipts of only $7,000,000.[11] Even individually, some corporations were big enough to dominate state governments, and if they should combine among themselves, they might come to dominate the federal government as well.

The existence of the industrial combinations and the threat that under one auspice or another—perhaps that of the investment bankers—there would come about some day a combination of the combinations that would be stronger than civil government itself, provoked a fear that haunted the minds of the writers of the industrial era, including many whose social views were as conservative as Eliot's. The fundamental fear of private power was well put by William Jennings Bryan, in a speech delivered at the Chicago Conference on Trusts in 1899:

> I do not divide monopolies in private hands into good monopolies and bad monopolies. There is no good monopoly in private hands. There can be no good monopoly in private hands until the Almighty sends us angels to preside over the monopoly. There may be a despot who is better than another despot, but there is no good despotism.[12]

And the general sense that the dire economic and political consequences of monopoly were as one was incorporated in the Democratic platform of 1900:

> Private monopolies are indefensible and intolerable. . . . They are the most efficient means yet devised for appropriating the fruits of industry to the benefit of the few at the expense of the many, and unless their insatiate greed is checked, all wealth will be aggregated in a few hands and the Republic destroyed.[13]

The most articulate expression of the Progressives' case against the political power of monopoly was made by Woodrow Wilson in 1912. It was the burden of his argument, against T.R., that once the existence of large-scale combinations is accepted, regulation of them by government becomes impossible, because the political power of business combination will be great enough to nullify all attempts at controlling it. Wilson played artfully on the fears and suspicions of the small entrepreneurs. . . . He pictured concentrated capital as being already in control of the government: "The masters of the government of the United States are the combined capitalists and manufacturers of the United States. . . . The government of the United States at present is a foster-child of the special interests."[14]

Of necessity this would continue to be the state of affairs until the combinations not only were unseated by the people but also were dissolved—until "this colossal 'community of interest' " was disentangled. It was a thing that the laws must "pull apart, and gently, but firmly and persistently dissect." Otherwise, under Roosevelt's plan for accepting and regulating monopolies, there would only be a union between monopoly and government: "If the government controlled by the monopolies in its turn controls the monopolies, the partnership is finally consummated." "If monopoly persists, monopoly will always sit at the helm of the government. I do not expect to see monopoly restrain itself. If there are men in this country big enough to own the government of the United States, they are going to own it."[15]

The third objective of antitrust action, hardly less important than the others, was psychological and moral. It sprang from the conviction that competition has a disciplinary value for character, quite aside from its strictly economic uses. America was thought to have been made possible by the particular type of character that was forged by competitive individualism, a type that had flourished in the United States because competitive opportunities had been so widespread that alert men could hardly fail to see them, to grasp and use them, and hence, to be shaped by them. The American male character was believed to have been quickened and given discipline by the sight and pursuit of opportunity. For this process to take place it was important that business be carried on fairly— the sporting vocabulary was never far below the surface—and that newcomers be able to enter the game as entrepreneurs on reasonably open terms.

The significance of this faith that competition could be relied upon to form character can be fully grasped only if we bear in mind the Protestant background of our economic thinking. Economists themselves had not been in the habit of analyzing economic relationships in purely mechanical and secular terms, and what may be said of them on this count can be said with greater force about laymen, when they thought about economic issues. Behind the American way of thinking there lay a long Protestant tradition, which tended to identify economic forces with religious and moral forces and which regarded economic processes from the standpoint of their contribution to the discipline and development of character. The economic order was not merely an apparatus for the production of goods and services; it was a set of rules for forging good conduct. . . .

The inherited belief that small property and opportunity for small business have forged the American character, which might well lose its form without the discipline imposed by a particular variety of entrepreneurial competition, is one that has never died out. Near the end of the Second World War the Small Business Committee of the Senate put this faith clearly when it said that the pursuit of opportunity by the small business owner

> has been a great motive force among our people. It stimulates expression of the fundamental virtues of thrift, industry, intelligence, schooling, home ties, and family pride—in short, those fireside virtues which have counted for so much in developing our strength and character.[16]

The preservation of opportunities for small business, as a member of the S.E.C. put it in 1945, is more important than any economic goal; it is "a goal which transcends economic and political forms and processes as such, and remains fundamentally concerned with the character of the men and women who comprise the nation."[17]

. . .

The Origin of the Sherman Act

GEORGE J. STIGLER

If consensus were proof, there would be little uncertainty about the origin of the Sherman Act. A depressed agricultural sector—still in 1890 a major part of the American economy—was casting about for sources of its economic troubles. One source was found in the deflation of the 1879–93 period and in the gold standard which brought it about. But monopolies—especially railroads for the farmer and the flourishing industrial trusts for everyone—were equally popular targets of complaints. The Republicans passed the Sherman Act to head off the agrarian (Granger and Populist) movements. So, in brief outline, goes the most popular explanation for the emergence of our antitrust policy. . . .

1. The Agrarian Movements

The Granger movement, which began in 1867 and reached its maximum strength about 1873, gave rise at one time or another to political parties with antimonopoly programs (and in one case the name "Anti-Monopoly"). State laws seeking to control railroad rates were passed under the influence of this movement.[1] In the late 1880s, numerous western and southern states passed antimonopoly laws.[2] . . . . "[T]he initial impetus of post-bellum opposition to mo-

Reprinted from 14 Journal of Legal Studies 1 (1985). University of Chicago Press: Chicago, Illinois.

nopoly stemmed mainly from the agrarian element.''[3] The agrarian movement, on this reading, first attacked the railroads and then expanded the attack to include all (other) monopoly.

To a believer in the rational behavior of political participants, the "agrarian distress" explanation for the appearance of an antitrust policy is a real puzzle. The railroads aside, there is no reason to expect that farmers were more vulnerable to monopolistic exploitation than the remainder of the population: they were not extensive purchasers of anything else besides land and credit. Were the railroads a suitable villain?

I have made admittedly crude estimates of the ratio of all railroad "profits" (chiefly return on equity investment) to semi-net farm receipts, and that ratio is only about 1–1.5 percent for all farming and reaches 5 percent only in the area between Nebraska and Montana. The utmost regulation of railroad rates compatible with survival of the railroads would have made an almost negligible addition to farm incomes.

Nor was the trend in rates such as to incite unusual complaints in the 1880s. One vast source of reduced transportation costs was the extension of the railroad network. The mileage of roads west of the Ohio or Mississippi is instructive (see unnumbered table below).[4] A second source was the secular decline in transportation rates from at least 1880 to 1900.[5] The low level of railroad rates in the United States was a source of much comment by European students.[6] It is highly probable that the railroads made the incomes of farmers more stable as well as larger than they would have been without the roads.[7]

Year	Mileage West of the Ohio or Mississippi Rivers
1870	25,000
1880	53,000
1888	95,000

There is a deeper reason for not finding the main support for antitrust policy in a distressed agricultural class: antitrust policy became stronger after 1900 as agricultural distress (and a separate political movement by farmers) passed away. For the farmers to combat the railroads—which were major benefactors of western agriculture—was in fact perverse behavior.

The farmers were an inappropriate special group to launch an antitrust policy on grounds of self-interest. They were no more vulnerable than other groups to industrial monopolies, and to the minor extent that they had special concern with railroads, the recently created Interstate Commerce Commission was a selective instrument to deal with them. The ICC had not achieved much by 1890, no doubt, but how much did the Sherman Act achieve in its first three years? Econometrics may never achieve the precision necessary to detect an influence of the Sherman Act in 1893 on *anything*. I shall not consider the inevitable suggestion that the frustrated farmers did not seek a rational explanation for their attack on monopolies; they *believed* in the devil.

2. The Self-Interest Hypotheses
. . .

In [the first twenty years of the Sherman Act] . . . the vigor of enforcement of the act grew, pari passu with the decline of agrarian political power and discontent.

The Sherman Act was potentially applicable to all interstate commerce, which had not yet swallowed all commerce, as the *Knight* decision was to show.[8] Who were its beneficiaries and its victims?

Economic theory tells us, as it told Adam Smith, that output is at a maximum under competition, so it would appear that most people would be beneficiaries of a rule commanding competition. It would be difficult to conjure up any redistributions of income consequent on the effective enforcement of a competitive rule that would systematically run against any important part of the economy in 1890.

The obvious losers from an antitrust policy would be the present (1890) and prospective possessors of monopoly power. This is a select group: for example, it surely does not include the business community or manufacturing at large. The average business is not capable of achieving effective cartelization or monopoly, simply because the small relative size of an efficient enterprise and the absence of entry barriers make such goals unattainable. Hence the average business is not among the prospective losers of an antitrust policy.

In order to identify the most likely losers, we have gone to the list of industries that were highly concentrated in 1899. There is a measure of paradox in identifying as victims of antitrust policy those industries which often became highly concentrated *after* the passage of the act, but at least those industries were capable of (possibly temporarily) high concentration, and with foresight could fear a vigorously enforced Sherman Act. . . .

The actual and potential monopolists would be the opposition on self-interest grounds to the passage of the Sherman Act. The small business sector would be the set of possible beneficiaries of the Act: an anti-big business statute would possibly hamper the growth of large enterprises whose greater efficiency threatened the small business sector in many industries. This small business support clearly led to the passage of the Robinson-Patman Act in 1936, and there is evidence of the political effectiveness of this group in earlier times. The Capper-Volstead Act of 1922 exempted agricultural cooperatives from the antitrust laws. The Clayton Act (1914) displayed a concern with predatory competition which probably reflects the same opposition to big business. It is easy to believe that the concerns of small business were already present in 1890, although the actual inroads of large enterprises on small business were still in an early stage.

I have sought to identify this small business constituency by elimination. The agricultural sector could not have seen any threat to the small farm enterprise from big business, nor could the large handicraft occupations (carpenters, plumbers, and so forth). In addition I exclude other areas with large-scale enterprises: railroads, public utilities, and employees in mining and manufacturing industries whose establishments had more than one hundred employees in 1890, on the grounds that these areas were already big business.

If one compares these two groups with a possible self-interest in the defeat or passage of the Sherman Act—would-be monopolists and small business, respectively—they prove to be highly and inversely related. The correlation across states in the two groups, each measured as a function of the state's nonagricultural labor force, is $-.86$. Accordingly I am unable to distinguish between the two interpretations.

3. The Evidence on Support for the Act

I possess two bodies of evidence on the support for the Sherman Act. Neither source is powerful, and they do not even have the decency to agree strongly with each other.

The first is the attitudes of the individual states toward antitrust policy. Well before 1890 some states had passed antitrust law, and in some cases also had constitutional prohibitions on monopolies. . . . Five states, all southern, passed laws before 1880. A full dozen (chiefly in the North) passed laws in 1889, and three more in both 1890 and 1891.[9] Thereafter the intense movement subsided.

The second evidence is the vote in Congress. The House vote was 242 for, none against, the passage of the Act; the Senate vote was 52 for and one against. These votes are hardly eloquent on the distribution of support for the law, but I have sought to deduce some information from the following ground.

TABLE I.   State Antitrust Laws by Date of Passage*

State	Date of Passage	State	Date of Passage
Before 1890:		1890–1900:	
Maryland	1867	Kentucky	1890
Tennessee	1870	Louisiana	1890
Arkansas	1874	Mississippi	1890
Texas	1876	Alabama	1891
Georgia	1877	Illinois	1891
Indiana	1889	Minnesota	1891
Iowa	1889	California	1893
Kansas	1889	New York	1897
Maine	1889	1900–1929:**	
Michigan	1889	Connecticut	...
Missouri	1889	Florida	...
Montana	1889	Massachusetts	...
Nebraska	1889	New Hampshire	...
North Carolina	1889	Ohio	...
North Dakota	1889	South Carolina	...
South Dakota	1889	Vermont	...
Washington	1889	Virginia	...
		Wisconsin	...

*For forty-two states obtaining statehood prior to 1890; states also in this group but with no antitrust legislation as of 1929 are Colorado, Delaware, Nevada, New Jersey, Oregon, Penn-

I interpret an abstention as an expression of less support for, or even opposition to, a legislative act. This approach, . . . provides a second measure of the variation across states in the support for the Sherman Act.

Consider the pattern of state antitrust laws passed before 1890. . . . Here the evidence suggests that potential monopolists' opposition to the Act, or small business support for the Act, was operative in the manner predicted by the self-interest theory.

	Below Average Share of Potential Monopolists	Above Average Share of Potential Monopolists
State law before 1890	14	3
No law before 1890	12	13
	26	16

I find that the percentage of a state's congressional delegation who vote (affirmatively) for the act is higher, the lower the fraction of the state's nonagricultural labor force in "monopolizable" industries but that the relationship has no statistical significance. This second, and more conjectural, test neither supports nor contradicts the evidence of the state antitrust laws.

4. Conclusion

I have found modest support for the view that the Sherman Act came from small business interests or that opposition came from areas with potential monopolizable industries, or both. A study of the later history of antitrust laws would have yielded explicit small

sylvania, Rhode Island, and West Virginia. Date of passage is defined here as year of constitutional or legislative antitrust provision, whichever was earlier, but ignoring constitutional provisions prior to 1860.

**Exact dates for this group are not readily available. Omits a Colorado statute found unconstitutional in 1927 and a New Jersey statute repealed in 1920.

business support for the Clayton Act and its amendments and, indeed, a strong element of populism in these laws.

Perhaps the chief reason I am not more successful in explaining the passage of the Sherman Act is that I am seeking to explain a moderate, not a major, change in public policy. The common-law opposition to restraints of trade, and to monopolies (which customarily had been conferred by the state), was part of our English heritage, and in the nineteenth century Americans adhered to this opposition considerably more strongly than the English. The Sherman Act implemented this policy by its provisions for public and private (treble-damage) enforcement of prohibitions against restrictive practices, where the common law usually had treated restrictive contracts as simply unenforceable. The statutory changes were not minor, but they represented no change in general goals or philosophy. The reader will recognize the convenience of this explanation for my failure to find strong evidence for any explanation for the passage of the Sherman Act.

Several other nations which shared our common-law tradition against restraints on trade slowly followed our precedent. Britain itself waited until the 1930's to begin policies against restrictive practices. It is a cliche of British history that the policy of free trade protected the domestic economy against monopoly until that time, but it is a cliche lacking specific evidence and possibly lacking general plausibility.[10] Canada passed ineffective legislation as early as 1889, but serious antitrust actions began in 1923.[11]

If a nation wished to foster competition, it would be at least a tenable position that the common-law rule of nonenforceability of restrictive agreements was sufficient legal action. Certainly the proponents of an active antitrust policy would not be heavily burdened, even today, with evidence for the success of our antitrust policy.[12] If a nation wished to protect its small business (including family farms), it could employ traditional instruments such as protective tariffs and governmental subsidies (including credit subsidies). With such competent substitute policies, this emergence of an antitrust statute may be only a minor puzzle.

Legislative Intent and the Policy of the Sherman Act

ROBERT H. BORK

Despite the obvious importance of the question to a statute as vaguely phrased as the Sherman Act, the federal courts in all the years since 1890 have never arrived at a definitive statement of the values or policies which control the law's application and evolution. The question of values, therefore, remains central to controversy about this basic law and its interpretation. More than one factor bears upon the answer to the question. Courts do not and should not, for example, attempt to administer any policy a legislature may seek to thrust upon them. Nevertheless, a starting point is the question of legislative intent. In this paper I propose to examine that question. My conclusion, drawn from the evidence in the Congressional Record, is that Congress intended the courts to implement (that is, to take into account in the decision of cases) only that value we would today call consumer welfare. To put it another way, the policy the courts were intended to apply is the maximization of wealth or consumer want satisfaction. This requires courts to distinguish between agreements or activities that increase wealth through efficiency and those that decrease it through restriction of output.

. . .

It would be possible to illustrate the use of values other than

Reprinted from 9 Journal of Law and Economics 7 (1966). University of Chicago Press: Chicago, Illinois.

consumer welfare in a number of cases, but the fact of judicial reliance upon such values is surely not in dispute, and excerpts from two well-known opinions of Judge Learned Hand may therefore suffice to illustrate the point. Values other than consumer welfare apparently played large roles in Judge Hand's reasoning in both the *Alcoa* and *Associated Press* cases.

In *Alcoa*, the Court of Appeals for the Second Circuit judged illegal Aluminum Company of America's large market position in virgin aluminum ingot. In an assertion seemingly important to his argument, Judge Hand said:

> We have been speaking only of the economic reasons which forbid monopoly; but... there are others, based upon the belief that great industrial consolidations are inherently undesirable, *regardless of their economic results*. In the debates in Congress Senator Sherman himself ... showed that among the purposes of Congress in 1890 was a desire to put an end to great aggregations of capital because of the helplessness of the individual before them.[1] [Emphasis added.]

Without pausing to explain what the noneconomic helplessness of the individual might consist of, what category of individuals was involved, or how the concept applied to the facts of the case before him, Judge Hand moved on to another formulation of noneconomic values supposedly embedded in the statute:

> Throughout the history of these statutes [the antitrust laws, including the Sherman Act] it has been constantly assumed that one of their purposes was to perpetuate and preserve, for its own sake and *in spite of possible cost*, an organization of industry in small units which can effectively compete with each other.[2] [Emphasis added.]

. . .

The italicized phrases in each of the foregoing quotations indicate that Judge Hand was asserting that the nebulous values he derived from the legislative history, or from prevalent assumptions about the legislative history, were powerful enough to require a court to override considerations of consumer welfare. He did not inform us whether that was true in all cases where the "economic" value of consumer welfare conflicted with these other values or, if not, how to predict the cases in which one or the other of these conflicting values would take precedence.

But Judge Hand went further even than this. In his *Associated*

Press opinion he asserted that the Fifty-first Congress had given the federal courts virtual carte blanche to choose the values they would implement through the Sherman Act. Approaching his topic through a rapid survey of antitrust doctrine and using a cluster of trade association cases for his springboard, Judge Hand said:

> [T]he injury imposed upon the public was found to outweigh the benefit to the combination, and the law forbade it. We can find no more definite guide than that.
>
> Certainly such a function is ordinarily "legislative"; for in a legislature the conflicting interests find their respective representation, or in any event can make their political power felt, as they cannot upon a court. . . . But it is a mistake to suppose that courts are never called upon to make similar choices: i.e., to appraise and balance the value of opposed interests and to enforce their preference. The law of torts is for the most part the result of exactly that process, and the law of torts has been judge-made, especially in this very branch. Besides, even though we had more scruples than we do, we have here a legislative warrant, because Congress has incorporated into the Anti-Trust Acts the changing standards of the common law, and by so doing has delegated to the courts the duty of fixing the standard for each case.[3]

The liberating potential of this judicial equivalent of free verse or "tennis with the net down" was demonstrated as Judge Hand went on to note that Associated Press' by-laws made attainment of membership more difficult for newspapers in competition with present members, that non-members were disadvantaged by being unable to get Associated Press news, that the First Amendment expresses an important value in our society, and, finally, that this value weighed against the Sherman Act legality of the by-laws. The method by which Judge Hand moved from First Amendment values to the illegality of the by-laws left a great deal—in fact, almost everything—to be desired. Passing that, however, the propriety of Judge Hand's consideration of First Amendment values at all demands that Congress' "incorporation" of "the common law" into the Sherman Act have been intended to delegate a value-choosing role to the federal judiciary.

I do not wish to focus upon Judge Hand. He is cited here merely as an authoritative and persuasive spokesman for positions which are widely held and which I wish to dispute. There would be little point in reviewing here all of the positions that have been advanced

concerning the broad social, political, and ethical mandates en-
trusted to the courts through the Sherman Act, or in naming the
persons who have urged them, for there is not a scintilla of support
for most such views anywhere in the legislative history. The only
value other than consumer welfare which is even suggested by the
record is protection of small businessmen, but, as will be argued,
that value was given only a complementary and not a conflicting
role. The legislative history, in fact, contains no colorable support
for application by courts of any value premise or policy other than
the maximization of consumer welfare. The legislators did not, of
course, speak of consumer welfare with the precision of a modern
economist but their meaning was unmistakable.

A point which requires emphasis at the outset is the distinction,
alluded to above, between conflicting and complementary values.
I recognize that many of the legislators who voted for the Sherman
Act may have had values in mind in addition to or other than
consumer welfare. There was, for example, repeated expression
of concern over the injury trusts and railroad cartels inflicted upon
farmers and small businessmen. It by no means follows, however,
that Congress intended courts to take such concerns into account
under the statute. A legislator may be moved to vote for a statute
by his perception that it will affect a range of values which are not
reflected in the criteria that the law requires the courts to use. In
the case of the Sherman Act it seems quite clear that this was the
situation. Not only was consumer welfare the predominant goal
expressed in Congress but the evidence strongly indicates that, in
case of conflict, other values were to give way before it. This means
that such other values are superfluous to the decision of cases since
none of them would in any way alter the result that would be
reached by considering consumer welfare alone. For a judge to
give weight to other values, therefore, can never assist in the correct disposition of a case and may lead to error. In short, since
the legislative history of the Sherman Act shows consumer welfare
to be the decisive value it should be treated by a court as the only
value.

Following these guidelines, then, the following arguments, which
will be supported by evidence from the record, seem to me, when
taken together, to establish conclusively that the legislative intent
underlying the Sherman Act was that courts should be guided

exclusively by consumer welfare and the economic criteria which that value premise implies.

1. Both in the bills introduced and in the debates there are a number of explicit statements that the purpose of antitrust legislation was consumer welfare and that that policy was to guide the courts.

2. The rules of law which Congress foresaw are inconsistent with any value premise other than consumer welfare. Congress contemplated that the statute would strike at three basic phenomena: cartel agreements; monopolistic mergers; and predatory business tactics.

a. A rule of *per se* illegality for cartel agreements (agreements whose purpose is not to produce efficiency but merely to eliminate competition) discloses a policy judgment that firms should fare well or ill according to the standards consumers impose in a competitive marketplace. Such a rule leaves a court no discretion to weigh other values which might legitimate the cartel: for example, the preservation of existing small businessmen, or the welfare of those businessmen who would prefer a shorter work day if their rivals would agree to close down too. The flat prohibition of cartel agreements which Congress envisaged seems fully consistent only with the idea that output should not be artificially restricted, and that desire is in turn explained only by a concern for consumer well-being.

b. A rule against monopolistic mergers, taken by itself, may appear less unequivocally to imply a consumer welfare rationale. The fact that the rule is phrased in terms of monopoly rather than absolute size suggests such a rationale, but the rule could conceivably reflect values of the sort Judge Hand sketched in his *Alcoa* opinion. The argument for this rule in Congress, however, shows that it derived in large measure from a desire to protect consumers from monopoly extortion. Insofar as other classes, such as small producers who sold to or bought from monopolists, were to be benefited, that benefit was not seen as conflicting with the consumer-welfare rationale but rather as reinforcing it. Where producer and consumer welfare might come into conflict, as will be seen under point 3 below, Congress chose consumer welfare as decisive.

c. A similar policy ambiguity may seem at first glance to accompany a rule outlawing predatory business practices. A law against "unfair" commercial tactics could be rooted in moral or humane considerations, a wish to introduce Marquis of Queensbury rules into the commercial arena, either for the sake of the combatants or of the spectators. An alternative hypothesis is provided, however, by an economic theory widely held then as now. Business firms with large capital or low ethics were thought capable of gaining or preserving monopoly positions by crushing rivals with tactics, such as selling below cost, which do not reflect superior efficiency. This theory leads the legislator who entertains it to outlaw injury to competitors only when it is a step toward monopoly and does not result from the exercise of efficiency. The terms of the arguments made in Congress as well as the attitude of Congress toward efficiency indicate that this second hypothesis explains the congressional antipathy to "unfair" practices. The rule thus rests on a consumer-welfare rationale.

3. Congress was very concerned that the law should not interfere with business efficiency. This concern, which was repeatedly stressed, was so strong that it led Congress to agree that monopoly itself was lawful if it was gained and maintained only by superior efficiency. Thus the desire to protect small firms from annihilation by monopoly-minded rivals did not extend an inch beyond the bounds of the consumer-welfare rationale. Small producers would be equally threatened by a rival on its way to monopoly through superior efficiency. The noneconomic helplessness of the individual to which Judge Hand referred would, moreover, seem to be the same before any monopoly, no matter how gained. Only a consumer-welfare value which, in cases of conflict, sweeps all other values before it can account for Congress' willingness to permit efficiency-based monopoly. To break up such monopolies because rivals could not meet their low prices would be to impose lower output and higher prices upon consumers.

4. That Congress did not wish courts to apply criteria expressing values other than consumer welfare is also strongly suggested by its preferred method of dealing with situations in which consumer welfare was not to be controlling. The primary examples were farm and labor organizations. Most of the congressmen who spoke to this issue favored the complete exemption of such organizations from the coverage of the statute. Senator Edmunds, who appears

to have played the primary role in drafting the bill which became the Sherman Act, wished to include such groups within the law's sweep. The Act as passed was silent on the issue. It may be uncertain, therefore, whether Congress had an intention on this issue and, if it did, what that intention was. But it is clear that those who did not wish farm and labor organizations judged by consumer-welfare criteria adopted the technique of exempting them from the bill altogether. No one suggested that the matter be handled by letting the courts balance the values that these congressmen thought were in play. This raises a fairly strong inference that no values other than consumer welfare were to be considered in those cases which were intended to come within the statute's coverage.

5. Given the narrow view of the commerce power that prevailed in 1890 it is extremely unlikely that the Fifty-first Congress intended to give the courts the power to make broad social or political decisions through the Sherman Act. The federal commerce power was circumscribed not merely by the wide category of commerce that was intrastate but also by its nature as a commercial power. It was generally assumed, that is, that the ends to be accomplished by the exercise of the commerce power must themselves be of a commercial nature. This assumption would not impose a consumer-want-satisfaction rationale upon the statute—the category of commercial purposes comprises more than that—but it does tend to rule out an intention to achieve the broad noncommercial goals that are sometimes attributed to the Sherman Act. The discussions of the commerce power in Congress, as well as the phrasing given the statute by the Judiciary Committee, bear out this thesis.

6. Congress recognized that broad areas of discretion were being delegated to the courts but not one speaker suggested that that discretion included the power to consider any values other than consumer welfare. Senator Sherman, on the other hand, was as explicit as could be desired that the criteria by which the delegation was to be controlled were those relating to consumer welfare. The statute's incorporation of a highly artificial version of "the common law" further demonstrates the consumer-welfare limits of the discretion delegated to the courts.

7. The complete absence of any expression of values which con-

flict with consumer welfare among those urging antitrust legislation is itself compelling evidence that no such values were intended. Those few legislators who urged that producer welfare override consumer interests in some cases did so, significantly, in opposing the bills drafted by Senators Sherman and Reagan.

Finally, an objection to the thesis advanced here will be discussed. This consists of the argument that the legislative intent underlying the statute is essentially unknowable because the Judiciary Committee draft which was enacted was totally different from Sherman's and Reagan's drafts which were discussed. It can be shown, however, that the policies of the drafts were the same so that the debates are fully applicable to the Act as it stands today.

. . .

Senator Sherman introduced S.1 in December 1889. It was called up for debate before the Senate in Committee of the Whole on February 27, 1890, and subjected to a detailed, scathing attack upon its constitutionality and efficacy. The Finance Committee, of which Sherman was the leading member, responded by reporting a modified version of S.1 on March 18. Neither the criticisms nor the modifications concerned the bill's criteria for illegality. Debate on the modified bill began on Friday, March 21, with a lengthy explanation of S.1 and its policies by Sherman. The process of discussion and amendment continued through Thursday, March 27, when the bill was referred to the Judiciary Committee for redrafting. The Judiciary Committee's redraft of S.1, which ultimately became the Sherman Act, was reported back on April 2 and passed the Senate, by a vote of 52 to 1, on April 8. House debate followed and a proposed House amendment, with a Senate amendment in response, led to two conferences before both houses receded and the bill was enacted as it had first come from the Senate. President Harrison signed the bill on July 2, 1890.

Prior to the redraft of S.1 by the Senate Judiciary Committee the Senate in Committee of the Whole had adopted so many amendments in the nature of additions that the bill had become a monstrosity. The more important additions for our purposes were those proposed by Senator Reagan (D., Texas), which dealt with the same problems as Sherman's bill, and Senator Ingalls (R.,

Kansas), which placed a prohibitive tax upon dealings in options and futures. These and a host of minor amendments made the bill so complex as to be incomprehensible. It was for this reason, as well as because of widespread doubt concerning the constitutionality of the various measures as framed, that the Judiciary Committee was asked to write a new draft.

. . .

1. Explicit Policy Statements

The views of Senator Sherman (R., Ohio), are crucial to an understanding of the intent underlying the law that bears his name. Sherman was the prime mover in getting antitrust legislation considered and pressed through the Senate. He was also by far the most articulate spokesman for antitrust in Congress. It will be seen, moreover, that though Sherman's bill was completely rephrased by the Judiciary Committee, of which he was not a member, the final bill, in its substantive policy aspects, embodied Sherman's views.

Sherman's views on the policy to be served by antitrust legislation are clear. They appear on the face of the bill he drafted and reported from the Committee on Finance, S.1. Section 1 of that bill declared illegal two classes of "arrangements, contracts, agreements, trusts, or combinations": (1) those "made with a view, or which tend, to *prevent full and free competition*," and (2) those "designed, or which tend, *to advance the cost to consumer*" of articles of commerce. Sherman employed these two criteria of illegality in every measure he presented to the Senate. The first test, which subjects all firms to market forces, is hardly a means of preserving social values that consumers are not willing to pay for. It can be reconciled only with a consumer-welfare policy. The second test is even more explicit. The touchstone of illegality is raising prices to consumers. There were no exceptions. Sherman wanted the courts not merely to be influenced by the consumer interest but to be controlled completely by it.

Sherman's speeches in support of his bill fully bear out this reading. He said, for example, that his bill sought "only to prevent and control combinations made with a view to prevent competition, or for the restraint of trade, or to increase the profits of the producer at the cost of the consumer";[4] that a combination which embraced "the great body of all the corporations engaged in a particular industry" tended "to advance the price to the consumer," and was "a substantial monopoly injurious to the public";[5] and, speaking of the trusts, "If they conducted their business lawfully, without any attempt by these combinations to raise the price of an article consumed by the people of the United States, I would say let them pursue that business."[6]

Though an economist of our day would describe the problem of concern to Sherman differently, as a misallocation of resources brought about by a restriction of output rather than one of high prices, there is no doubt that Sherman and he would be talking about the same thing. Indeed, Sherman demonstrated more than once that he understood that higher prices were brought about by a restriction of output. In defending his bill's constitutionality, for example, he asked, wholly rhetorically, whether Congress had not the power to "protect commerce, nullify contracts that restrain commerce, turn it from its natural courses, increase the price of articles, and thereby diminish the amount of commerce?"[7] This and other remarks suggest that Sherman and his colleagues identified the phrase "restraint of commerce" or "restraint of trade" with "restriction of output." If this identity can be carried over to the wording of the Sherman Act, as I believe it can, the meaning of that statute becomes clear and its consumer orientation indisputable.

After Sherman in importance in the legislative career of the statute stand the members of the Senate Judiciary Committee which reworded the bill after most of the debate had taken place. The members of that Committee were Edmunds (R., Vermont); Hoar (R., Massachusetts); Ingalls (R., Kansas); Evarts (R., New York); Wilson (R., Iowa); Coke (D., Texas); Vest (D., Missouri); George (D., Mississippi); and Pugh (D., Alabama). Of these men, four—George, Coke, Vest, and Pugh who comprised the Democratic minority—gave explicit evidence that they agreed with the consumer-welfare rationale offered by Sherman. Of the five Republicans, none gave evidence of disagreement with that policy and several gave indirect evidence.

George was a vociferous critic of the constitutionality and efficacy of Sherman's bill on such issues as the inability of the commerce power to deal with manufacturing and the difficulties of
proving intent, but his agreement with that bill's value premise is
shown by the bill he drafted. George's bill employed the same
tests for illegality as Sherman's—the prevention of competition
and the advancement of costs to consumers. George's speeches
showed him to be concerned with the effect of the trusts upon the
small producers who sold to or bought from them, but his bill
confirms the internal evidence in his speeches that he did not wish
the courts to protect small producers at the expense of consumers.
George's concern for producers was entirely complementary to his
concern for consumers.

Coke offered his own bill, very similar to Reagan's, and Reagan's
bill, as will be shown, appeared to reflect the same policies as
Sherman's bill. But Coke criticized Sherman's draft for omitting
criminal sanctions. His argument that private damage suits would
not provide adequate relief confirms his agreement with Sherman
concerning the policy the law should serve.

. . .

Vest accepted Sherman's goals but doubted the effectiveness of
his bill, saying, after he had heard Sherman's lengthy exposition
of his views, that if the bill "would effect what he [Sherman] claims
for it, I should vote and speak for it until my strength was exhausted
in this Chamber."[8] He preferred Coke's bill as likely to prove more
effective. Vest's acceptance of the consumer-welfare rationale was
also shown by his argument that the real remedy for the evil of
the trusts was the elimination of the protective tariff because "We
know very well that competition always reduces prices." He said
it was no argument for tariffs, even if it were true, that steel rails
were as cheap in England as in the United States: "I say if you let
these two manufacturing interests compete together and create
competition, you then secure lower prices to the consumer."[9] He
spoke of American manufacturers coming together to "create these
combines at the expense of the consumer in order to enhance their
own profits."[10]

Pugh supported Sherman's bill on a consumer-welfare rationale
and perceived the connection between artificially raised prices and
restriction of output:

[T]he existence of trusts and combinations to limit the production of articles of consumption entering into interstate and foreign commerce for the purpose of destroying competition in production and thereby increasing prices to consumers has become a matter of public history, and the magnitude and oppressive and merciless character of the evils resulting directly to consumers and to our interstate and foreign commerce from such organizations are known and admitted everywhere. . . . [11]

Two other senators not on the Judiciary Committee—Gray (D., Delaware) and Teller (R., Colorado)—also stated explicitly that antitrust legislation should serve consumer welfare. Gray did so by introducing an amendment which employed the same consumer-interest tests for illegality as Sherman's bill. Teller disclosed his policy objectives when he stated he might vote for Sherman's bill, though he was "not very much moved by it" because of its lack of an adequate remedy:

Now, how does this bill reach the great evil against which it is aimed? The Standard Oil Trust has been spoken of. . . . But what can we do about it? We do not dissolve the corporation. What do we do? Anybody who is damaged can sue them. When they interfere with somebody who has sunk a well in Ohio and they run down the price of oil until they shut him up, he may have his remedy against them. But that is not what we are complaining of. We are complaining that Standard Oil Company has a tendency to reduce and destroy competition, and thereby, by destroying competition, to put up improperly the price of oil. Who suffers by that? The sixty-five millions of people in the United States who use oil; and how do they suffer? How much damage have they sustained? It is inconsequential individually, but great to the whole mass of the people. [12]

In this passage Teller also shows that predatory attacks by the trusts upon their smaller rivals were not to be outlawed simply to preserve competitors but because of the effect of the resulting monopoly upon consumers.

The debate in the House of Representatives contains similar evidence of the purpose of the Sherman Act, though the debate there was shorter and less enlightening concerning the question of values than was the debate in the Senate. One of the clearest statements of the evil which the bill was designed to cure was made by Representative Heard (D., Missouri) in his excoriation of the "dressed-beef combine":

[T]his giant robber combination, while perhaps the most damaging of all of its class to the interests of our people, is only one of many which by their methods extort millions from the citizens of this Republic without adding one cent of value to our productions or one iota of increase to our prosperity. In fact, the very object of these giant schemes of combined capital is not to increase the volume of supply, and thus lessen the cost of any useful commodity, but rather to repress, reduce, and control the volume of every article that they touch, so that the cost to consumers is increased while the expenditure for production is lessened, and thereby their profit secured.[13]

Heard clearly envisaged the law as one which would prohibit market control that led to restriction of output. He correctly stated that such restriction injured those who sell to trusts as well as consumers, but his concern for such small producers was limited to the restriction-of-output situation and thus did not contradict or add to his consumer-welfare rationale. . . .

Additional evidence of the intent of the House of Representatives is provided by the bills introduced there. In the Fifty-first Congress no antitrust bill introduced in the House—or the Senate, either, for that matter—mentioned a value other than consumer welfare. I have counted ten House bills which related explicitly to consumer welfare, and the remainder, given the economic theories of the time, were fully consistent with that value. . . .

Explicit value statements in the Senate and the House, then were overwhelmingly in favor of the proposition that Congress intended the Sherman Act to be interpreted in accordance with the principles of consumer welfare. Those few legislators who spoke against that value were . . . in opposition to Sherman's bill and also, significantly, to the bill introduced by Senator Reagan (D., Texas).

2. The Proposed Rules of Law

I have already indicated the policy which underlies rules against cartel agreements (sometimes referred to as loose combinations), monopolistic mergers (tight combinations), and predatory tactics. In this section I will attempt to show that those rules were in fact contemplated by Congress.

a. Cartels

Doubt has been expressed about the clarity of the congressional intent with respect to cartels. Yet is seems plain that Congress intended to outlaw "loose combinations" of the sort typified by price-fixing and market-division agreements between competitors. (I am speaking here of agreements not involving any significant efficiency-creating integration.) The evidence for this intent is of several sorts.

The language of the Sherman Act itself seems to distinguish between cartels and tighter arrangements similar to mergers. Section 1 refers to "Every contract, combination in the form of trust or otherwise, or conspiracy." Aside from the differing connotations of the words "contract," "combination," and "conspiracy," there is the obvious point that the drafters chose to modify only the word "combination" with the phrase "in the form of trust or otherwise." The word "trust" originally gained currency to describe anticompetitive combinations because the trust device was used to gather industries or large parts of them under single ownership and control. It is arguable, therefore, that its use in the Sherman Act indicated that the "trust" was but one member of the general class of close-knit "combinations" while it was not a member of the classes of "contracts" or "conspiracies." The distinction between the latter two terms may have been that between formal agreements and informal, probably secret, understandings. In any event, the obvious setting apart of the word "combination" in a way which seems to indicate common ownership and control suggests that something else was meant by the other two words, and that something else could hardly have been anything other than cartels. This argument is rather speculative, however, and clearer evidence exists.

Sherman's original draft of S.1, as well as Reagan's and the other bills, supports the theory that Congress intended to prohibit cartels by employing words that suggest every range of coordination from the loosest general understanding to the tightest-knit integration. In the debates, moreover, Sherman plainly demonstrated an intention to outlaw cartels. He expounded his legislative aims, for instance, by reading to the Senate at great length from judicial opinions which he stated were representative of the common law he said his bill would enact. The cases he read from or described held illegal a market-division cartel agreement as well as monopolistic mergers and the predatory extraction of railroad rebates by the Standard Oil Trust.

Sherman's intention to outlaw cartels was understood by his colleagues, and the remarks of Senators Stewart (R., Nevada) and Platt (R., Connecticut), who favored certain cartels show that not only Sherman's bill but Reagan's would enact such a rule. Stewart objected to both bills because they would ban competitors' agreements to limit output during periods of "overproduction" and depression. Platt attacked Sherman's measure because, "Unrestricted competition is brutal warfare. . . . "[14] He favored a rule that would permit agreements to charge prices that were "just and reasonable and fair." The Senate paid no attention to either Platt or Stewart and, in the Committee of the Whole, adopted Reagan's amendment and reported Sherman's bill with its various additions and amendments to the Senate.

The intention of both houses of Congress to outlaw cartels is also shown by the extended sparring that took place over the Bland amendment the House added to the Senate bill. Representative Bland (D., Missouri) offered a two-part amendment to make clear that the bill covered "every contract or agreement entered into for the purpose of preventing competition in the sale or purchase of any commodity, or to prevent competition in transportation."[15] The House had before it then the Senate Judiciary Committee's draft which may have seemed less clear than the Sherman and Reagan bills to those who had not followed the Senate debates. The House adopted Bland's amendment but the Senate Judiciary Committee objected to the first part as beyond Congress' power under the commerce clause. Indeed, the switch from Sherman's and Reagan's wording to the Judiciary Committee's seems originally to have been motivated largely by the very doubts of constitutionality which Bland's amendment provoked. Senator Hoar (R., Massachusetts), who reported the Judiciary Committee's reaction to the Bland amendment stated he thought the remainder of the amendment concerning transportation was covered in the Senate bill already, but there was no harm in adding Bland's proposal. Had matters stopped there it would have been clear that cartels were illegal. If the Senate bill, which became the Sherman

Act, covered railroad rate cartels (which was what the House was driving at in the second part of the Bland amendment), it certainly covered other cartels. But for the question of the reach of the commerce power, the first part of the Bland amendment was surely covered by a bill which made no distinction between transportation and other goods or services.

A day later, however, Hoar said some members thought the Judiciary Committee's revision of the Bland amendment was not as precise and well guarded as it might be. He did not explain, but his motion to recommit was agreed to. The committee came back with a very different amendment under which agreements preventing competition in transportation were illegal only if rates were "raised above what is just and reasonable." The Senate agreed, perhaps because this approach to transportation seemed more in keeping with the railroad rate philosophy of the recently enacted Interstate Commerce Act. The House refused to accept the Senate amendment and ultimately both the Senate and the House agreed to recede from their respective amendments, leaving the bill as it had first come from the Senate.

The inference from this maneuvering is that all cartels were to be illegal, regardless of the price they set. The Senate Judiciary Committee's objection to the first part of the Bland amendment is probably to be taken at face value. Hoar's statement that the bill already covered the second part of the Bland amendment indicates not only that the unamended bill made railroad cartels flatly unlawful but that it had that effect upon all other cartels since there is nothing in the wording of the statute or the debates to suggest the Senate had intended a distinction. Indeed, Hoar's words may have been the factor that galvanized the senators who favored a different rule for railroads to press for a revision specifying a "just and reasonable" standard for railroad rate agreements. This move constitutes an admission that the general language of the bill permitted no such construction. By receding afterward the Senate appears to have indicated again that the flat rule applied to all cartels.

No contrary implication can be drawn from the House's recession. The House had not attempted to distinguish between railroad and other cartels. By the time of the recession, particularly in view of Hoar's first statement, it may very well have seemed that Bland's amendment was unnecessary to the House's purposes.

The evidence appears unmistakable that the Congress intended to outlaw cartels.

b. and c. Monopolistic Mergers and Predatory Practices

There is no need to spell out all the evidence that Congress intended to outlaw both mergers (or other forms of close-knit combination) that created monopoly and predatory business tactics. Sherman's description of the common law which his bill would enact, his other remarks, the speeches of a number of legislators, and the language of the bills introduced sufficiently establish this point. No one, to my knowledge, has ever challenged it. The important point is that these rules were typically justified in terms of consumer welfare. Sherman stated the general case against both monopolistic mergers and predatory practices:

> The sole object of such a combination is to make competition impossible. It can control the market, raise or lower prices, as will best promote its selfish interests, reduce prices in a particular locality and break down competition and advance prices at will where competition does not exist. Its governing motive is to increase the profits of the parties composing it. The law of selfishness, uncontrolled by competition, compels it to disregard the interest of the consumer. It dictates terms to transportation companies, it commands the price of labor without fear of strikes, for in its field it allows no competitors. Such a combination is far more dangerous than any heretofore invented, and, when it embraces the great body of all the corporations engaged in a particular industry in all the States of the Union, it tends to advance the price to the consumer of any article produced, it is a substantial monopoly injurious to the public, and, by the rule of both the common and the civil law, is null and void and just subject to restraint by the courts, of forfeiture of corporate rights and privileges, and in some cases should be denounced as a crime, and the individuals engaged in it should be punished as criminals. It is this kind of a combination we have to deal with now.[16]

The emphasis in this passage is upon the harm done to consumers. Sherman also mentions that a combination of the sort he describes allows no strikes but that is clearly an additional evil and not a test for illegality to be applied independently of consumer welfare. If there were any ambiguity in the passage, it would be removed by the wording of his bill which specifies only consumer-welfare tests. Other legislators spoke of the evils of the trusts in respects other than their harmful effect upon consumers, but, like Sherman, none of them suggested that these harmful effects could take place in any case not involving injury to consumers. The language is always fully consistent with the view that concern for farmers, laborers, or small businessmen was complementary to concern for consumers and not to override it in case of conflict between the interests of consumers and other groups. Other factors, particularly the one to be discussed in the next section, demonstrate that this interpretation is the correct one.

3. The Preservation of Efficiency; The Legality of Monopoly Gained Through Efficiency

Congress' position with respect to efficiency cannot be explained on any hypothesis other than that consumer welfare was in all cases the controlling value under the Sherman Act.

Sherman took great pains to stress that his bill would in no way interfere with efficiency. It would outlaw only those mergers which created great market power. "[The bill] aims only at unlawful combinations. It does not in the least affect combinations in aid of production where there is free and fair competition."[17] He stressed the legality of efficiency repeatedly,[18] citing partnerships and corporations as two forms of combination which were efficiency-creating and therefore lawful. He said corporations "ought to be encouraged and protected as tending to cheapen the cost of production."[19] He also praised the efficiency-creating corporate merger.[20]

Not once did Sherman suggest that courts should blunt or discourage efficient size or conduct in the interest of any social or political value. The only limit he urged to the creation of efficiency by combination was justified explicitly in terms of consumer welfare. He thought combinations of monopolistic size would not pass their efficiencies on to consumers:

> It is sometimes said of these combinations [the monopolistic trusts] that they reduce prices to the consumer by better methods of production, but all experience shows that this saving of cost goes to the pockets of the producer. The price to the consumer depends upon the supply, which can be reduced at pleasure by the combination.[21]

Here again Sherman identified injury to consumers as occurring through restriction of output by firms with market control.

The Senate later adopted an amendment to Sherman's bill offered by Senator Aldrich (R., Rhode Island) which stated:

> *Provided further*, That this act shall not be construed to apply to or to declare unlawful combinations or associations made with a view or which tend, by means other than be a reduction of the wages of labor, to lessen the cost of production or reduce the price of any of the necessaries of life, nor to the combinations or associations made with a view or which tend to increase the earnings of persons engaged in any useful employment.[22]

The adoption of this amendment by the Senate in Committee of the Whole indicates agreement with Sherman's position on efficiency, though Thorelli warns that at the time of adoption the Senate was concerned primarily with Ingalls' amendment to prohibit trading in futures and options.[23] The last clause of the amendment appears merely to reflect the Senate's desire to exempt labor unions from the scope of the law.

The most dramatic illustration of Congress' agreement with Sherman's position, however, was the decision to make legal the gaining of monopoly by superior efficiency. The Judiciary Committee draft made it an offense to "monopolize," not to have a monopoly. The wording itself suggests that an activity rather than a status was to be outlawed, and that in turn suggests that there were lawful means of gaining a monopoly position. . . .

. . . Hoar's answer, then, [was] that monopolies gained by merger or predatory tactics are illegal but monopolies gained by superior efficiency are not. Edmunds then explained further and supported Hoar's position. No contrary position with respect to the desirability of legalizing monopoly gained through efficiency or the meaning of the statute was expressed. Apparently satisfied with the construction put on Section 2 by Hoar and Edmunds, the Senate promptly passed the bill, 52 to 1.

Congress' decision to permit monopoly achieved by efficiency is completely inconsistent with the view that courts should use the Sherman Act to ameliorate the noneconomic "helplessness of the individual" before "great aggregations of capital" or that they may take into account the alleged desirability of preserving for its own sake an economy of small business units. Monopoly by efficiency is as effective as monopoly by predation in driving smaller rivals from an industry, and it would seem to have whatever undesirable social or political side effects that any monopoly or large industrial size may be thought to imply. Monopoly by efficiency, however, is probably beneficial to consumers and to small business suppliers and customers of the monopolists—at least by comparison with the policy alternative. Breaking up monopoly gained by efficiency is likely to impose higher costs at that level of the distributive or productive chain to the detriment of consumers and all vertically related firms. The Senate's conscious election to legalize monopoly by efficiency, therefore, is highly significant—a clear choice of consumer welfare and those values consistent with it over competing values, including that of preserving small business units in the same market.

. . .

5. The Narrow Scope of the Commerce Power

The notion abroad today that the Fifty-first Congress breathed broad social and political values into the Sherman Act is an anachronism. The Congress and the Supreme Court of 1890 had no such expansive view of federal power generally, and of the commerce power in particular, as has become familiar in recent times. The limitations upon Congress' commerce power were thought to be of two sorts—the reach of the power, defined by the interstate-intrastate distinction, and the nature of the power, defined by the commercial-noncommercial distinction. These limitations are related, both being based on concepts of federalism and limited central government. For that reason it is logically and psychologically probable that men who favored a short reach in the commerce power would favor a narrow definition of the goals for which the power could be exercised. There is ample evidence in the Congressional Record that the Fifty-first Congress took a limited view of the reach of the interstate concept and it is correspondingly unlikely that they took a broad view of the values the power could be used to implement directly.

More direct evidence of Congress' view of the goals to be directly implemented through the commerce power comes both from the general trend of legislation under that clause and statements made in the course of the passage of the Sherman Act. The first major commerce clause legislation was the Interstate Commerce Act of 1887. Congress there confined its law to matters bearing directly upon the movement of commerce—terms and conditions of interstate transportation by railroad. It apparently believed that the commerce power did not enable Congress to prevent the starting of unnecessary railroad enterprises or to regulate railroad financial operations such as fictitious capitalization. Up to 1890 Congress had not even attempted to exercise a general "police power" under the commerce clause, and it was not until 1895 that a very modest beginning was made with a statute barring lottery tickets from movement in interstate commerce. In 1903, the Supreme Court, divided five to four, upheld that statute as within the commerce power. Even then the majority felt obliged to use a "pollution-of-commerce" rationale, analogizing the statute to the prohibition of the interstate movement of diseased cattle.[24] Congress moved slowly into the field of social legislation, and the Supreme Court struck many such laws down for over forty years after the passage of the Sherman Act. Since Congress was experimenting timidly with the commerce power as a vehicle for social reform well after 1890, and the Supreme Court was resisting well into the 1930's, it seems farfetched to suppose that Congress intended to enact broad social welfare measures through the Sherman Act.

This general argument is borne out by the legislative history of the statute. Sherman's argument for the constitutionality of his bill rested entirely on the theory that it would facilitate the flow of interstate commerce: "[Congress] may 'regulate commerce'; can it not protect commerce, nullify contracts that restrain commerce, turn it from its natural courses, increase the price of articles, and therefore diminish the amount of commerce?"[25]

Edmunds, who proposed the final phrasing of the statute's relation to commerce in the Judiciary Committee, took a very limited view of federal power. He said the Constitution did not give and ought not to give Congress "power to enter into the police regulations of the people of the United States."[26] Edmunds maintained that Congress lacked the power under the commerce clause to abolish the sugar trust. He opposed Ingalls' proposal to tax dealings in options and futures because it was essentially a "police measure" and the Supreme Court would say that Congress had no power "to regulate the good order of society." It is hardly conceivable that a man with such views could have drafted a bill intended to hand over to federal courts, operating under a delegation of the commerce power, the right to adjust social and political ills of a noncommercial nature.

The Judiciary Committee dropped the wording of Sherman's and Reagan's bills and instead employed the phraseology not merely of the common law but of Sherman's reasoning about Congress' power over commerce. The redrafted bill spoke in terms of the diminution or lessening of the flow of commerce which Sherman had said resulted from control of the market—that is, in terms of contracts, combinations, and conspiracies "in restraint of trade or commerce" and monopolizations of such trade or commerce. This adroit phrasing not only imported the substantive criteria which Sherman had proposed but was calculated to satisfy both broad and narrow constructionists of the commerce power's reach. The Act's reach would depend upon the Supreme Court's demarcation of the line between interstate and intrastate. But the wording also indicated that the test for illegality was entirely the effect upon commerce, not an effect upon some other thing or condition, such as a supposed social or political evil, which had merely some requisite jurisdictional effect upon commerce.

This evidence of the Fifty-first Congress' view of the scope of the commerce power is of course not conclusive of the point sought to be established here. But it does tend strongly to indicate the improbability of the proposition that Congress intended to delegate noncommercial criteria to the federal courts. More than that, Sherman's commerce clause argument and the wording of the final bill suggest not merely that the statute's intended goals were commercial but that they related entirely to safeguarding the flow of commerce against diminution, against, in a word, a restriction of output. Edmunds' views on this point were shared by other members of the Judiciary Committee and the Senate. Edmunds told the Senate that the Judiciary Committee had unanimously determined to "frame a bill that should be clearly within our constitutional power." What discussion there was on the topic in the House of Representatives paralleled the majority position in the Senate.

6. The Criteria Delegated to the Federal Courts

Those who have described the Sherman Act as the delegation of broad discretion to the courts, in some respects comparable to the powers delegated to or assumed by the courts under the great clauses of the Constitution, are of course quite correct. Congress specified a value, a core of meaning, and left it to the courts to elaborate a framework of subsidiary rules in the course of examining great numbers of market structures and forms of market behavior over a period of many years. But those who, like Judge Hand, think the delegation essentially unconfined are in error. Many legislators in the Fifty-first Congress remarked the fact of delegation, but none suggested that it was without standards. The standards intended can easily be found.

As always John Sherman provides the clearest and best statement on the subject. Speaking of his own bill, whose policy, as we shall see, is to be equated with that of the subsequent Judiciary Committee draft that became law, Sherman said:

> The first section, being a remedial statute, would be construed liberally, with a view to promote its object. It defines a civil remedy, and the courts will construe it liberally; they will prescribe the precise limits of the constitutional power of the Government; *they will distinguish between lawful combinations in aid of production and unlawful combinations to prevent competition and in restraint of trade....* [27] [Emphasis added.]

Sherman could hardly have said more clearly that the law was to delegate to the courts the task of distinguishing between those agreements and combinations which increase efficiency and those that restrict output.

Judge Hand was correct, of course, in viewing the Sherman Act's common law terminology as expressing the delegation of discretionary powers to the courts, but he and many other commentators appear to have misinterpreted the role of "the common law" in Sherman Act adjudication. The problem seems at first more difficult than it is because there was in 1890 no unitary body of common law doctrine which could give meaning to the statute. The common law of restraints of trade and monopolies has been a variable growth, composed of diverse and even contradictory strains, many of them obviously irrelevant to the concerns of the Sherman Act. Yet Sherman and many of his colleagues repeatedly assured the Senate, without objection by anyone, that they proposed merely to enact the common law.

There is no mystery, for Sherman and the others also repeatedly stated what the common law was. The fact that their statements did not accurately mirror that confused body of precedent does not obscure what they intended to convey. It is clear from the debates that "the common law" relevant to the Sherman Act is an artificial construct, made up for the occasion out of a careful selection of recent decisions from a variety of jurisdictions plus a liberal admixture of the senators' own policy prescriptions. It is to this "common law," holding full sway nowhere but in the debates of the Fifty-first Congress, that one must look to understand the Sherman Act.

I have already mentioned that the only cases cited by Sherman as representative of the common law held illegal the predatory extraction of railroad rebates by the Standard Oil Co., cartel agreements, and monopolistic mergers. But this extensive discussion of "the" common law was by no means the only occasion upon which Sherman told the Senate what that law was. He identified his bill— which struck at agreements preventing full and free competition or tending to advance costs to consumers—with the common law. The first point in Sherman's first speech on behalf of his bill was the categorical assertion that the bill "does not announce a new principle of law, but applies old and well recognized principles of the common law to the complicated jurisdiction of our State and Federal Government."[28] And later: "It is the unlawful combination, tested by the rules of common law and human experience, that is aimed at by this bill, and not the lawful and useful combination."

Sherman defined "monopoly" with a quotation from one of his selected common law cases: "Any combination the tendency of which is to prevent competition in its broad and general sense, and to control, and thus at will enhance, prices to the detriment of the public, is a legal monopoly."[29] And he concluded his review of the decisions by claiming for the common law generally a policy uniformity despite a variability in the law itself:

> I might add to the cases cited innumerable cases in nearly all the States and in England, and in all of them it will appear that while the law in respect to contracts in restraint of trade and combinations to prevent competition and to advance the price of necessaries of life has varied somewhat, but in all of them, whether the combinations are by individuals, partnerships, or corporations, when the purpose of the combination or its plain tendency is to prevent competition, the courts have enforced the rule of the common law and have vigorously used the judicial power in subverting them.[30]

The internal inconsistency of this passage may suggest that Sherman was quite conscious that "the" common law upon which he based his bill did not in fact exist and that he was deliberately imposing a fictitious uniformity upon the precedent.

In his discussion of trusts Sherman identified consumer welfare as the policy of the common law in this area:

> [W]hen [a combination] embraces the great body of all corporations engaged in a particular industry in all of the States of the Union, it tends to advance the price to the consumer of any article produced, it is a substantial monopoly injurious to the public, and, by the rule of both the common and the civil law, is null and void and the just subject of restraint by the courts. . . . [31]

No senator challenged Sherman's representations of the common law, and two—Vest and Teller, the former a member of the Judiciary Committee—supported it . . . .

. . .

There can hardly be any question that the discretion delegated to the courts by the Sherman Act was that of determining the consumer interest in particular cases and assessing legality accordingly. This is shown by Sherman's explicit statement that the task of the courts would be to distinguish between combinations which create efficiency and those which restrain trade. We have seen that by "restrain trade" Sherman meant "restrict output." . . .

7. The Absence of Expressed Values Other Than Consumer Welfare

Of those senators who supported the policy of Sherman's bill (as distinct from its constitutional footing or the remedies it provided), and they comprised the great majority of all who expressed views, not one suggested that the courts should in any case give weight to a value inconsistent with consumer welfare. It may be useful to examine some of the passages in the debates which have upon occasion been cited as expressive of conflicting values. A showing that these passages do not require, or in many cases even allow, such an interpretation should assist in establishing the intended exclusivity of the consumer welfare policy.

In the passage from the *Alcoa* opinion quoted first at the beginning of this paper, it will be recalled, Judge Hand attributed to Sherman "a desire to put an end to great aggregations of capital because of the helplessness of the individual before them." This helplessness was a noneconomic reason why "great industrial consolidations are inherently undesirable, regardless of their economic results." For this proposition Judge Hand relied upon two passages excerpted from Sherman's speeches. In the first, Sherman, speaking of trusts, said:

> If the concentered powers of this combination are intrusted to a single man, it is a kingly prerogative, inconsistent with our form of government, and should be subject to the strong resistance of the State and national authorities. If anything is wrong this is wrong. If we will not endure a king as a political power we should not endure a king over the production, transportation, and sale of any of the necessaries of life. If we would not submit to an emperor we should not submit to an autocrat of trade, with power to prevent competition and to fix the price of any commodity.[32]

It is at once apparent that Sherman's language not only fails to require Judge Hand's reading but refutes it. Sherman here analogizes the form of economic tyranny practiced by the trust to a political form, the "kingly prerogative." The latter is "inconsistent with our form of government," and so, by analogy, is the trust, the "autocrat of trade." If there were any doubt whatever about Sherman's meaning, it would be removed by the last sentence quoted. The thing which Sherman denounces is the "power to prevent competition and to fix the price of any commodity"—the power, in short, to injure consumers.

The second passage quoted by Judge Hand came as part of a rhetorical crescendo in Sherman's opening speech urging adoption of his bill:

> The popular mind is agitated with problems that may disturb social order, and among them all none is more threatening than the inequality of condition, of wealth, and opportunity that has grown within a single generation out of the concentration of capital into vast combinations to control production and trade and to break down competition. These combinations already defy or control powerful transportation corporations and reach State authorities. They reach out their Briarian arms to every part of our country. They are imported from abroad. Congress alone can deal with them, and if we are unwilling or unable there will soon be a trust for every production and a master to fix the price for every necessity of life.[33]

It is rather difficult to see what it is in this passage that might support the interpretation given it by Judge Hand. Either in or out of context, Sherman's words here are entirely consistent with his constant reference to the effect of the trusts upon consumers as the touchstone of illegality under his bill. Sherman does speak of inequalities of condition, wealth and opportunity, but it is abundantly clear that he does not suggest that the courts will or should use the law he proposes to create greater equality by dissolving large aggregations of capital regardless of the adverse impact this may have upon consumers by destroying efficiency. Sherman specifically complains only of those inequalities which are created by "the concentration of capital into vast combinations to control production and trade and to break down competition." He had explained already that these were to be forbidden because of their harmful impact upon consumers. If Sherman can be construed in this passage to welcome other forms of equality which would follow from the dissolution of monopolistic mergers, such results are clearly no more than a welcome by-product of a decision arrived at upon consumer welfare grounds. The same is clearly true of Sherman's remark that the combinations "reach State authorities." He was obviously not suggesting that, contrary to its explicit terms, the sanctions of his bill would be invoked upon proof that a trust had bribed or otherwise improperly influenced a state authority. The most that can be said of this passage is that Sherman took occasion to recount all of the sins of the trusts. To find in these words a mandate for a court to make a decision counter to the consumer welfare—in contradiction to everything else he had said on the topic—requires an effort beyond the merely heroic.

Senator George frequently expressed concern over the plight of the small producer, and Judge Hand cited a page of one of his speeches which does contain some oratory that sounds as if it might support Judge Hand's thesis:

> It is a sad thought to the philanthropist that the present system of production and exchange is having that tendency which is sure at some not very distant day to crush out all small men, all small capitalists, all small enterprises. This is being done now. We find everywhere over our land the wrecks of small independent enterprises thrown in our pathway. So now the American Congress and the American people are brought face to face with this sad, this great problem: Is production, is trade, to be taken away from the great mass of the people and concentrated in the hands of a few men . . . .[34]

There is, in truth, a great deal of sympathy for small producers expressed in George's speeches. It seems abundantly clear, however, that George did not propose that the law's impact should ever be altered by that sympathy. He viewed the small producer interest and the consumer interest as complementary rather than conflicting and demanded action in the name of small producers only in situations where the same action would be required by the prevalent theory of consumer welfare. George agreed with Sherman's policy of protecting consumers,[35] and mentioned only two other situations as justifying, questions of constitutional power aside, the intervention of law: the imposition of lower prices upon small sellers by monopsonistic combinations; and the extraction of higher prices from small producers by monopolistic suppliers.

These are all cases which would call for the same legal intervention on a consumer-welfare rationale. That George's concern for small producers was entirely complementary to his concern for consumers is further shown by the fact that the bill he drafted employed precisely the same consumer-welfare criteria as Sherman's bill. No man who proposed that the courts should favor producers over consumers in some cases would draft a law which made it illegal in every case to advance the cost of goods to consumers. This reading also squares with George's participation as a member of the Judiciary Committee in the decision to permit monopoly gained by efficiency.

There are scattered remarks by other legislators which might suggest to a casual reader that preservation of small business for its own sake was advocated. Analysis demonstrates, however, that, with the exception of those few men who favored a reasonable-price test for cartels, in no case did the speaker intend that courts in deciding cases should ever prefer the preservation of small business to consumer welfare. Beyond this, it is impossible to find even colorable language suggesting most of the other broad social or political purposes that have occasionally been suggested as relevant to the application of the Sherman Act.

. . .

Having presented the evidence that leads me to conclude the Fifty-first Congress intended courts to apply a consumer-welfare policy exclusively, I turn to consider an objection. This is that the views of Senator Sherman and the discussion that turned on his and Reagan's proposals are irrelevant to the bill which the Judiciary Committee drafted and Congress enacted.

The view that the debates which swirled around Sherman's draft of S.1 are largely irrelevant to the statute which ultimately emerged results from overestimating the severity of the break represented by the Judiciary Committee's redrafting of the bill. Walton Hamilton and Irene Till phrased this misunderstanding succinctly:

> The great bother is that the bill which was arduously debated was never passed, and that the bill which was passed was never really discussed. . . . The [Judiciary] committee turned a deaf ear to all that the Senate had said and done and went its own way. Intent, therefore, forsakes the Congressional Record for the capacious recesses of that flexible corpus called the common law.[36]

The authors also state that the law "is to this day strangely enough called the Sherman Act—for no better reason, according to its author [Hoar], than that Senator Sherman had nothing to do with it whatever." These assertions are provocative, to say the least, and it is unfortunate that Hamilton and Till do not indicate the evidence upon which their statements rest.

My own study of the Congressional Record leads me to conclude that the policy of the bill so "arduously debated" was carried forward into the Judiciary Committee's draft and enacted. The popular name of the statute correctly attributes paternity to Sherman. There is no reason to doubt this other than the fact that the Judiciary Committee recast S.1 in common law terms. Common sense alone, moreover, makes the Hamilton-Till thesis dubious. The shortness of the Senate debate over the Judiciary Committee's redraft certainly suggests that the Senate thought it knew what the draft meant, and that can be explained only on the theory that the preceding discussions of Sherman's policy were fully applicable to the new draft. In fact, when Hoar brought the redraft in he told the Senate, "I shall not undertake to explain the bill, which is well understood." There are other good reasons to believe that the Senate thought the Judiciary Committee draft represented the basic policies espoused by Sherman. He was by far the most articulate and thorough speaker on the question of what goals antitrust should serve. Those who spoke overwhelmingly agreed with his position on this issue. Disagreement was largely confined to questions of remedies and the constitutional reach of Sherman's measure. The reference to the Judiciary Committee was finally made, after having been voted down twice, because of concern with those matters as well as the meaning and constitutionality of the various additions, such as the Ingalls amendment, which had been made to S.1. The one major issue which arose in connection with the Judiciary Committee draft, the issue of monopoly due to efficiency, was, moreover, explained by Hoar and Edmunds and resolved in a manner consistent with Sherman's consumer-welfare rationale.

Even more clear-cut evidence is supplied by the role of "the common law" in the Senate's deliberations. Prior to the Judiciary Committee reference Sherman's bill and policy were firmly and repeatedly identified with the common law. Sherman gave the

Senate an extended discussion of common law cases and principles which he said his bill would enact for federal enforcement. He repeatedly used common law terminology, "restraint of trade," as interchangeable with his bill's reference to prevention of full and free competition and advancement of costs to consumers. Even the title of his bill made the point: "A bill to declare unlawful trusts and combinations in restraint of trade and production." That title not only identified the consumer-welfare tests of the bill with the common law of restraints of trade, but, by adding the term "restraint . . . of production" suggested that the evil was restriction of output. We have seen that Sherman made the same point in defending his bill as a proper exercise of the commerce power and in identifying the mechanism by which trusts advanced costs to consumers. No senator challenged Sherman's version of the common law or his assertion that his bill merely enacted it. Senators Vest and Teller explicitly agreed with Sherman.

When the Judiciary Committee, which had not been asked to alter or amend Sherman's policy in any way, reported back a redraft that made the test of illegality the "restraint of trade or commerce" members of the Senate had every reason to think that this use of the common law phrase carried Sherman's policy views with it. This is particularly true because Vest, who had agreed with Sherman on this point, was a member of the committee. In reporting the redraft, moreover, Hoar three times identified it with the common law. He said the committee had "affirmed the old doctrine of the common law in regard to all interstate and international commercial transactions." In reply to Kenna on monopoly by efficiency he said the offense of monopolizing prohibited by section 2 of the bill was defined by the common law, and, in an argument very like that of Sherman's, he said:

> The common law in the States of the Union of course extends over citizens and subjects over which the State itself has jurisdiction. Now we are dealing with an offense against interstate or international commerce, which the State can not regulate by penal enactment, and we find the United States without any common law. The great thing that this bill does, except affording a remedy, is to extend the common law principles, which protected fair competition in trade in old times in England, to international and interstate commerce in the United States.[37]

· · ·

The Senate was thus told what "the common law" was and then repeatedly assured that both Sherman's bill and the Judiciary Committee's redraft were enactments of that law. According to a well-known axiom, Sherman's policy and the Judiciary Committee's policy, being equal to the same thing, are equal to each other.

· · ·

The construct we call "legislative intent" must be used with care. If for no other reason than its inherent artificiality, "legislative intent" cannot properly be used to settle all questions about the bounds of judicial discretion. I offer this paper, therefore, less to demonstrate that Sherman Act issues are only those relevant to consumer welfare—though such weight as "legislative intent" may have surely pulled in that direction—than to rebut contrary claims which purport to rest upon a discernible congressional intention. If values other than consumer welfare are to be made legitimate criteria for Sherman Act litigation, the legitimation will have to proceed from some base other than the "purpose" of the Fifty-first Congress.

· · ·

Courts charged by Congress with the maximization of consumer welfare are free to revise not only prior judge-made rules but, it would seem, rules contemplated by Congress. The Sherman Act defines the class of situations to which it may be applied, but it does not freeze into statutory commands the rules of legality about predation, mergers, and so forth, that many congressmen contemplated. Sherman and others clearly believed that they were legislating a policy and delegating to the courts the elaboration of subsidiary rules. Nothing in the legislative history or in the language of the statute suggests that courts are required to hold any specific type of agreement or behavior unlawful regardless of its probable impact upon consumers. In terms of "law," therefore, the Sherman Act tells judges very little. A judge who feels compelled to a particular result regardless of the teachings of economic theory deceives himself and abdicates his delegated responsibility. That responsibility is nothing less than the awesome task of continually creating and recreating the Sherman Act out of his understanding of economics and his conception of the requirements of the judicial process.

Wealth Transfers as the Original and Primary Concern of Antitrust: The Efficiency Interpretation Challenged

ROBERT H. LANDE

Considerable dispute over the goals of the antitrust laws has surfaced in scholarly commentary on the subject. While it is unanimously agreed that Congress enacted these laws to encourage competition, disagreement continues over Congress' ultimate goals. . . .

The prevailing view is that Congress intended the antitrust laws only to increase economic efficiency. Others, however, contend that Congress was largely motivated by a number of social, moral, and political concerns. This Article presents a third view, one suggested by the antitrust laws' legislative histories. This Article will argue that Congress passed the antitrust laws to further economic objectives, but primarily objectives of a distributive rather than of an efficiency nature. In other words, Congress was concerned principally with preventing "unfair" transfers of wealth from consumers to firms with market power. This Article will also demonstrate that Congress intended to subordinate all other con-

Reprinted from 34 Hastings Law Journal 67 (1982).

cerns to the basic purpose of preventing firms with market power from directly harming consumers.

. . .

The view expressed in this Article is that the antitrust laws were passed primarily to further what may be called a distributive goal, the goal of preventing unfair acquisitions of consumers' wealth by firms with market power. It should be stressed, however, that Congress did not pass the antitrust laws to secure the "fair" overall distribution of wealth in our economy or even to help the poor. Congress merely wanted to prevent one transfer of wealth that it considered inequitable, and to promote the distribution of wealth that competitive markets would bring. In other words, Congress implicitly declared that "consumers' surplus"[1] was the rightful entitlement of consumers; consumers were given the right to purchase competitively priced goods. Firms with market power were condemned because they acquired this property right without compensation to consumers. This Article contends that the antitrust laws embody a strong preference for consumers over firms with market power.

The Article begins by defining possible economic goals of the antitrust laws. Turning to the specific antitrust statute, the Article first analyzes the legislative history of the Sherman Act to demonstrate Congress' motivations. . . . [2]

Economic Effects of Monopoly Power: A Brief Overview

The observation that monopolies cause increased prices and reduced output is hardly new. This conclusion finds expression in early English common law[3] and in classical economic theory. Adam Smith noted that "The monopolists, by keeping the market constantly under-stocked, by never fully supplying the effectual demand, sell their commodities much above the natural price, and raise their emoluments, whether they consist in wages or profit, greatly above their natural price."[4] By the time the Sherman Act was passed, economists were able to prove that a monopolist pursuing its own best interests would normally follow this course of conduct.

Modern economists have, of course, made many important advances in the theory of monopoly. The most important development may be the modern analysis of the implications of monopoly self-interest, long recognized as including higher prices and restricted output. These effects can be divided into three categories. The first, allocative inefficiency, describes the misallocation of resources, which diminishes the total wealth of society. A second effect is a transfer of wealth from consumers to monopolists. The third involves the effect of monopolies, and antimonopoly statutes, on firms' productive efficiency. . . .

Transfer of "Consumers' Surplus" from Consumer to Monopolists

The most visible and obvious result of monopoly pricing is a transfer of wealth from purchasers to the monopolist; consumers become poorer while the monopolist becomes richer. The relative size of the transferred wealth and the allocative inefficiency will vary considerably from case to case depending upon a number of factors. Under market conditions most likely to be encountered, however, the transferred wealth usually will be between two and forty times as great as the accompanying allocative inefficiency. Thus, the redistributive effects of market power generally exceed the allocative inefficiency effects by a substantial amount.

The two principal effects of monopolistic pricing, the transfer of wealth from consumers to monopolists and the decrease in allocative efficiency, are different in one fundamental manner: the latter represents a decrease in society's absolute wealth, while the former merely redistributes that wealth. As Professor Williamson has observed, "[t]his [redistributive] transformation of benefits from one form (consumers' surplus) to another (profit) is treated as a wash under the conventional welfare economics model."[5]

Nevertheless, this transfer of wealth raises a very controversial question: is the transfer a "good," "bad," or neutral result of monopoly pricing? The value-laden answer in large part is determined by whether anyone is thought to be entitled to the economic benefit of the "consumers' surplus." Under monopoly pricing, some consumers' surplus is acquired by the monopolist. Depending on one's perspective, one can be entirely indifferent to the result, or one can conclude either that the monopoly is "unfairly taking" property from consumers, or that the monopoly is only reaping its just reward.

The redistributive effects of monopoly power are clearly good or bad only with respect to the assumptions and welfare criteria that are used to evaluate them. Condemnation of the direct consumer impact of monopoly power is therefore normally and properly termed "subjective" or a "value judgment," because it is based upon a preference for consumers over monopolists.

. . . Congress decided that consumers were entitled to the benefits of a competitive economic system. Consumers were deemed entitled to the "consumers' surplus" because Congress regarded the competitive scenario as the normal one. Monopoly pricing represented a change from the norm which Congress condemned as an "unfair" taking of consumers' property.

This congressional decision does not, moreover, violate the important principle of Pareto optimality. Before one can evaluate an improvement under the Pareto principle, the initial distribution of entitlements or property rights must be defined. Assuming that Congress decided consumers were entitled to consumers' surplus, condemnation of monopolistic extractions of wealth does not violate Pareto optimality because the monopoly is unfairly taking property from consumers and, as a practical matter, no compensating transfer payments by monopolists to consumers are made. Condemnation of monopoly pricing can thus be justified as the only practical method of preventing monopolies from "unfairly" taking property that, in the view of Congress, belongs to consumers.

Even if a condemnation of monopolistic transfers from purchasers to producers does violate Pareto optimality, this violation would not undermine the thesis of this Article. Pareto optimality, on which the condemnation of allocative inefficiency is based, is itself a subjective standard which almost every modern economist is willing to accept. No member of Congress, however, when subjectively designing or voting for any antitrust law, was, or is, under any compunction to be held to the Pareto principle. Similarly, it may or may not be wise social policy to design antitrust laws to prevent certain transfers of wealth; the decision, however, belongs to Congress.

In summary, considerable controversy exists over the proper

treatment of monopolistic transfers of wealth. . . . Congress believed consumers were entitled to products priced at competitive levels and to the opportunity to buy the quantity of products a competitive market would offer. . . . [W]hen Congress passed the antitrust laws it condemned the use of market power to interfere with these property rights or entitlements out of an explicit antimonopolistic, proconsumer bias.

. . .

Congressional Goals

It is axiomatic that when the words of a statute are clear and unambiguous, courts need go no further in their interpretation of that law. Ambiguous, doubtful, or undefined words or phrases require interpretation, however, by reference to the statute's legislative history. Examination of a legislative history generally seeks determination of legislative intent regarding particular applications of the statute. The analysis often goes one step further in an attempt to determine what legislative intent "would have been" had Congress considered situations never actually contemplated.

The antitrust laws are among the least precise statutes enacted by Congress. The central terms, including "competition," "unfair methods of competition," "conspiracy in restraint of trade," and "monopolize," are inherently vague and not self-defining. One commentator has observed that antitrust legislation has, perhaps more than any other field, stimulated the courts to consider, as an interpretative aid, the history of the era that gave rise to the legislation.[6]

It is not possible to ascertain with certainty the original goals of the antitrust laws. Not only are there conflicting statements of legislative purpose, but it is often difficult to decide whether certain statements represent isolated, unimportant views or infrequently mentioned but nevertheless significant motivating factors. . . .

The Sherman Act

From the language of the Sherman Act, its legislative history, and the history of late nineteenth century America, it is clear Congress was concerned about those activities of trusts and monopolies that unduly restrained trade or caused a monopolization of interstate commerce. It is equally clear that with the Sherman Act " 'Congress was dealing with competition, which it sought to protect, and monopoly, which it sought to prevent.' "[7] These truisms do not, however, reveal why Congress passed the Sherman Act, or what goals it attempted to implement. If the goals of the antitrust laws are to be understood, the crucial issue is the explanation behind Congress' effort to protect competition.

. . . [T]he legislative history of the Sherman Act reveals a total lack of concern for allocative inefficiency. Trusts and monopolies were condemned principally because they "unfairly" extracted wealth from consumers. Productive efficiency also was an aim of the Act. Congress wanted the economy to function efficiently primarily to provide consumers the benefits of free competition. . . . [I]n balancing the competing considerations, Congress condemned firms with monopoly power despite their acknowledged efficiencies, and with the knowledge that this condemnation might not maximize society's economic efficiency. Indeed, the evidence suggests that Congress was unwilling to subordinate its distributive-based distaste for trusts and monopolists to the goal of corporate efficiency when the efficiency gains would be retained by the monopolist. . . . [T]he legislative history shows that Congress passed the Sherman Act because it believed that trusts and monopolies possess excessive social and political power, and reduce entrepreneurial liberty and opportunity.

Improving Economic Efficiency
. . .

Although modern economists often eschew economic value judgments, the 1890 Congress may have been more willing to make them. The legislative history of the Sherman Act indicates that Senator Sherman and other legislators condemned trusts for raising prices and restricting output, but no evidence has ever been found to suggest that any legislator understood that monopoly pricing causes allocative inefficiency. It is extremely unlikely that the legislators' distaste for monopoly pricing could have been based upon its impact on allocative efficiency: The concept of allocative efficiency was, at best, on the verge of discovery by leading economic theorists when the Sherman Act was passed.[8]

More importantly, leading economists of the day had very little influence on the passage of the Act.[9] It is unlikely, then, that the legislators who passed the early antitrust laws were aware that monopoly pricing led to allocative inefficiency. Nothing in the legislative history of the Sherman Act suggests that they were. No commentator has pointed to any economic testimony that referred to a concept resembling "allocative efficiency," nor is there the slightest evidence that any member of Congress was even remotely familiar with this type of welfare loss.

Given the state of economic theory at that time, the assertion that legislators supporting the Sherman Act were influenced by considerations involving allocative efficiency is without credibility. Congressional distaste for the pricing and output consequences of monopoly pricing must therefore be rooted in other concerns. These concerns include the distribution of wealth between consumers and producers and, secondarily, the maintenance of productive efficiency, preservation of economic opportunities for small enterprises, and the concentration of economic, social, and political power in a few hands.

Productive Efficiency

Although the legislative history of the Sherman Act never alludes to any concept resembling allocative efficiency, it does repeatedly praise corporate productive efficiency and recognize that free competition leads to efficient competitors. The productive efficiency of free competition was especially encouraged when gains were passed on to consumers. Nevertheless, there is little basis for suggesting that the Sherman Act was passed primarily to improve or even to preserve productive efficiency; indeed, the trusts were viewed as extremely efficient. Rather, Congress wanted to pass a law for other purposes which hampered productive efficiency as little as possible.

Many scholars have suggested that the trusts existing in 1890 were efficient at production.[10] Even their harshest critics admit this. Senator Sherman appreciated the efficiencies of large corporations generally:

> Experience has shown that they are the most useful agencies of modern civilization. They have enabled individuals to unite to undertake enterprises only attempted in former times by powerful governments.

The good results of corporate power are shown in the vast development
of our railroads and the enormous increase of business and production
of all kinds.[11]

But congressional endorsement of trusts' efficient operations
stopped when consumer prices rose, and the legislature withheld
approval from combinations that, while yielding more efficient
methods of competition, also produced higher consumer prices.
The trusts were condemned despite their efficiency in large part
because they kept the fruits of such efficiency. As Senator Sherman
pointed out in qualification of his praise for efficiency, "It is sometimes said of these combinations that they reduce prices to the
consumer by better methods of production, but all experience
shows that *this saving of cost goes to the pockets of the producer*."[12]
Congressional condemnation of monopolistic extractions of wealth
was so strong that it is even unlikely that Congress meant to provide
an exception for a monopoly based solely upon superior efficiency.

Although Congress was aware that trusts and monopolies raised
prices and restricted output, the legislators were unaware that this
caused allocative inefficiency. They thought that monopolies were
relatively efficient producers and that breaking them up could decrease productive efficiency. Yet, Congress enacted the Sherman
Act largely to prohibit and condemn them. Clearly, the chief economic concern was not productive efficiency; if Congress' main
goal was to encourage that form of industrial organization that
was, in 1890, most efficient, it would have praised the trusts, not
condemned them. Rather, the Sherman Act was intended to insure
that consumers obtained their "fair share" of the benefits of free
competition.

Protecting Consumers from Unfair Transfers of Wealth

In the legislative debates over the Sherman Act, Congress clearly
condemned the use of market power to raise prices and restrict
output. This condemnation, however, did not arise from concern
with allocative efficiency. The debates strongly suggest that Congress condemned trusts and monopolies because they had enough

market power to raise prices and "unfairly" extract wealth from consumers, turning it into monopoly profits.[13]

In the legislative debates, Congress discussed at length price increases by trusts and the resulting higher consumer prices. For example, Senator Sherman, defending the bill's constitutionality, asked that Congress protect the public from trusts that "restrain commerce, turn it from its natural course, increase the price of articles, and therefore diminish the amount of commerce.... "[14]

The debates strongly suggest that higher prices to consumers were condemned because they unfairly extracted wealth from consumers and turned it into monopoly profit. For example, during the debates Senator Sherman termed monopolistic overcharges "extortion which makes the people poor," and "extorted wealth."[15] Congressman Coke referred to the overcharges as "robbery."[16] Representative Heard declared that the trusts, "without rendering the slightest equivalent," have "stolen untold millions from the people."[17] Congressman Wilson complained that the beef trust "robs the farmer on the one hand and the consumer on the other."[18] Representative Fithian declared that the trusts were "impoverishing" the people through "robbery."[19] Senator Hoar declared that monopolistic pricing was "a transaction the direct purpose of which is to extort from the community . . . wealth which ought to be generally diffused over the whole community."[20] Senator George complained that "They aggregate to themselves great enormous wealth by extortion which makes the people poor."[21]

Congress condemned monopolistic overcharges in strong moral terms, rather than because of their efficiency effects. Purchasers, whether resellers or ultimate consumers, were entitled to purchase competitively priced products. Members of Congress also condemned the unequal distribution of wealth resulting from monopolistic overcharges. The legislators decided that competitive prices were "fair" whereas monopoly prices were not; therefore, consumers were entitled to own that quantity of wealth known today as "consumer surplus." The unfair prices, in effect, robbed consumers of that wealth. As a result, Congress was willing to risk some immediate efficiency losses in order to benefit consumers ultimately. Congress was willing to pass the Sherman Act in large part in an attempt to prevent such "unfair" transfers of wealth from consumers to monopolies.

Other Goals

CURBING THE SOCIAL AND POLITICAL POWER OF TRUSTS AND MONOPOLIES

Evidence also suggests that more than economic considerations motivated Congress to curb the power of trusts and monopolies. Although the concerns discussed thus far relate to the economic power of monopolies and trusts, Congress was also motivated by a desire to curb the social and political power of large businesses. This additional purpose is demonstrated by analyzing the history of the Sherman Act in light of the economic, social, and political context in which the law was passed.

The legislative history demonstrates that Congress condemned monopolies in part because they increased the cost of goods to consumers. Logic would seem to indicate that pressure from consumers burdened by higher prices contributed to the passage of the Sherman Act. This cannot be the complete explanation, however, because just prior to the passage of the Act, price levels in the United States were stable or slowly decreasing. In 1890, American consumers paid less for goods than at almost any time since the end of the Civil War.

Despite the then-recent rise of trusts, this phenomenon of falling prices is easily explained. The first trusts of any significance probably did not achieve their full power until a few years before passage of the Act. Although some trusts did raise prices in the years immediately before 1890, overall consumer prices decreased dramatically from the end of the Civil War until approximately 1884, when they leveled off. In addition, the last half of the nineteenth century witnessed a great industrial revolution; large-scale production, new technology, and increased production speed resulted in tremendous efficiencies. The industries that spawned some of the most notorious trusts also benefitted most from the new efficiencies. As a consequence, prices often fell despite the existence of the trusts.

Falling prices during this period in fact contributed to the formation of the trusts. Viewing falling prices and increased production with alarm, producers sought to arrest this trend by combining or entering agreements to stabilize or raise prices, restrict output, and suppress competition. This trend was only beginning, however, by 1890. Most large and significant trusts were formed or achieved full power after and in spite of the passage of the Sherman Act.

While prices might have fallen more rapidly had the trusts not attempted to halt their decline, it seems unlikely that consumers would strongly condemn the trusts only because prices were not dropping as rapidly as they should have been. It is possible that even though overall prices were stable or decreasing, Congress or the public could have focused their attention on those prices that were rising and concluded that trusts were, on the whole, causing higher prices. It is more likely that other factors were at work. Consumers probably were angered less by the reduction in their wealth than by the way in which the wealth was extracted.

The legislative history reveals that a major factor leading to the passage of the Sherman Act was a congressional desire to curb the power of trusts. While Congress was concerned about the uses of this power to raise prices and restrict output, it also desired, as an end in itself, the prevention of accumulation of power by large corporations and the men who controlled them. Alarm over corporate aggrandizement of economic, social, and political power pervaded the debate. The legislators feared not only the economic consequences of monopoly power, but potential social disruptions as well. Moreover, this apprehension has been recognized repeatedly by courts interpreting the legislative history of the Act.

A review of the social history of the period illuminates the reasons underlying Congress' alarm. The post-Civil War period saw a rural agricultural nation transformed into an increasingly urban and industrial society. Work patterns changed. By the end of the Civil War individual yeoman farmers had all but vanished. In their places stood entrepreneurs and commercial farmers who shipped their goods to markets and then used the resulting cash to purchase goods from small businesses. Thus, traditional independence gradually changed into interdependence.

With the rise of trusts, interdependence became impotence. Decisionmaking was transferred from traditional power centers to the great industrialists. Self-reliant farmers, business owners, and local leaders became dependent on the discretionary power of a few very rich men. Local control of society ended as numerous small power centers were swept away by the new class, one perceived as greedy and evil. This transfer of power generated hostility towards the trusts and resulted in political pressure on Congress to pass antitrust legislation.

The political and social evils of accumulated power, recited in the legislative debates and reiterated by the cases and historians, probably engendered more public resentment toward the trusts than did an isolated rise in prices during an era of stable and declining prices. The congressional complaint, therefore, was directed not solely at the effects of monopoly power—higher prices and poorer consumers—but also at the process that produced them. The Sherman Act was intended not only to achieve competitive prices but also to restructure the economy in ways ensuring a "fair" process for economic, social, and political decisionmaking by reducing the unfairly accumulated power of the trusts.

Protecting Small Businesses

Congress also expressed concern for preserving business opportunities for small firms. The opportunity to compete has been viewed as particularly important for small entrepreneurs, perhaps because of their vulnerability to predatory activities. Carrying this goal to its extreme, Representative Mason alone would have condemned trusts even if they lowered prices to consumers because they could financially ruin small businesses.

Judicial statements of congressional intention to assist small businesses have been frequent. Courts have even occasionally viewed congressional interest in protecting small businesses as overriding its consumer-oriented goals.

Despite clear judicial recognition, close examination reveals relatively little support in the legislative history, beyond the few references above, for the "small producer" rationale. Although there are a few statements suggesting that the protection of the opportunity of small business to compete was one motivating factor for the legislators, these statements do not imply that protection of small businesses was meant to override other goals. Congress probably did not intend to go further than establishment of an economic system providing free opportunities for entry and enough producers to ensure vigorous competition, a system in which no company became large enough to dominate.

Additionally, the congressional intent to assist small businesses can be interpreted as promoting distributive, rather than efficiency, considerations. Passage of the Sherman Act may have been intended, in part, to transfer wealth to small businesses. The legislative history does not indicate, however, that Congress intended to help small businesses as a means of improving the overall efficiency of the economy. The debate suggests only a possible intent to assist small businesses as an end in itself, not as a means of increasing total economic output.

Sympathetic to the plight of small businesses harmed by trusts, Congress expressed a desire to create an environment in which small businesses could effectively compete. It can fairly be said that one of Congress' goals was to assist small businesses; although consumers' interests were meant to be paramount, and conflicts between the welfare of consumers and small businesses were generally to be resolved in favor of consumers, Congress' desire to help small businesses certainly extended to those circumstances in which small businesses would be helped but consumers would not significantly suffer.... [T]his expression of sympathy did not amount to a congressional directive to assist small businesses in ways conflicting with the essential purpose of the Act, the protection of consumers.

Summary

Congress passed the Sherman Act to further a number of goals. Its main concern was with firms acquiring or possessing enough market power to raise prices artificially and to restrict output. Congress' primary aim was to enable consumers to purchase products at competitive prices. Artificially high prices were condemned not for causing allocative inefficiency but for "unfairly" transforming consumers' wealth into monopoly profits. All purchasers, whether consumers or businesses, were given the right to purchase competitively priced goods. All sellers were given the right to face rivals selling at competitive prices.

Concurrently, Congress was interested in encouraging efficient behavior in firms. Congress wanted a competitive economy to encourage the greater efficiencies resulting from competition. Efficiency gains were particularly desired when benefits passed through directly to consumers. A concern with productive efficiency could not, however, explain why Congress passed the Sherman Act. Congress condemned the relatively efficient trusts and monopolies for redistributive reasons. With the unlikely possibility of an exception for the "efficient monopolist," monopolizing conduct was not permitted merely because it produced efficiency gains for the monopolist.

The Act also involved efforts to decentralize economic, social, and political decisionmaking to ensure that narrow private interests would be unable to override the public good flowing from free competition. The corporate power that the free market inadequately curbed was the target of the Act. Thus, the Act was also aimed at curbing the social and political power of large corporations and at encouraging opportunities for small entrepreneurs to compete, both thought to flow from the desired economic order as expressed in the Act.

The Sherman Act, the first antitrust law, set the tone for future antitrust legislation. Subsequent antitrust laws represented either extensions of the same ideas to different economic arenas, or attempts to better implement the same fundamental principles.

The Sherman Act and The Balance of Power

DAVID MILLON

> I have not learned the doctrine that cheapness is the only thing in the
> world we are to go for. I do not believe that the great object of life is
> to make everything cheap.[1]

Most Americans accept the economic and political power of big
business as a natural, inevitable feature of life in what they would
describe as a free society. We have trouble imagining desirable
alternative forms of economic organization because significant re-
structuring is assumed to involve unacceptable public intrusion on
personal liberty. These assumptions about naturalness, inevitability, and freedom confer legitimacy on the position of big business
in American society, so that criticism of economic concentration
is erratic and eccentric.

Americans have not always shared this complacent attitude or
subscribed to the ideology that legitimated it. Instead, Americans
once believed that large concentrations of privately controlled economic power were dangerous and viewed them with suspicion and
hostility. Not only did these great creatures threaten to deprive
ambitious, hard working citizens of the opportunity for prosperity,
but democracy itself could not survive their corrupting influence.

Reprinted from 61 S. Cal. L. Rev., 1219–92 (1988). Reprinted with the permission
of the Southern California Law Review.

Economic power meant political power, and plutocracy meant the end of government for all the people.

These ideas found expression during the eighteenth century among English and then American opponents of the British monarchy. They were part of our revolutionary heritage and continued to inform political, economic, and legal thought during the nineteenth century. At the core was an ideology that emphasized decentralized, balanced economic power. Only if wealth were dispersed could Americans be secure from the capture and abuse of governmental power by selfish factions.

The importance of balanced economic power required that government must refuse participation in efforts to create monopoly power. Further, where government sought to promote economic opportunity, its efforts must benefit all citizens indiscriminately. As long as government avoided favoritism, America's seemingly unlimited abundance appeared simultaneously to guarantee material success for those who deserved it and to deny anyone the ability to establish a permanently entrenched position of wealth. Preservation and promotion of competitive opportunity would ensure a balance of economic power, and thus protect society from monopoly and its incidental social and political evils.

Opposition to monopoly power and faith in the efficacy of competition to prevent it shaped political and economic theory as well as public policy until the last years of the nineteenth century. . . . [T]he Sherman Act of 1890 was a final effort on behalf of this long-standing, deeply rooted ideology. The statute's two succinct, unequivocal sections were the dying words of a tradition that aimed to control political power through decentralization of economic power, which in turn was to be achieved through protection of competitive opportunity. This legislation ignored the question of potential efficiencies to be gained through concentrated production. The abiding strength of the traditional ideology would have rendered such claims irrelevant.

By 1890, the magnitude of the wealth concentrated in the great trusts far exceeded what anyone could have imagined a hundred years earlier. Just as Congress was passing the Sherman Act, defenders of this new order were beginning to devise social, economic, and legal theories asserting its legitimacy. One element of this effort was the claim that large-scale concentration was the inevitable consequence of a "free" market. This "fact" was then taken to establish the legitimacy of big business and the illegitimacy of governmental intervention. The noninterventionist argument scored its greatest victory as early as 1911, when the United States Supreme Court announced an unprecedented distinction between reasonable and unreasonable monopoly.[2] Courts have since applied the so-called Rule of Reason in several areas, with economic ideas supplying the content of reasonableness. The result has been constriction of the Sherman Act's broad proscriptions. . . .

Economic theory has thus played a key role in support of a "hands-off" antitrust policy. The so-called "Chicago School"[3] has led the way in this campaign, using microeconomic analysis and the concept of economic efficiency in support of its policy views.[4] According to these views, the purpose of antitrust law should be the maximization of aggregate consumer welfare, defined as optimal satisfaction of consumer preferences. Courts should not apply the law's proscriptions unless the challenged conduct harms consumer welfare thus defined. Where concentrated production yields efficiencies that on balance exceed welfare loss caused by absence of competition, courts should not intervene.

The argument has two interconnected elements. The first purports to define the conditions under which maximization of consumer welfare will occur and asserts that maximization is a desirable policy goal. The second element emphasizes that maximization can only occur if antitrust law is interpreted and applied without regard for other values that conflict with the efficiency norm. These might include concerns about the impact of concentrated production on other would-be participants in the market, or the effect of concentrated economic power on the political process.

. . .

. . . [T]he language of the Sherman Act meant something far different to those who approved it than it does under [economic efficiency] analysis.[5] Congress reacted to a particular problem: pervasive public outrage over the great trusts, and popular demand for the restoration of a balance of economic power in American society.

Congress and the American public viewed the great trusts in light of a traditional conception of the connection between individual liberty and economic organization. Liberty was the freedom to pursue one's self-defined goals to the greatest extent consistent with the liberty of others. Trusts threatened this liberty in two ways. First, they possessed the economic power to exclude people from opportunities to seek material success through competition in the market. Second, the trusts' immense wealth provided the ability to corrupt the legislative process so as to benefit their owners at the expense of the rest of society. Liberty therefore depended on the decentralization of economic power; the possibility that concentration may have been more efficient in some circumstances could not justify its evils. It is within this ideological context that we must seek the meaning of the legislators' statements and the statutory language.

1. The Concentration Crisis

Economic growth in the United States accelerated dramatically after the Civil War. Technological innovation, the growth of national transportation and communications systems, population expansion, and legal developments all contributed to a massive increase in industrial productivity. Business enterprises of unprecedented size grew through horizontal and vertical combination. The railroads were the first of these huge consolidations, followed by processing and distribution firms, and then by massive integrated manufacturing enterprises. By 1890, great "trusts" dominated the petroleum, cottonseed oil, linseed oil, sugar, whiskey, and lead processing industries. . . .

. . .

The advent of big business on this massive scale was a traumatic event. "[T]he old gentry, the merchants of long standing, the small manufacturers, the established professional men, the civic leaders of an earlier era" saw themselves deprived of economic power, opportunity, personal independence, and social status.[6] This urban middle class, the backbone of the progressive reform movement, was profoundly antagonistic to big business,[7] and no one complained more bitterly than the owners of small businesses.[8] Agrarian populism also identified big business, particularly the great railroad combinations, with the farmer's increasingly tenuous control over his livelihood.[9] Labor sought strength in collective organization to protect itself from the power of massed capital.[10] Thus, a broad spectrum of American society complained bitterly about the evil powers of the trusts. Monopoly had "always meant some sort of unjustified power, especially one that raised obstacles to equality of opportunity. The trust was popularly regarded as nothing but a new form of monopoly, and the whole force of the tradition was focused against it immediately."[11]

Antimonopoly sentiment grew out of concerns far more profound than the perceived impact on individual fortune. The trusts' enormous wealth and economic dominance presented the specter of uncontrollable, selfishly exercised power, immune from regulation by the market or the modest powers of government.... Huge concentrations of wealth represented the rise of "a great, unscrupulous, powerful plutocracy."[12]... The growth of monopolies threatened the vitality of democracy itself:

> Modern Feudalism is most apparent in the erection of great and irresponsible rulers of industry, whose power, like that of the feudal barons, burdens the people, and even overshadows the government which gave it existence. The only important distinction is, that in the old days of force, the power of feudalism was measured by the thousands of warriors; in the days of modern plutocracy, its power is measured by millions of dollars.[13]

Clearly, there was more at stake than destruction of individual economic opportunity. Americans judged these menacing developments against a traditional vision of America as a democratic republic of independent producers and property owners and decentralized political and economic power. The rise of the great monopolies decisively upset the balance of economic power on which a true democratic republic depends.

. . .

... [S]tatements regarding the importance of competition are significant not only because of concerns about impact on consumers, but also because they reveal Congress' belief in the importance of competitive opportunity and decentralized economic power. There is no reason to believe that Congress would have preferred a single efficient monopolist to several less efficient smaller businesses. Indeed, there is express evidence in the legislative history to the contrary. Nor do statements about promotion of competition or enhanced consumer prices necessarily demonstrate that efficiency was the Sherman Act's sole concern. The record contains statements expressly rejecting the view that low consumer prices were the statute's primary goal.

. . .

3. The Political Theory of Balanced Power

To Americans during the later nineteenth century, the meaning of the concentration crisis depended on a deeply rooted ideology that was obsessed with the destructive potential of political and economic power. In particular, this tradition warned Americans of government's susceptibility to the corrupting forces of concentrated wealth. Selfish plutocracy was not the only fear; excessive disparities of wealth might also lead to mob rule and governmental redistribution. Protection from the uses of governmental power for sectarian purposes rather than public purposes required a balance among the various private interests at large in society. Emphasizing the connection between the social environment and the legitimacy of the political process, Americans relied on a vision of atomized, kinetic economic activity as the guarantor of this balance of power. Atomization did not connote rigidly equal distribution of wealth. However, it did assume that at any given time the gap between rich and poor would have to be relatively narrow. Furthermore, economic opportunity would make all disparities only temporary; mobility would prevent the creation of entrenched concentration or of a permanent underclass.

This ideology grew originally out of liberal political theory, modified by classical republican ideas articulated in England and then America during the eighteenth century. This theory provided the intellectual basis for the American Revolution and for the constitutions of the new state and federal governments. It also shaped public policy and legal doctrine respecting monopoly power and defined the relationship between government and economy throughout the nineteenth century.

A. Liberalism and the Control of Power

Classical liberal political theory's primary contribution to the ideology that informed the Sherman Act was a profound sense of the coercive threat to others inherent in the possession of power. This idea was based ultimately on a particular vision of human psychology.

Liberal theory conceived of personal welfare as entirely self-defined but essentially materialistic owing to human nature's basic acquisitive impulses. Liberty therefore required individual freedom to pursue these material goals. At the same time, however, liberty depended upon protection from coercion by others motivated by their own pursuits of self-interest. Government was therefore necessary to protect the individual's personal security and property interests from the ceaseless aggressions of fellow citizens, while nevertheless allowing all persons to realize their legitimate ambitions in an orderly manner.

The market was the appropriate arena for the individual's pursuit of acquisitive goals. The medium of freedom of exchange would allow the pursuit of these goals to the fullest extent consistent with the liberty of each other member of society. All voluntary transactions were legitimate and enforceable by the state. A system of legal rules distinguished between enforceable transactions, on the one hand, and illegitimate coercion and interference with personal security and property interests on the other.

Defining government's proper functions was not the only problem. The very existence of governmental power presented the danger that selfish elements might capture the state machinery and use it to promote their private goals. Because of the central importance of property, the greatest threat of all was the coercive redistribution of wealth for the benefit of some faction. Therefore, governmental power had to be sharply limited so as to eliminate opportunities to seize one person's wealth in order to bestow a benefit on someone else.

Strictly limiting governmental power to appropriate functions would result in greater general welfare as well as individual liberty. Through the operation of natural laws, the sum of each individual's orderly pursuit of self-interest would yield the greatest benefits to all of society, as if "led by an invisible hand."[14] The nation would achieve maximal wealth and a natural harmony of interests among all members of society would result.

B. *Republicanism and the Balance of Power*

American political theorists of the late eighteenth century took for granted the liberal preoccupation with the control of power. Recently, however, scholars have rediscovered the importance of another set of ideas, which were adapted from classical republican political theory. This political tradition was at odds with liberalism in certain important respects. In particular, while liberal theory tended to emphasize natural processes and governmental nonintervention as the source of general welfare, republicanism stressed government's role in the definition and promotion of the common good. Republicanism also conceived of human personality as essentially civic minded rather than selfish.

The essence of republican government was its dedication to the welfare of all citizens. The common good was more than merely the outcome of private pursuit of self-interest. While republican theorists emphasized the importance of governmental structure in achieving this goal, they also stressed the relationship between social environment and effective governance. Their fundamental concern was the idea of civic virtue—the citizenry's willingness and ability to place the good of the commonwealth before competing selfish objectives. Only if society were made up of citizens exercising this quality could government function in the interests of all and thereby promote general welfare.

. . .

Once freed from British tyranny, Americans confronted the problem of designing a form of government that would avoid the dangers of corruption and protect individual liberty from human nature's inevitable lust for power and self-aggrandizement. Power within government must be divided and subject to an effective system of internal checks and balances. However, Great Britain's recent decline into corruption demonstrated that a constitutional structure alone was not sufficient to guarantee a government dedicated to the common welfare. Past republican policies had avoided monarchical despotism or the anarchy of pure democracy by investing a broadly defined but socially responsible electorate with ultimate political authority. Because the American republic was believed to be grounded on democratic participation, its success depended ultimately on the virtuous character of its citizenry.

Republican theorists emphasized property ownership as the precondition for civic virtue. Only an electorate composed of independent, self-sufficient real property owners would be willing and able to pursue the public good. Those who worked for others were, to that extent, dependent upon them and, lacking independence, would have no choice but to support those upon whom they depended for survival. This is the meaning of Jefferson's well known paean to the virtues of agrarian independence:

> [W]e have an immensity of land courting the industry of the husbandman. Is it best then that all our citizens should be employed in its improvement, or that one half should be called off from that to exercise manufactures and handicraft arts for the other? Those who labour in the earth are the chosen people . . . [in] whose breasts he has made his peculiar deposit for substantial and genuine virtue. . . . Dependence begets subservience and venality, suffocates the germ of virtue, and prepares fit tools for the designs of ambition. . . . It is the manners and spirit of a people which preserve a republic in vigour. A degeneracy in these is a canker which soon eats to the heart of its laws and constitution.[15]

A nation composed of sturdy yeoman farmers would possess the independence necessary for civic virtue, while remaining immune to the corrupting influences of greed and luxury.

The broad distribution of property would not by itself guarantee the republic's future. Extreme differences in wealth would endanger its survival. An impoverished majority might obtain legislation to benefit itself at the expense of property owners. Alternatively, an aristocracy of wealth would possess the resources to capture and subvert governmental power to its own selfish goals. A large fortune would discourage the willingness to subordinate private interests to general welfare. Significant disparities of wealth and the resulting differences in social class would generate disagreements about goals as well as occasions for selfish factionalism. Unless the electorate was reasonably homogeneous, this clash of differing interests would impede the government's pursuit of the common good.

. . .

Had republican ideology insisted on independent agrarianism as the basis for civic virtue, it would have failed to accommodate the increasingly commercial, capitalist nature of the American economy. The robust expansion of commercial opportunities during the early years of the nineteenth century saw a subtle but crucially important shift in focus. Americans increasingly came to appreciate that a virtuous republic might be grounded on commercial activity, even including wage labor.

The key to this development was the rejection of the identification of commerce with dependency. While personal advancement might require an individual to work for another for a period of time, thrift and industry in the pursuit of the seemingly boundless opportunities offered by the American market would ensure the achievement of independence. The absence of a legally privileged hereditary aristocracy possessing entrenched, unassailable wealth and influence, allowed individual initiative to prevent a replication of the old world's static hierarchies of dependency. Engaged assiduously in the pursuit of wealth, the American worker's abundant prospects for success provided a self-interested stake in the public's interest in security of property. Equality of opportunity therefore replaced broadly egalitarian distribution of land as a sufficient condition for individual economic independence and civic virtue.

Commercial opportunity meant more than just personal independence. Equally important, it guaranteed a balance of economic power in society. As it had in the context of egalitarian land distribution, the emphasis on balance addressed fears about seizure of governmental power by a wealthy minority or an impoverished majority. Opportunity generated mobility and mobility in turn prevented lasting accumulations of massive wealth or establishment of a permanent underclass. Furthermore, this opportunity ensured that the gap between rich and humble would remain relatively narrow. . . .

Opportunity created atomization rather than concentration, and fluidity rather than entrenchment. A vision of limitless economic potential seemed to guarantee both personal independence and social balance. Classical economic theorists described the natural

laws that governed this inexorable process. Thus, Jefferson's austere republicanism embraced Adam Smith's optimistic capitalism.

The great appeal of this vision of balanced power was the perception that it was firmly grounded in social reality. The continuing
multiplication of commercial opportunities fueled faith in the lev-
elling power of the market. Americans noted the absence of significant inequality of fortune. De Tocqueville was also struck by
the general equality of condition. . . . As de Tocqueville observed,
"[w]ealth circulates with inconceivable rapidity, and experience
shows that it is rare to find two succeeding generations in the full
enjoyment of it." As Americans around the turn of the nineteenth
century revised their thinking about the conditions necessary for
economic balance, social reality seemed to confirm the strength of
their vision of balance maintained through opportunity.

C. The Legacy of Republicanism
. . .

There are two clearly identifiable historical points at which
Americans chose to compromise republican principles in favor of
ideas that might be characterized as liberal. The first was the
triumph of the Federalists over the Anti-Federalists following the
controversy over ratification of the United States Constitution.
This dispute centered on the structure and processes of government, particularly the significance of direct self-government and
active citizen participation. Pessimism over the inability or unwillingness of the commoner to subordinate self-interest to general
welfare and related fears of "mob tyranny" led the Federalists to
reject a republican vision of true participation. The Federalists
instead advocated a broadly based electoral process designed to
mediate conflicting private preferences through the mechanism of
representation.

The second occasion was the victory of the Jeffersonian Republicans over the Federalists in the election of 1800. Here the issue
was not the structure of government, but its role in American
society. The choice was between a republican conception of government actively engaged in and responsible for promotion of the
common good, and a minimalist state that could best promote
social welfare by interfering as little as possible with private activ-

ity. The Jeffersonian "Revolution" signalled a repudiation of the republican ideal of an active, affirmative state. In Jefferson's words, good government was "a wise and frugal government, which shall restrain men from injuring one another, which shall leave them otherwise free to regulate their own pursuits of industry and improvement, and shall not take from the mouth of labor the bread it has earned."

Despite the apparent triumph of liberalism, republican ideas about the crucial importance of balanced economic power survived and indeed flourished during the nineteenth century. Three important aspects of republican theory that provided key elements of the ideology that eventually shaped the Sherman Act deserve emphasis. First was the persistent emphasis on the subversive effects of great wealth on the political process. Economic power meant political power because wealth provided the means to create dependence and thereby collect political influence. Across the nineteenth century, recurrent denunciations of plutocracy echoed the republican distinction between the common good and purely factional interest. They assumed that the clash of private interests would not sufficiently protect the public interest where private power was significantly unbalanced. Furthermore, extreme imbalance generated dependence, which likewise threatened the legitimacy of the political process.

Second, if Americans continued to identify excessive wealth as politically subversive, republican theory continued to offer the remedy. A balance among fragmented sources of power would prevent any element from achieving dominance. Balance through separation was the primary constitutional mechanism for control of governmental power and the prevention of, in Madison's words, "tyrannical concentration." The survival of this model was one of republican political science's legacies. This structural solution to the problem of oppression through concentrated power extended beyond the internal workings of government to provide a vision for the control of economic power in society. Coupled with relentless social mobility, atomization would assure balanced economic power. Eventually, of course, reliance on private economic activity to control political power yielded grotesque disparities of wealth and power, and Americans later found ways to assure themselves that balance was unimportant. Nevertheless, the republican commitment to balanced economic power lasted through the nineteenth century and provided a basic component of the thinking that went into the Sherman Act.

The third republican survival was the use of governmental power affirmatively to promote social welfare, particulary through expansion of economic opportunities and regulation of concentrated economic power. These policies, pursued throughout the nineteenth century in the contexts described below, continued to take for granted the republicans' insistence on balanced economic power as the key to control of governmental power, as well as their commitment to the use of government to achieve that result. The Sherman Act was part of this tradition.

4. The Balance of Power and Public Policy

The fundamental political importance of balanced economic power and the commitment to preservation of opportunity as the means for its achievement were republicanism's contribution to the ideology of the Sherman Act. Liberal economic thought taught that natural processes tended to produce balanced economic power, while liberal political theory cautioned against affirmative exercise of governmental power in any event. These ideas provided objections to redistributive policies intended to level differences in wealth. They did not, however, preclude uses of governmental power in situations less threatening to individual property interests. Faithful to their republican heritage, nineteenth century governments never pursued rigidly laissez-faire economic policies. For example, President Jefferson, despite his commitment to minimal government, approved the use of public funds for the Louisiana Purchase in order to provide free land "for our descendants to the hundredth and thousandth generation." Governmental interference in the market presumptively tended to generate suspicion, but state governments implemented a wide range of policies intended to expand the range of individual economic opportunity through the removal of barriers to productive activity. Government also dismantled or regulated significant concentrations that threatened to upset the balance of economic and political power. Atomization through facilitation of competitive opportunity would ensure "dispersion of the powers of decision in the community" and prevent any individual or group from attaining lasting dominance. As government pursued these goals, political discourse and judicial opinions routinely justified policy in the ideological language of balanced economic power. The willingness to use governmental power to guard against the political evils of economic concentration is a consistent theme in nineteenth century public policy.

A. Government Franchised Monopoly

The original legal definition of a monopoly was a state grant of an exclusive right to pursue a particular trade. In nineteenth century America, government sponsorship of monopolistic privilege continued to be the clearest instance of abuse of power for the benefit of private rather than public interest. Several states included antimonopoly provisions in their constitutions, and efforts were also made to include such a provision in the federal Constitution or Bill of Rights. Legislation establishing a monopoly was illegitimate because it concentrated economic power in a favored person or group and then granted immunity from competitive pressures. Those who would otherwise have entered that market were denied the opportunity to do so. Accordingly, destruction of the Charles River Bridge monopoly removed a barrier to entrepreneurial activity. In such situations law served "to enlarge the range of options open to private individuals and groups."

. . .

[Court] opinions stressed the individual's right to unrestricted opportunity and the illegitimacy of governmental action denying this right. In this respect, these decisions echoed traditional English common law rhetoric. Among the offensive aspects of monopoly . . . was the belief that, all trades being "profitable for the commonwealth," monopolistic grants violated "the benefit and liberty of the subject." . . .

Not only was publicly created monopoly a denial of individual opportunity. By upsetting the balance of economic power, monopoly threatened the integrity of the political process. These concerns emerged clearly in Andrew Jackson's campaign against the second Bank of the United States—the most celebrated attack on government franchised monopoly. . . .

It was not government's responsibility to ensure material equality through redistribution, but, if unrestricted by governmental favoritism of special interests, opportunities for economic success were so abundantly available that all who were willing to apply themselves might achieve material prosperity. Under these circumstances, private efforts to achieve monopoly power were doomed. Government must therefore remain vigilant against efforts to obtain monopoly through grants of special privileges. As long as it did so, a balance of economic power was assured.

B. *Promotion of Economic Opportunity*

State governments actively promoted transportation enterprises deemed necessary to remove impediments to individual productive capacity. Such undertakings were defensible only if they would benefit the public generally—government efforts on behalf of some special group were illegitimate.

. . . Besides outright subsidization, state and local governments provided tax abatements, debt guarantees, and public subscriptions to stock issues. The federal government played a similar role through its land grant and postal subsidy programs.

Probably of greatest importance in the promotion of transportation was the widespread state delegation of eminent domain powers. Here the states in effect forced sales of privately owned property at prices determined by publicly administered appraisal procedures. State courts and legislatures sought to control the potentially harsh effects of eminent domain delegations on individual landowners. The public purpose requirement limited exercise of eminent domain powers to transportation projects undertaken for a public purpose rather than for purely private benefit. Meanwhile, those individuals whose property was taken would not bear the costs of the public benefit alone, but would instead receive just compensation from the state. While seeking to promote the general welfare, states might not unjustly impose the costs on certain individuals by denying compensation for damage to property resulting from exercise of eminent domain powers where the result was to destroy its economic value. Thus, delegation of eminent domain powers represented efforts to expand economic opportunities for all through improved transportation, while recognizing the importance of spreading the burdens as well as the benefits among all members of the community.

Governmental efforts to expand economic opportunity prompted concerns that the actors might be seeking only to benefit some special interest group. For example, critics of governmental corruption and corporate power in the early nineteenth century repeatedly argued that entrepreneurs bribed legislators to obtain the advantages conferred by special incorporation acts. The potential for corruption that seemed inherent in the requirement of a special act led some extremists to conclude that all corporations were products of illicit alliances between government and private interests, and to urge their elimination. Nevertheless, promoters sought increasingly to organize their businesses as corporations rather than partnerships, and public opinion came to view the corporation as a useful vehicle for capital accumulation and encouragement of productive risk taking through limitation of liability.

Rather than responding to charges of favoritism by limiting special chartering, states instead passed general incorporation statutes. Their purpose was to make the advantages of incorporation readily available to all who desired them by removing the requirement of a special legislative act.

. . . By 1870, general incorporation laws had begun to supplant special chartering in most states, and the corporation soon became the common vehicle for many business ventures. The general incorporation movement thus sought to eliminate potential government corruption through removal of legislative discretion over grants of corporate status. These statutes facilitated opportunity for competitors in order to address concerns about concentrated economic power. As with state franchised monopoly, promotion of economic opportunity required sensitivity to the maintenance of balanced economic power.

C. Regulation of Monopoly Power

Where government created a monopoly, competition would be prevented by law. Such legislation would upset the balance of power by rendering the monopolist's power immune from competitive challenge, and therefore was illegitimate. In contrast, if unprotected by law, economic power was subject to competition and could only be short lived. However, the nature of the industry might render an enterprise immune from competition—a de facto monopoly. The monopolist's economic power would enable it to exert a corrupting influence on the governmental process, and it would possess the same dictatorial powers over workers, suppliers, and consumers as would a legally protected monopoly. Public regulation of such monopolies resulted from an appreciation of the threat they posed to the balance of power.

In addition to chartering corporations involved in manufacturing and other enterprises in which competition was feasible and desirable, states chartered corporations in industries in which opportunities were inherently limited, such as transportation, water supply, insurance, and banking. The states did not confer de jure monopoly status on these businesses. The charters rarely granted explicit monopolistic privileges, and courts refused to find a right to monopoly by implication. Nevertheless, the concerns about the danger of monopolistic abuse were often present because these were essential services, and control over transportation and finance represented possession of great and ominous power over the community. Since competitive opportunities were inherently limited, facilitation of competition was not a suitable means of controlling this power. Instead, these corporations generally were singled out for regulation to protect the public interest.

During the special charter period, transportation company charters typically required fair and reasonable rates within certain ranges, while banking and insurance charters included analogous provisions. By 1850, states turned to statutory commissions for railroad regulation. In 1869, Massachusetts established a commission with broad supervisory powers over rates and also over each firm's "mode of operating its road and conducting its business." In response to farmers' and small merchants' outcries over extortionate practices, several midwestern states during the 1870s passed Granger laws creating even broader regulatory powers. For example, the Illinois legislature decreed maximum railroad rates, and also provided for rate regulation of grain warehouses and elevators.

These actions reveal clearly that even in those few special situations where monopoly appeared to be "natural" and therefore unavoidable, its power was sufficiently threatening to require protection of the public interest through governmental action. Regulation served the dual purpose of protecting the public from extortionate pricing and limiting the monopolist's ability to acquire excessive wealth that might have been used for illegitimate political influence.

D. Private Efforts to Create Monopoly Power

Private attempts to eliminate competition were no more legitimate than governmental action. Common law doctrine refused to sanction such private conduct, even where there was no legal or practical immunity from competitive pressures. The legal responses to these efforts underscore the preoccupation with concentration of economic power, and the belief in government's responsibility to police the balance of power.

Individual efforts to eliminate competition could be ignored because they were believed not to possess monopolistic potential. For much of the nineteenth century, agriculture and business continued to be conducted on a relatively small scale. As long as there were no legal barriers to competition and the industry was not somehow inherently monopolistic, there was no reason to believe that an individual could achieve a position of entrenched monopoly power.

Concerted private action, however, might pose a greater threat. Two or more competitors might agree among themselves to suppress competition and thereby create monopoly in a market in which there had previously been rivalry. Again, it was unlikely that they could achieve a lasting monopoly. Nevertheless, the danger of such power, even if relatively short lived, was greater than that posed by the individual actor. Accordingly, courts refused to lend their assistance to such schemes by declining to enforce cartel and other agreements in restraint of trade.

Cases concerning agreements in restraint of trade presented an apparent conflict between the individuals' presumptive right to freedom of contract and the public's interest in protection from the threat of uncontrolled economic power. The governing principle was that such agreements were unenforceable if the resulting combination tended to create monopoly power. In other words, courts subordinated the individual "right" to contract to the public interest. Even though subject to competitive pressures, such agreements offended the public policy against creation of significant concentrations of unregulated economic power.

. . .

The results in [the cases] depended on the courts' perception of the extent of the threat to the public posed by the cartel arrangement. Restraints on competition were acceptable as long as they were loose enough to preclude extortionate behavior in the short term, but American courts drew the line at agreements characterized as having a tendency monopolistically to suppress competition.

Decisions about covenants in restraint of trade reflect similar solutions to the problem of protecting the public from monopoly power. Courts were willing to enforce limited promises not to compete where the promises were incident to sales of business assets. Some courts justified their holdings through denial of any monopolistic potential. A single individual's promise not to compete with another generally would not establish monopoly power in the way that a restrictive agreement among all competitors would. In other decisions, the emphasis was on the parties' purpose. If the restrictive covenant was only ancillary to an otherwise legitimate transaction, such as a sale of a business or secret process, then it would be enforced even though potential competition would be lessened. Restriction on the seller's activity was justified by the public's legitimate interest in the transferability of such property, which might require protection for the buyer; also, in the typical case, there was no reduction in actual competition. American courts were careful, however, to proscribe restrictive covenants that were monopolistic.

Common law doctrine governing monopolistic agreements was limited to the question of their enforceability against the parties to the contract. Those claiming to have been injured by such agreements were denied judicial relief. After the Civil War, several states enacted regulatory solutions that addressed the problem directly. Seeking more vigorously to control monopoly power, these states included monopolistic cartels within their regulatory schemes. . . . There was evidently no efficiency argument to be made, and in any event, the relevant point was that monopoly power, however created and regardless of efficiency, was dangerous and had to be controlled.

Suppression of competition through merger rather than cartel presented the same monopolistic potential. However, because the public policy issue typically arose only in cases of attempts to enforce contractual undertakings, a wholly executed contract— like a consummated merger—generally would not come under judicial scrutiny. Responding to increasing merger activity in the years just prior to passage of the Sherman Act, several states began prosecuting corporations that entered into monopolistic mergers. These cases responded to fear of the dangers of privately created monopoly power and the public's interest in its control, and paralleled Congress' response to the same problem through passage of the Sherman Act. The specific legal basis for these prosecutions was the states' regulatory authority over their chartered corporations. The goal was to prevent concentration of economic power by invalidating participation in monopolistic trusts or partnerships. As creatures of state government, corporations existed for the good of the public. Private agreements to facilitate monopoly power by restraining the corporation from continuing to act as an individual entity violated the corporation's responsibility to the public. Other decisions held that participation in a monopolistic trust was an *ultra vires* act warranting forfeiture of the corporate charter.

Judicial opinions in monopoly cases typically focused on the immediate issue of economic harm to the community.

. . . The vitality of republican government itself depended on correction of such imbalances of economic power.

Acting through judicial application of common law rules denying the enforceability of monopolistic agreements, direct regulation of the power of monopolistic cartels, and attacks on monopolistic mergers, the states recognized clearly their obligation to preserve the balance of power. Concerns about efficiency never tempered this commitment. As with the preceding public policy contexts in which the monopoly problem was presented, there was no suggestion that anything akin to . . . consumer welfare theory could legitimate monopolistic concentration.

5. The Monopoly Problem in Economic Theory

The most important contributions of economic doctrine to the ideology behind the Sherman Act were the theories of the inevitably harmful nature of monopoly and the efficacy of competition to preserve a balance of economic power. As late as 1890, conventional American economists continued to write in the classical tradition about the social evils of monopoly power. The economists' main focus was on economic injury to individuals, as would-be rivals were excluded from competitive opportunities and as consumers were forced to pay extortionate prices. This emphasis complemented political theory's focus on the significance of balanced power as the guarantor of legitimate governmental activity.

Conventional learning also emphasized the "artificial" character of trusts. They were the products of deliberate conduct, either by government or by private parties, that subverted the competitive process and resulted in concentrated economic power otherwise unattainable. This analysis encouraged belief in the efficacy of opportunity and mobility as checks on concentration. It also legitimated use of governmental power to prevent private efforts to achieve consolidation since it suggested that law might reverse developments that were not the inevitable result of "natural" processes. Around 1890, a new generation of economists began to rethink the trust problem and concluded that the trusts might in certain respects be natural rather than artificial. Nevertheless, these theorists continued to insist upon the illegitimacy of uncontrolled monopoly power.

A. Classical Theory

1. THE EVILS OF MONOPOLY

According to classical liberal economic theory, competition preserved the balance of economic power in society. It prevented any individual from attaining a position from which he or she could dictate the terms of exchange—that is, coerce a reluctant buyer or seller. This was so because there would always be rivals eager to make a profit by offering to trade on competitive terms. Competition thus checked private power and guaranteed personal autonomy. A competitive market also provided freedom for all individuals to use their resources according to their own calculations of value. No person had a prior claim of right to exclude others from pursuing their goals in the market. No person could force others to enter into a transaction against their will.

Virtually all American economists in 1890 continued to advocate the classical view of the wrongfulness of monopoly and the benefits of competition. Monopoly represented denial of opportunity. It was thought typically to result from predatory activities aimed against would-be competitors. For example, the giant trusts were accused of having gained their power by using localized price discrimination to compel rivals to join the combination or face destruction. Denial of economic opportunity was "a monstrous crime against public trade and against individual right."

Economists also stressed the inevitably harmful effects of monopoly power on consumer prices and product quality. . . . Thus even superior efficiency could not have justified monopoly, because there was nothing to prevent the monopolist from abusing its power and appropriating to itself all of efficiency's benefits.

2. CAUSES AND CURES

According to classical theory, monopoly would always be elusive if the state allowed natural processes to operate freely. Any successfully exploited advantage would attract self-interested competitors eager for a share of the profits. Only governmental interference (or certain unique situations of naturally limited opportunity) could present effective barriers within which the monopolist could build an empire. Monopoly could not result solely from internal expansion through superior productive efficiency.

. . .

[T]he classical model did not consider whether market imperfections such as disparities in access to technology, capital, labor, or materials, might prevent competition with larger, established firms. . . . Some of the American classicists did discuss how economies of scale might allow some larger producers to compete more effectively than smaller ones. . . .

Despite such views, these theorists never suggested that there may be situations in which greater efficiency through increasing scale might result in monopoly. It was a standard assumption that very large firms could never be as efficient as moderately sized ones. . . .

Furthermore, the process of competition would itself prevent any firm from achieving a position of entrenched market power. The influential English economist Alfred Marshall, whose *Principles of Economics* first appeared in 1890, described a cyclical process of ongoing growth and decay among competing firms of modest size:

> On the whole then the small [manufacturing] factory can seldom compete on equal terms with a larger establishment which is organized on the ideally best plan. But as a rule a large business is itself only the development of a smaller one which has prospered under good management: after a time the management becomes incompetent, or for some other reason the business is broken up; and again the cycle is renewed by other small businesses pushing their way upwards.[16]

The vision is of constant mobility and fluctuation rather than static, entrenched power.

If very large firms were inherently inefficient and subject to inexorable erosion by competition, some explanation was needed for the rise and apparent success of the great trusts. American classicists addressed this problem through elaboration of the "natural" and "artificial" monopoly theories. The former would arise under circumstances that inhibited the simultaneous existence of two or more competing firms, either because supply itself was unavoidably limited or because capital requirements discouraged rival entrants. Railroads were the prime example, but natural monopolies also included public utilities and other transportation and communication enterprises.

Artificial monopolies resulted from governmental interference in the market, for example, through tariff policy or grants of exclusive privileges like patents. Even in the absence of governmental interference, it was recognized that a monopoly could be created by conspiracies among rivals to restrain competition. Since inefficiency and competition would prevent a single firm from growing naturally into a monopoly, collusion was the only option available to firms seeking to achieve monopoly power. When later nineteenth century economists spoke of the monopoly problem, they referred to large-scale combinations—the so-called trusts. None had arisen "naturally" through internal growth. As the products of deliberate anticompetitive conduct, these monopolies were therefore considered to be artificial.

Viewed as the artificial products of collusive behavior rather than the inevitable results of market forces, the trusts lacked the legitimacy that a theory of natural formation might have offered. Furthermore, as creatures of antisocial human efforts, they might be prevented through legal rules proscribing the offensive behavior. The common law traditionally denied enforceability to monopolistic agreements, and several states had initiated prosecutions against monopolizing conduct. The artificiality theory encouraged faith in the efficacy of a legal solution to the trust problem. Reinvigoration of competition would then restore a balance of economic and political power in American society.

· · ·

B. New Ideas

For the new generation of economists who attained prominence during the 1890s, traditional faith in competition no longer offered a convincing solution to pressing social problems. They rejected sanguine assumptions about the efficacy of competition as a check upon concentration. Nevertheless, they shared the classical economists' deep antipathy toward monopoly.

According to this new generation, "excessive" or "cutthroat" competition resulted in over production and below cost pricing. To avoid mutual destruction, competitors combined to control output. . . .

Confronted with these apparently inevitable developments, some of the new generation reiterated conventional thinking about "natural" as opposed to "artificial" monopoly. . . . Natural monopolies included transportation, communication, and public utility enterprises. Other monopolies were artificial, facilitated through governmental grants of patents, copyright privileges, or through private combinations. . . . Thus, monopolies in manufacturing and processing industries did not enjoy superior efficiency and were merely artificial products of anticompetitive combinations.

· · ·

The view that the trusts enjoyed superior efficiency undermined the classicists' faith in the rigors of market competition as a check on monopoly power. . . . Even though "monopoly prices are about certain to be higher than competitive prices," because they are not controlled by costs, effective competition might not be feasible. Excessive profits would not necessarily induce rivals to enter the market; they may lack knowledge of the amount of those profits as well as access to capital and other resources. Even if a rival did enter, the dominant firm could drive out the interloper by selling below cost. Thus, "in a great variety of industries, perhaps a majority of all, permanent monopolies may be maintained, apart from any legislative or special aids. . . . No economic laws prevent the permanent existence of monopolies."

None of these new theorists argued that the inevitability or naturalness of concentration in some industries rendered monopoly legitimate. Instead, they reiterated the standard belief that self-interest dictated that monopoly power would always be wielded in an antisocial manner. . . . Efficient or not, a monopoly still presented the specter of uncontrollable economic power and political corruption.

. . .

Assuming the need for state action of some kind, economists debated the appropriate form it should take. . . .

Ownership was preferable to regulation because regulation "means interference with private business, and this begets corruption." Public control would also eliminate private artificial monopolies created through preferential arrangements with natural monopolies. . . .

Thus, while traditional classical economists believed that the trusts were artificial and inefficient, the new generation suggested that they might be the results of severe competitive conditions, and that combinations might in fact yield efficiency gains. There was no disagreement, however, regarding the unacceptability of these huge, privately controlled monopolies. The younger economists shared the classical liberals' profound distrust of concentrated private power. However, they preferred a regulatory (or even public ownership) approach over reestablishment of a balance of power based on competition. A regulatory response to the dangers of economic power was not unprecedented, but the breadth of the problem would have required extremely far reaching uses of governmental power. While the solutions offered by the new generation may have been politically unacceptable, it is important to see that their analysis of the naturalness of concentration did not serve a legitimating function in 1890. Their insistent hostility towards uncontrolled monopoly therefore reinforced traditional attitudes.

6. The Meaning of the Sherman Act

The political theory of balanced power, together with classical economic ideas about the evils of monopoly and the significance of competitive opportunity, provided the ideological context that defined the meaning of words used by the legislators who created the Sherman Act. Their pronouncements reveal unequivocal hostility to monopolistic concentration because of its connection with governmental corruption and the economic injuries inflicted on individual citizens. Virtually all legislators accepted classical economic assumptions about the inevitability of the great manufacturing and processing trusts and about monopolies in general. The remedy was the reinvigoration of competition. The means to this end were legal rules facilitating attack upon the techniques of combination and other deliberate efforts to obtain monopoly power. Congress showed no appreciation for recent and novel ideas about the inevitability of concentration or monopoly based on efficiency. It did not occur to any legislator—any more than it had to any academic economist—that efficiency might somehow legitimate controlled monopoly power. Instead, Congress turned to conventional concepts and language in order to understand the trusts' impact on social life. These familiar ideas yielded the familiar conclusion that the trusts threatened the political process as well as personal prosperity. In designing a response to these concerns, the legislators did not create a new theory. Instead, they relied on traditional, deeply rooted assumptions about opportunity and mobility as the vehicle for achieving atomization and balance. Their words can only be understood if read within their original context.

A. The Dangers of Uncontrolled Economic Power

The debates reveal that the traditional concern about the destruction of balanced economic power was at the heart of the Sherman Act. As amended on March 18, 1890, Senator Sherman's bill attacked the great nationwide trusts as well as other monopolistic combinations. The evil of the trusts was their immunity from the natural regulatory forces of competition. According to Senator Sherman, such a monopoly "can control the market, raise or lower prices, as will best promote its selfish interests, reduce prices in a particular locality and break down competition and advance prices at will where competition does not exist."[17] Even if massive enterprise might theoretically be able to reduce prices through "better methods of production . . . , all experience shows that this saving of cost goes to the pockets of the producer."[18] Senator Sherman thus reiterated the standard belief that the power to raise prices would always be exercised extortionately. Only the monopolist would benefit from any gains in efficiency. Any monopoly, efficient or not, would be socially harmful.

Hostility to the trusts was not limited to their economic power over individual citizens. The trusts were capable of using their power to influence state governments selfishly:

> The popular mind is agitated with problems that may disturb social order, and among them all none is more threatening than the inequality of condition, of wealth, and opportunity that has grown within a single generation out of the concentration of capital into vast combinations to control production and trade and break down competition. These combinations already defy or control powerful transportation corporations and reach State authorities. They reach out their Briarean arms to every part of our country. They are imported from abroad. Congress alone can deal with them, and if we are unwilling or unable there will soon be a trust for every production and a master to fix the price for every necessity of life.[19]

. . .

Senator Sherman equated the trusts' uncontrolled economic power with illegitimate political domination:

> If the concentrated powers of this combination are intrusted to a single man, it is a kingly prerogative, inconsistent with our form of govern-

ment, and should be subject to the strong resistance of the State and national authorities. If anything is wrong this is wrong. If we will not endure a king as a political power we should not endure a king over the production, transportation, and sale of any of the necessaries of life. If we would not submit to an emperor we should not submit to an autocrat of trade, with power to prevent competition and to fix the price of any commodity.[20]

Congress' condemnation of monopoly was unequivocal. . . . The breadth of [the legislative] statements and the statutory language is a measure of the extent of Congress' hostility to the trusts, and its concern about the injuries they were inflicting on society.

B. Restoring the Balance

Congress appreciated the trusts' threat to the integrity of the political process as well as their economic power over all who were forced to deal with them. Seeking to fashion a concrete response to the problem, the legislature hoped to restore a balance of power in society through reinvigoration of economic opportunity. Atomization and mobility would then prevent the creation of entrenched concentration.

. . .

Sympathy for individual cases of hardship surely played an important role in the legislators' thinking. However, [legislative] statements . . . meant more than simply a desire to protect owners of small businesses from predation or their own inability to compete. . . . Atomization suggested a nation of independent individuals, while concentration meant domination and dependence. There was more at stake here than merely the economic interests of a particular commercial class. The imbalances created by the trusts had fundamentally altered the structure of American society and the character of the relationships among its citizens.

. . .

C. The Sherman Act and Economic Efficiency

On several occasions legislators explicitly rejected the values underlying [a] consumer welfare policy. In express terms they denied that consumer prices were the focus of their attention. Lower prices due to enhanced efficiency could not legitimate a monopoly. . . .

Conventional economic theory denied that the competitive process could generate a large, powerful monopoly. The ebb and flow guaranteed by competition would always take place within a relatively narrow range of possibilities because large firms could not compete effectively with those of moderate size. Even innovative theorists of the "naturalness" of monopoly had before them only examples of huge monopolies achieved through combination, which might then be resistant to competition due to economies of scale. No one imagined that internal growth accomplished without "artificial" means could result in a large scale monopoly. . . .

. . .

Conclusion

Congress in 1890 was concerned about power, not efficiency. The legislators confronted the concentration crisis from the perspective of an ideological tradition that equated excessive economic power with political corruption as well as oppression of competitors and consumers. This tradition grew out of classical liberal assumptions about the threat to individual liberty inherent in public and private power. Republican theory explained how wealth could be used to create dependence, which then provided the means for diversion of government from pursuit of the common good. Governmental dedication to general welfare therefore required a citizenry possessing personal independence grounded in economic security. Unless there were a balanced distribution of wealth, extreme disparities would inevitably destabilize governmental processes. Initial ideas about the importance of an egalitarian distribution of property gave way to a vision of self-interested pursuit of America's abundant economic opportunities as the basis for personal independence and balanced distribution. Robust, unrestricted economic opportunity would generate mobility and prevent entrenched accumulation. It also prevented any individual from achieving a position of dominance over competitors or consumers.

These assumptions shaped the legislators' thinking about the significance of the concentration crisis. In accordance with contemporary economic thought, existing legal doctrine, and a long tradition of public policy, they readily ignored the possibility that enhanced efficiency might justify concentrated production. Even if monopoly were capable of creating social benefits, the lack of competitive pressure or governmental regulation coupled with the monopolist's pursuit of self-interest could only result in abuse of power. Consumers would pay extortionate prices while the owners of ruined smaller businesses watched from the sidelines. More fundamentally, the enormous wealth of the great trusts represented massive, uncontrolled power that would inevitably subvert the integrity of the political process and result in plutocracy. In their economic power as well as their political influence the trusts symbolized tyranny and despotism. There could be no "welfare trade-off" because they offered nothing of value to society.

Just as separation and balance within government prevented concentration of power in any single constituent element, so too was atomization of economic power the solution to the crisis brought on by the concentrated power of the trusts. Believing that the trusts were unnatural products of deliberate efforts to avoid the rigors of competition, Congress attacked the techniques of combination and monopolization. By requiring all actors to submit to the natural forces of the market, balance would be restored.

The point is not that Congress examined [a] consumer welfare policy and rejected it in favor of a competing value. The normative theory of allocative efficiency did not exist in 1890. Instead, the legislators approached the concentration crisis with an entirely different set of assumptions and concerns about the nature of the problem. They were not worried about maximization of wealth. While several senators expressed unwillingness to temper their opposition to concentration for the sake of economies of scale, that should not lead us to construe their views in terms of our modern debate over whether all competing values should be sacrificed for efficiency. That was not what they were worried about.

Looking back at reactions to the rise of the trusts, the outrage and unequivocal hostility of politicians, economists, and the general public seem the products of a different world. Fears of corrupt plutocracy and faith in diffusion of wealth as the guarantor of governmental legitimacy appear as quaint as the belief that competition yields mobility and balance rather than inequality and rigid class division. A profound change in our thinking about these matters has made it extremely difficult to recapture and appreciate the ideology that shaped the Sherman Act.

Even as the United States Senate tried vainly to shore it up, that ideology was beginning to crumble under the weight of social reality. Economic imbalance, only embryonic a hundred years previously, was by 1890 swallowing up the mass of American citizens. The Senate's conservative approach to the concentration crisis failed to appreciate the magnitude and complexity of the problem. The Sherman Act thus had little impact on the rapidly accelerating consolidation of big business.

. . .

An important consequence of this ideological revolution is the tendency to view proposals to dismantle economic concentration as threats to individual liberty. Concentration is seen to be the natural result of activity in the market. The Chicago School of antitrust analysis advocates a noninterventionist approach that allows private citizens to define the optimal allocation of economic resources through their individual market decisions. This value renders legitimate the resulting distribution of wealth and power. If inequality is the result, it is because equality is inconsistent with liberty.

. . .

. . . In 1890, the legislators did not perceive this dichotomy: the modern argument about liberty cast no cloud of illegitimacy over their attack upon the trusts. Instead, their ideological tradition identified personal liberty with economic balance. Liberty—freedom to compete—meant opportunity and mobility, which were thought to ensure a general equality of condition and to protect the individual from selfish abuse of public or private power. The Sherman Act sought to reinvigorate competition in order to put to an end the nascent monopolistic giants of the day. Competition thus restored promised freedom from monopoly and, ultimately, individual liberty. Grudging acceptance of concentration was no part of the bargain.

The "Rule of Reason" in Antitrust Law: Property Logic in Restraint of Competition

RUDOLPH J. PERITZ

. . .

A strikingly different history emerges from this Article's reformulation of legislative and judicial history. First, the legislative debates chronicle a conflict between commitments to fostering competition and commitments to protecting property rights, a tension that produced the Sherman Act of 1890. From the earliest moments of federal antitrust history, assuring competitive markets never constituted the sole concern of legislators or judges. Second, it was this tension between competition and property, this struggle between two logics, that motivated the well-known jurisprudential disagreement between the "literalist" and "rule of reason" factions on the Court. The literalists were not naive; they developed a scheme based on the familiar categories of direct and ancillary restraints, a scheme that we continue to use today. Compromise with the proponents of the rule of reason was not possible, however, because the literalists' competition-driven views were profoundly incompatible with their colleagues' property-directed commitments. Third and most surprisingly, the emergence of the rule of reason represented the triumph of a property-driven logic,

Reprinted from 40 Hastings L. J. 285 (1989).

not the competition-directed analysis universally associated with the rule today. Thus, when Justice Oliver Wendell Holmes wrote that the Sherman Act "says nothing about competition," he represented the rule of reason's position in the early battle over the foundations of antitrust law.

. . . Redefining the framework to reflect a tension between competition and property logics brings to light the other half of this history. The so-called literalist opinions and their rule of reason successors make more sense reinterpreted within this new historical framework. Perhaps most importantly, the new framework allows us to understand modern antitrust law and its relationship to both the Sherman Act and the early cases. Finally, in destabilizing the previously unquestioned link between antitrust and competition, and in authenticating the importance of property logic to antitrust law, this Article also raises a new set of questions about the relationship between competition and the efficiency norm.

. . .

1. The Legislative Debates: Industrial Liberty and Fair Price

. . . For more than two years, the Senate and the House debated a bill, originally introduced in 1888 with the following operative language: "*Be it enacted* . . . that all arrangements, contracts, agreements, trusts, or combinations . . . made with a view, or which tend, to prevent full and free competition . . . or which tend, to advance the cost to the consumer . . . are hereby declared to be against public policy, unlawful, and void. . . ."[1] While a number of amendments were offered and discussed, most of the congressional debate centered on three issues: the proper constitutional reach of congressional authority under the commerce clause, an explicit labor exemption, and the desirability of state court jurisdiction. Eventually, the 1888 bill was referred to the Committee on the Judiciary for revision. Six days after the 1888 bill's referral, Committee Chairman Edmunds introduced an amended bill that was quite different from its predecessor. In place of the 1888 language of "full and free competition" and "cost to the consumer," the 1890 Bill substituted "contract . . . in restraint of trade or commerce," and "monopolize, or attempt to monopolize . . . trade or commerce."[2] The 1890 Bill was passed in a matter of days. . . .

A. The Competition Logic of Industrial Liberty

. . . Following is a sampling of references to competition in the *Congressional Record*. Senator Sherman himself stated:

> This bill, as I would have it, has for its single object to invoke the aid of the courts of the United States . . . in dealing with combinations that affect injuriously the industrial liberty of the citizens. . . . It is the right of every man to work, labor, and produce in any lawful vocation. . . . This is industrial liberty and lies at the foundation of the equality of all rights and privileges. . . .
>
> The sole object of . . . [a trust] is to make competition impossible. It can control the market, raise or lower prices, as will best promote its selfish interests, reduce prices in a particular locality and break down competition and advance prices at will where competition does not exist. Its governing motive is to increase the profits of the parties composing it. The law of selfishness, uncontrolled by competition, compels it to disregard the interest of the consumer.[3]

Although Senator Sherman's references to competition sound familiar, his use of the term depended on a set of assumptions and beliefs that have grown unfamiliar to us in recent years. In talking about "full and free competition," Senator Sherman and others made frequent reference to something called "industrial liberty."[4] Although modern readers might understand this term to mean freedom from governmental regulation or other market intervention, Senator Sherman and his contemporaries were concerned with another kind of power. Their attentions focused on "combinations of capital" that "make competition impossible."[5] Such market power "advance[d] the cost to the consumer"[6] by the "ultimate fixing of a price."[7] The interest of the public was safe only so long as competition remained free of such market power.[8] In our terms, the primary strategy of Sherman and others was to limit market power and thereby to prevent monopoly pricing; their ultimate goal was to enhance the consumer's well-being.

While "full and free competition" may have been seen as the best way to protect consumers, the related notion of "industrial liberty" signified a broader set of assumptions and beliefs, which captured the congressional imagination. As Senator Sherman's statement above indicates, industrial liberty was valued not only for its potential downward push on prices. Senator Teller expressed as much when he said, "I do not believe that the great object in life is to make everything cheap."[9] Industrial liberty also embodied a sense of the public as competitors and employees of the new large combinations of capital, whose power rendered "the boasted liberty of the citizen . . . a myth."[10] Thus, in the House debate, Representative Mason pointed out that even if "trusts have made products cheaper, . . . [they] have destroyed legitimate competition."[11]

Senator Reagan first introduced his own antitrust bill[12] and later offered several amendments to Sherman's bill to assure a cause of action for the small competitors injured by large combinations of capital—a realistic "remedy for the great mass of people."[13] Industrial liberty (whether enjoyed by capital or labor) was thought to require rivalrous marketplace participants, and perhaps some supervision and control of industries characterized by firms with large cumulations of assets. In sum, the idea of industrial liberty demanded conditions of rough competitive equality.

In congressional debates, a distinction was drawn between industrial liberty and unrestrained competition, the belief being that some competition impinges on industrial liberty. For example, in the heated debate just prior to the 1888 bill's referral to committee and radical redrafting, Senator Platt articulated a tension between industrial liberty and that bill's language of free competition; he noted that the "bill proceeds upon the false assumption that all competition is beneficent to the country. . . ."[14] Later, in House debate over the Conference Report on the 1890 bill as enacted, Representative Stewart stated his understanding of the new language: "It is just as necessary to restrict competition as it is to restrict combination. . . ."[15] Thus, the congressmen shared the belief that "unrestrained competition" is not free competition because it diminishes industrial liberty. Rather, "free and fair competition" was seen as the victim of both unrestricted competition and unrestricted combination. The trusts were seen as embodying the forces of both unrestricted extremes.

The concern for consumer and producer liberty also implicated political liberty . . . . Senator Jones argued that if the trusts were allowed to continue, "the boasted liberty of the citizen is a myth . . . and our Government is a farce and a fraud."[16] Senator Sherman echoed these sentiments in stating that industrial liberty is "the foundation of the equality of all rights and privileges."[17] He believed that rough competitive equality was important not only for economic or vocational liberty, but for political liberty in a democratic society as well.

> They had monopolies and mortmains of old, but never before such giants as in our day. You must heed their appeal or be ready for the socialist, the communist, and the nihilist. Society is now disturbed by forces never felt before.
>
> The popular mind is agitated with problems that may disturb social order, and among them all none is more threatening than the inequality of condition, of wealth, and opportunity that has grown within a single generation out of the concentration of capital into vast combinations to control production and trade and to break down competition.[18]

Given the commitment to industrial liberty and the identification of trusts as the threat to it, the solution seemed simple enough. Whether by forfeiture of assets to the government or by private treble damage actions, political power in the form of antitrust legislation could protect the natural process of competition from the market power of unnatural combinations of capital. This seemingly rational and natural alignment of legislation and competition, however, remained problematic even after the 1890 Bill's passage, not because of concern over governmental intervention into some sacred arena called "the competitive market,"[19] but because of deep convictions about something else. The alliance between political power and competition was undercut by the imaginative force and normative appeal of something called "fair price."

The desire to assure fair prices was not the only source of tension in the relationship between industrial liberty and private agreements such as trusts and price fixing cartels. Another area of conflict was over the role of government in ensuring industrial liberty. On the one hand, industrial liberty was taken to mean rough competitive equality. In this sense, it called for the restraint of trusts and other powerful combinations. Thus, governmental action to dissolve private agreements in restraint of competition is a legitimate way to achieve industrial liberty. This impulse to equalize market power constituted a movement toward the ideal of perfect competition. At the same time, this impulse generated the ideal's demise. Under this view industrial liberty could suggest that private agreements were a means of achieving countervailing power against trusts or cartels.[20] Thus, this impulse toward competitive equality could not provide an indisputable basis for deciding whether a private agreement in restraint of competition was a social evil.

On the other hand, industrial liberty was also taken to mean the freedom to enter into contracts to further one's own interests. This *laissez-faire* view of market conduct, unspoken in the debates, was founded in the social value of liberty. In this sense, industrial liberty involved freedom from political power and therefore, freedom from government dissolution of private agreements. Thus, industrial liberty could also mean enforcing private agreements, whether or not they restrained competition.

This tension in the notion of industrial liberty can be understood in two ways. First, "liberty" can mean either freedom from governmental power or freedom from market power. These views, with their radically different concerns, employed conflicting strategies to achieve their goals. The freedom from government power view required the government to enforce private agreements, whether or not they restrained competition. In contrast, where the goal was freedom from market power, the government was to intervene to enjoin private agreements that restrained competition. Second, the tension in industrial liberty can be understood in terms of two impulses—one toward equality and perfect competition and the other toward liberty and free competition (or *laissez-faire* competition). . . .

In spite of the tension, these two sides of industrial liberty did share one important tenet. For entirely different reasons, both views held that one benefit of industrial liberty was "fair price." Those who argued for equalization of market power called for governmental intervention to dissolve private agreements, such as trusts or price fixing cartels, in order to reinstate the "full and free competition" necessary to produce fair prices. Those who claimed the liberty to enter into private agreements in restraint of competition characterized their combinations as contracts to charge fair prices in the face of ruinous competition. Thus, each side of the industrial liberty tension claimed fair price as its own product.

B. The Property Logic of Fair Price

Both views of industrial liberty—freedom from market power and freedom from government power—had many proponents at the time. Yet, the congressional speeches employing the rhetoric of industrial liberty championed only the freedom from market power view. These speeches called for governmental intervention to dissolve trusts and other private agreements in restraint of competition. But other speeches by freedom from market power advocates deployed a very different form of argument. For example, Senator George stated:

> These trusts and combinations are great wrongs to the people. . . . They increase beyond reason the cost of the necessaries of life and business and they decrease the cost of the raw material, the farm products of the country. They regulate prices at their will. . . . They aggregate to themselves great, enormous wealth by extortion. . . . Then making this extorted wealth the means of further extortion from their unfortunate victims . . . they are fast producing that condition in our people in which the great mass of them are the servitors of those who have this aggregated wealth at their command.[21]

Senator Jones reiterated the negative impact of trusts on the public: "These commercial monsters called trusts . . . [are] preying upon every industry, and by their unholy combinations robbing their victims, the general public. . . . "[22] Senator Turpie agreed: "The conspirators of the trust . . . are hunting the prey, dividing the spoil in every market. . . . [If they] pirate upon the earnings of the people, justice may . . . strike down the offense and the offenders."[23]

Moreover, those speeches seeking enforcement of private agreements advanced the very same logic, founded in the notions of "fair profit" or "fair return." The following excerpts are examples of speeches using this logic. Senator Platt stated:

> The true theory of this matter is that prices should be just and reasonable and fair, that prices . . . should be such as will render a fair return to all persons engaged in its production, a fair profit on capital, on labor, and on everything else that enters into its production. . . . [E]very man in business . . . has a right, a legal and a moral right, to obtain a fair profit upon his business and his work; and if he is driven by fierce competition to a spot where his business is unre-

munerative, I believe it is his right to combine for the purpose of raising prices until they shall be fair and remunerative.[24]

Representative Stewart also emphasized a notion of fair return on investment:

A rate war between railroads is absolutely injurious to the community. Why, it cannot be otherwise. In the first place the doctrine of fair play requires, and everybody concedes, that the railroads should have a just compensation for their services. We ought not to ask them to do anything for less than will pay the interest on the investment and the running expenses. That is only reasonable and fair.[25]

Representative Morse echoed these concerns for a fair price:

[If this Bill] proposes to deny to manufacturers and merchants the right to control the price at which their goods shall be sold, the right to say they shall not enter into ruinous competition, the right to exact a fair and living profit on the sale of their goods by the merchant who handles them, it will be unwise legislation and injurious to the manufacturer, to the merchant, to the consumer, and the whole people, and strike a blow at the business interests of the country, because it will violate a sound business principle, to "live and let live."[26]

These speeches representing the freedom from government view illustrate the workings of a logic very different from the competition rhetoric of industrial liberty. They describe the contours of a property rhetoric whose foundation is the notion of a "fair profit" or "fair return." Briefly, the argument is as follows: It is an independent social good that those who work, those who put their labor or capital into the market, should get a fair return on their input. This social good benefits both producers and consumers. "Fair profit" or "fair return" is a social good that the government should enforce, whether the evil be competition or combination and whether the harm be low profits or high prices. It is a social good to be enforced in much the same way that one's possession of property is protected from theft or extortion.

Like the competition rhetoric of industrial liberty, the property rhetoric of fair price embodied a tension. Fair price could be characterized as the consequence of competition as well as the consequence of combination. . . .

[The] notions of fair return or fair profit appear alien in statements about competition. In contrast, they comfortably inhabit statements about protecting the value of one's property—whether labor, rolling stock, manufacturer's goods, or retailer's goodwill. With this rehearsal of the tension between competition and property as an epilogue, debate on the 1888 Bill ended.

C. Property Logic and the Language of the Common Law

Six days after the debate's closure, Senator Edmunds introduced a new bill. The 1890 Bill replaced the previous Bill's language of "free competition" and "cost to the consumer" with language of the common law—"restraint of trade or commerce" and "monopolize."[27] One week after the new Bill's introduction, after only a few hours of floor debate, both Houses quickly passed the new Sherman Act.[28] Aside from Congress' well-known concerns about the earlier Bill's constitutionality, what other significance can be attributed to the radical change in language?

There is much evidence to suggest that Congress intended to codify the common-law meaning of the terms used in the new Bill. For example, Senator Hoar, who first asked that the new Bill be taken up by the full Senate, immediately expressed hope of an early vote. His reason for anticipating such expedited treatment of an entirely new Bill was that the Bill was already "well understood." The obvious implication of this assertion is that much off-the-record negotiation and compromise had accompanied the new Bill and had already familiarized everyone with the Bill's content. Beyond this familiarity with the Bill's language, however, there was also a common ground for the Senators' understanding of the new Bill's language. Apparently, it was taken for granted that there was a common law that would provide the groundwork for the development of a federal common law of monopoly and restraints of trade.[29] This assumption is suggested in Senator Hoar's statement in the *Congressional Record*: "We have affirmed the old doctrine of the common law . . . and have clothed the United States courts with authority to enforce that doctrine. . . . "[30] Senator Edmunds later added that the Committee took the new Bill's language—"monopolize," for example—"out of terms that were well known to the law already."[31] In response to a question about an ingenious rancher's monopoly of short-horn cattle trade with Mexico, Senator Edmunds stated, "Anybody who knows the meaning of the word 'monopoly,' as the courts apply it, would not apply it to such a person at all. . . . "[32] He continued:

> "[M]onopoly" is a technical term known to the common law. . . . [A] man who merely by superior skill and intelligence . . . got the whole business because nobody could do it as well as he could was not a monopolist. . . . [Monopoly] involved something like the use of means which made it impossible for other persons to engage in fair competition. . . . [33]

This common-law "meaning" upon which Congress seemed to rely came from the states or from sources outside the United States, as there was no federal common law of monopoly or restraints of trade prior to the Sherman Act. Under the common law developed in the several states, price fixing agreements were generally void and unenforceable, though there were a few notable exceptions.[34] State governments attacked some of the more visible trusts, typically arguing that their corporate charters did not permit the formation of such trusts[35]. . . .

In contrast to the states' treatment of private agreements in restraint of competition, the most recent and best known case under the British common law espoused a radically different view. In *Mogul Steamship Co. v. McGregor, Gow & Co.*, a "shipping conference" or cartel was not dissolved, even though it financed a "fighting ship" to carry cargo at prices that "would not repay a shipowner for his adventure."[36] Although Lord Bowen declared that "intentionally to do that which is calculated . . . to damage, and which does, in fact, damage another in that other person's property or trade, is actionable," this agreement was not a common-law restraint of trade because it did "nothing more . . . than pursue to the bitter end a war of competition. . . . "[37] Thus, the British court protected the freedom to enter into private agreements in restraint of competition, characterizing the agreement as an acceptable form of competition.

Though there is no record of how these and other statements formulating restraints of trade doctrine engaged the imaginations of individual congressmen, a great deal can be said about what they took for granted concerning classical legal doctrine and economics. From a sketch of the contours of classical economics and then classical contracts and property doctrine, a good likeness (for our limited purposes) of the shared cultural context of the Fifty-First Congress emerges. That cultural context included some sense[38] of monopolies and restraints of trade. Perhaps most salient here, it also included an account of the unnatural appearance of monopolies and restraints of trade in an otherwise lawfully and naturally competitive marketplace.

A naturalistic sense of lawfulness and rationality constituted the foundation of nineteenth century discourse, whether scientific, economic, or legal. Hence, when Representative Stewart spoke of "two great forces working in human society,"[39] he imagined competition and combination as two lawful and rational agencies contending with one another. This claim that there might be *two* natural tendencies—one to compete and the other to combine—rather than an unrivaled tendency to compete, was a recent development prompted by the changing face of American industry and labor. The nineteenth century belief in natural law and its rationality animated a desire to characterize the tendency to combine as natural and rational, because the alternative—asserting the unnaturalness of the widespread practice of combination—would call into question the very belief in natural law and its rationality. At the same time, a profound ambivalence gripped the nineteenth century attitude toward combinations. The success of such combinations was at odds with classical legal and economic doctrines, which espoused the inevitability of competition. Under these doctrines, if only the tendency to compete was natural, then competitive markets were inevitable, making governmental intervention unnecessary. In other words, the natural tendency to compete would overcome the current wave of combinations. In contrast, if Representative Stewart was correct, if there had evolved two natural tendencies and forces (competition and combination) then the prospects for competitive markets were indeterminable.

Representative Stewart's view was also tough to swallow because it challenged the classical view that a fair price derived from free exchanges between roughly equal individuals. Under this labor theory of value, since commodities embody a worker's labor, it is labor that imparts market value. Free exchanges among numerous independent trading partners produce "natural" or "market" prices. Moreover, since each party to such idealized transactions was imagined as getting something in return that was proportional to his contribution, the prices and the process were seen as not only natural and free, but also fair and just. Insofar as combinations charged prices higher or lower than the natural market price, classical economics considered them unnatural, and perhaps unjust, interlopers in the process of competitive markets.

Although classical economics permitted regulation of combinations, it required such governmental intervention to conform with the classical view of property law. Under this view, the state could interfere with an individual's property rights only in a very limited set of circumstances and through a very limited set of processes. This notion of property derived from the strongly held sentiment, still powerful today, that a person has a right to the product of her labor. . . .

This battle had already been fought on constitutional grounds. As discussed above, *Munn v. Illinois* (and other "Granger" cases) recognized a state's right to regulate profit when there was a public interest in the industry.[40] In that case, the Supreme Court upheld an Illinois statute that set maximum prices farmers could be charged for wheat storage in Chicago's grain elevators. But what about all those industries that were not clothed in something called the "public interest"? . . . It was not clear that government could preserve or impose competitive conditions—that is, indirectly control monopoly pricing in those industries not clothed in the public interest.

Such controls would have to overcome strong commitments to the sanctity of property. In particular, any governmental intervention, even indirect price regulation by imposition of competition, would have to confront a justification for monopoly profit couched in clearly classical terms. This justification held that a monopoly price for short-horn cattle was a competitive reward fairly won by "superior skill and intelligence." . . .

. . .

It is easy to see why monopolies or combinations in restraint of trade were so problematic. Their very existence called into question one of the basic tenets of classical economics and legal doctrine—the fairness of market price as derived from free exchanges between roughly equal individuals. Because actual market prices could mean monopoly price, predatory price, or competitive price, actual market transactions no longer seemed constrained by the competitive ideal of the market. Given the ubiquity of trusts and other sorts of combinations, countless trades could not be characterized as free exchanges between roughly equal individuals.

This dissonance between combinations and the competitive ideal did not go entirely unnoticed. In a scholarly critique of the classical view, influential economist Henry Carter Adams wrote that combinations, and corporations in particular, were destroying the "strategic equality" among classically conceived competitors.[41] Making the imbalance even more pronounced, he wrote: "[T]hese corporations assert for themselves most of the rights conferred on individuals by the law of private property, and apply to themselves a social philosophy true only of a society composed of individuals who are industrial competitors."[42] Motivated by similar concerns, other scholars, the popular "literature of protest," farmer and labor groups, as well as both the Democratic and the Republican Parties' platforms called for some antitrust action. Still, as Roscoe Pound has written, the classical economic vision continued to direct the production of legal doctrine:

> When in the last quarter of the nineteenth Century our courts were called upon with increasing frequency to pass on the validity of social legislation, in the transition from pioneer, rural, agricultural America to the urban, industrial America of today, they turned to an idealized picture of the economic order with which they were familiar, the principles of which had been set forth by the classical political economists. They pictured an ideal society in which there was a maximum of abstract individual self-assertion. This was "liberty" as secured in the Fourteenth Amendment.[43]

This repression of the impulse toward equalizing market power and its effects on liberty were reinforced by unquestioned belief in the principle that greater size always entails greater efficiency.[44] Thus, the wave of industrial combination, whether trusts, cartels, or pools, raised deeply troubling questions about the classical view that combinations would dissipate because competition was inevitable.

The impulse toward equality could also be repressed by invoking the classical view of competition as free exchange. Supporters of monopoly and combinations in restraint of trade could call upon the powerful idea of liberty. In much the same way that the individualist notion of liberty as "abstract individual self-assertion"[45] suppressed the tension within industrial liberty, it forged a connection between combinations and competition. In both instances, the impulse toward liberty overpowered a complementary commitment to equality. In both instances, this idealized notion of liberty legitimated private agreements, whether or not they restrained competition, by supporting the counterfactual image of typical market transactions as free exchanges between roughly equal parties. In this way, the impulse toward liberty constituted the foundation for a freedom of contract regime that relied on an ideal of equal competition and viewed social and economic reality as momentary aberrations from the ideal. Thus, the impulse toward liberty provided a powerful normative ground not only for the classical view of competition as free trade, but also for the freedom to enter into private agreements, without regard for their effects on competition. This idealized notion of liberty and its insinuation of equality within the classical view of competition as free trade was seen as justifying both competition and its restraint, both industrial liberty and fair price. It provided common ground for explaining and defending contradictory market conduct and conflicting social values.

These tensions produced profound economic and political implications. They encouraged the belief that monopolization and combinations in restraint of trade were justifiable. . . . In sharp contrast, perceptions of social and economic reality unconstrained by the classical images exploded popular and scholarly beliefs in naturally competitive markets and in natural connections between liberty and equality. Eventually, the loss of liberty itself became an issue:

> The power of groups of men organized by incorporation as joint-stock companies, or of small knots of rich men acting in combination, has developed with unexpected strength in unexpected ways, overshadowing individuals and even communities, and showing that the very freedom of association which men sought to secure by law when they were threatened by the violence of the potentates may, under the shelter of the law, ripen into a new form of tyranny.[46]

The Sherman Act passed through a Congress struggling with tensions between the political and economic mythology of artisans and local markets, and the reality of a new economic order of large scale enterprise and national markets. Despite the classical image of competition as free trade and the underlying view of human nature as embodying an irresistible tendency to compete, unregulated markets in reality seemed to produce combinations of capital without bounds. Industrial liberty, characterized in the debates as freedom from private (market) power, authorized governmental intervention to reestablish the competitive markets overrun by powerful combinations of capital. But a return to the classical image of perfect competition was not seen as an unalloyed good. A contrasting rhetoric of fair price as well as a contrasting sense of human nature as embodying a tendency to combine provided the logic for arguments that some combination was a social good.

Congress' eleventh-hour turn to the common-law language of monopolization and restraints of trade represents a retreat from the 1888 Bill's explicit and unmediated imposition of competition as the only natural and legitimate form of commerce. The 1890 Bill's common-law language of monopolization and restraint of trade carried with it familiar and stable images drawn from classical economic and legal thought—powerful though counterfactual images of mythic proportion. The classical views of economics and the common law proceeded on the assumption that competition was the natural state of society and markets. These classical ideals mediated the deeply felt fears engendered by the widespread experience of disruption in traditional social and economic patterns. The revised language proclaimed that trusts and restraints of trade, not competition, were the problem. Although criticism of the classical view of economics and departures from the common-law regime of freedom of contract began to appear, congressional repose in the traditional language of the common law suggests a retreat to the traditional doctrine and classical view. Moreover, economic and political impulses toward both liberty and equality were seen as best served by permitting this natural state to flourish. Finally, the idealized portrayal of commercial markets as free exchanges between roughly equal individuals also satisfied the social demand for a fair return on one's property or labor.

In the social and political turmoil of the new economic order, the Sherman Act's language of the common law sought shelter from, but only shifted the battleground for, the tension between the logics of competition and private property.... [The] confrontations between the rhetorics of industrial liberty and fair price, as well as their relationships to the social values of liberty and equality, characterize both the Sherman Act and the 1888 Bill, as well as the arguments favoring and opposing each version and its amendments....

. . .

4. The Logical Structure of Early Antitrust Law

. . .

Impulses toward liberty and equality have been seen in the workings of property logic as well. On the one hand, the property logic appearing in the congressional debates over the Sherman Act called for passage of a statute that would protect the fair profit of independent entrepreneurs from the extremes of competition and combination. This impulse toward equalizing market power to equalize wealth, not taken up in the early cases, seemed to authorize the courts to develop a common law of competitive torts to protect both consumers and independent entrepreneurs from cartels and trusts. On the other hand, the property logic driving the rule of reason called for government protection of monopoly power and profit, unless acquired by unreasonable means.... [T]his impulse toward liberty sometimes took the form of fundamental rights of contract, property, or liberty.

To give a fuller view of the implications of these logics as they appeared in antitrust's formative years, these logics are reorganized below according to their relationships to equality and liberty. "Equality," as it is used here, means the following: Having many competitors with roughly equal market power is, in and of itself, a social good because it makes the process of competition more fair or just. In addition, regulating the extremes of competition and combination produces a more equitable distribution of wealth. Market participants can expect a fair return on capital or labor put into the market, and consumers can expect to pay a fair price for goods and services. Finally, ... having many competitors and an equitable distribution of wealth encourages civic virtue. That is, a vibrant middle class of "small dealers and worthy men" is crucial to the workings of democratic government because their economic freedom allows them better opportunity to act independently in social and political matters.[47]

In contrast, the following is an abstraction of the notion of liberty as it appeared in antitrust's formative years: Liberty of contract and freedom in the use of one's property are, in and of themselves, fundamental rights in a democratic society. Further, these fundamental rights allow individuals to combine in commercial ventures. Consequently, individuals are able to shelter from the ravages of ruinous competition a reasonable return from property or labor put into the market. Protecting these fundamental rights as well as the expectation of reasonable profits is necessary for the maintenance of some competitive markets.

Employing these logics of competition and property, as well as impulses toward equality and liberty, a snapshot of the logical structure of early antitrust law might look like this:

P R O P E R T Y

		.E
L.	government protection	.Q
I. government protection of	of fair profit to the	.U
B. monopoly power and profit	independent entrepreneur	.A
E. _____	_____	.L
R.		.I
T. government sanction of	government imposition of	.T
Y. survival of the fittest	full and free competition	.Y

C O M P E T I T I O N

The field diagram represents relationships developed from the legislative debates, court opinions, and other textual materials from the early years of antitrust law. The top half of the diagram represents the domain of property and the bottom half represents the domain of competition. The line separating them, running across the diagram, can be thought of as the border, or battle line, between their incommensurate assumptions and beliefs. Whereas property logic evaluates market transactions according to their impact on individual ownership and exchange rights, competition logic judges market transactions based on their effects on the market process. The right half of the diagram reflects the impulse toward equality; the left half, the impulse toward liberty. The vertical line between them can be imagined as a barrier that both connects them and anchors their opposing impulses.

It is clear that *both* relationships—between property and competition, and between equality and liberty—are tensions, not simple oppositions. In other words, though property and competition logics have produced conflicting antitrust doctrine, they also support one another. For example, the rule of reason faction believed that protection of property rights drives competitive markets. The notions of liberty and equality share a similar relationship of tension, rather than simple opposition. For example, the literalists believed that a large class of independent businesspeople tends to disperse the power required to enjoy liberty. The inequality inherent in answering to one's superiors in large corporate hierarchies tends to limit the ways in which those with less power can exercise liberty. Freedom to make a choice requires freedom from the imposition of another's choice. In sum, the idea of a tension suggests that there is both conflict and mutual support in the two relationships.

The field diagram is also divided into four quadrants, each of which grounds the early antitrust policy produced by an interaction between the two tensions. The upper left quadrant, where the commitment to liberty influences property logic, represents the policy of government protection of monopoly power and profit. The rule of reason and its concern for freedom of contract were products of the interaction of these two forces in this area. The lower left quadrant, where liberty influences competition logic, represents the policy of government sanction of survival of the fittest. . . . The lower right quadrant, where competition logic acts instead on the impulse toward equality, represents the policy of government imposition of workable competition. Although Justice Holmes characterized this policy as atomization of rivals to impose perfect competition, the literalists countenanced some restraints, making their view closer to what we today might call workable competition. Finally, the upper right quadrant, where equality sentiments shape property logic, represents the policy of government protection of fair profit to independent entrepreneurs. The congressional debates included numerous calls for fair return on capital or labor put in the market.

While this field diagram was developed from antitrust's early years, it also represents the logical structure that supports modern antitrust law. . . . [T]he field diagram depicts a logical structure that makes sense of the seemingly haphazard movements of current case law, as well as its misunderstood connections to doctrinal antecedents. There may be other grounds for the production of antitrust law and for the production of other law or simply other discourse. Most likely, however, a statement located on another field diagram simply does not appear to us to be a statement about antitrust law, unless it also occupies a position on the diagram appearing above. . . .

Conclusion

In antitrust's formative years, shifting balances of power between rhetorical modes were evident from the earliest moments of the Sherman Act's legislative history, through the history of struggle between the "literalist" and "rule of reason" factions, to passage of the twin 1914 statutes. But those battles settled nothing. Nor could they prove that one logic was somehow better or stronger. Rather, those confrontations represented the very conditions of possibility for early antitrust law. . . .

. . .

. . . [I]t is important to make explicit an important implication regarding the relationship between competition and efficiency. This study introduces an analytical structure for understanding how the tensions between the competition policy and property rights has produced the efficiency norm in its various forms. In short, it shows a different mechanism at work in the production of antitrust doctrine, sharply different from the orthodox view that competition represents the only positive norm for antitrust and contrary to today's neoclassical view that efficiency is a proxy for competition. Placing competition into its logical and historical context allows us to recapture the positive values associated with combinations, small businesses, fair profit, and other doctrinal formulations that we currently associate with negative values such as "anticompetitive" practices or "anti-efficiency" policies. With an analytical structure that recognizes antitrust doctrine as a series of sociopolitical choices, we can start the Sherman Act's second century by making better informed judgments about antitrust doctrine and policy.

The Sherman Act and the Classical Theory of Competition

HERBERT HOVENKAMP

Ever since 1890 scholars have debated the relationship between the Sherman Act and the common law of trade restraints. Did the framers intend merely to enact the common law, or did they hope to do something more? Was there an identifiable "common law," or was it merely an "artificial construct?"[1] This essay examines the relationship between common law, economics and political theory at the time the Sherman Act was passed. It argues that the great difficulty we have had in understanding the relationship between the Sherman Act and the common law lies in the fact that in 1890 the common law of competition was itself undergoing a revolution—the same revolution that political economy experienced as classicism became neoclassicism.[2]

One of the great myths about American antitrust policy is that courts first began to adopt an "economic approach" to antitrust problems in the relatively recent past[3]—perhaps as recently as the late 1970's. At most, this "revolution" in antitrust policy represented a change in economic models. Antitrust policy has been forged by economic ideology since its inception.

But even the common law experienced economic revolutions. The notion of some[4] that antitrust can be freed of involvement in economic policy making if we can only rediscover its common law

Reprinted from 74 Iowa L. Rev. 1019 (1989).

roots is based on a misconception. The misconception is that the common law itself was somehow exempt from economic policy making. It never was, in any branch, and certainly not in the law of monopolies and restraints on trade. The common law responded dramatically to the death of mercantilism and the rise of classicism in the late eighteenth century. It responded equally as classicism collapsed a century later.

Courts realized this already at the time the Sherman Act was passed, as they wrestled with the problem of how much economic analysis was appropriate in judge-made antitrust policy. Judges preferred the relatively traditional approach of state corporate law to what they perceived as the excessively "economic" approach of the common law of trade restraints. . . . [The] . . . courts knew that in the process of applying the common law of trade restraints to the modern industrial trust they would be taking an "economic" approach. They were . . . reluctant to do so.

But the elite legal counsel who created the trusts proved to be skillful at evading state corporation law. Already in the 1890's it was clear that some trusts could be condemned, if at all, only under the relatively economic law of combinations in restraint of trade. At the same time Anglo-American economic theory was nearing the end of a great revolution that we identify today with the rise of neoclassicism. Classical political economy had become neoclassical economics, and by 1890 neoclassicism was already affecting judicial thinking. The important question for courts interpreting the Sherman Act, which was modeled on the law of combinations in restraint of trade, was not whether they would take an "economic approach." That question was settled decisively in Congress's selection of models. The only important question was whether courts deciding antitrust cases would draw their economic wisdom by looking back at one hundred years of classicism, or forward to emerging neoclassicism.

A. Competition and Politics

Political economy and law became technical and professionalized in the second half of the nineteenth century. Before they had been part of the same world view. Classical political economists were men of affairs, often lawyers. Political economists and lawyers were concerned with the same policy problems, they tended to view things the same way, and they read and wrote in the same journals. As Theodore Sedgwick, one of America's foremost treatise writers, observed already in 1836, the principal difference between law and political economy is that law is positive while political economy is normative. "The former teaches what the law is, which it is the business of the lawyer to learn; the latter teaches what law should be, which is the business of the public economist, or legislator to learn."[5] The great legal values of nineteenth century American lawyers—individualism, liberty of contract, abhorrence of forced wealth transfers—were also the values of classical political economy. To be sure, judges did not often cite works of political economy in legal opinions. But the etiquette of legal citation was a function of lawyers' technique, not of understanding or perception.

During the nineteenth century both law and economics began to develop theories of competition, and ideological defenses of competition as a social good. Perhaps for lack of self-confidence, lawyers and economists each had exaggerated notions about the ability of the other discipline to determine the appropriate limits of competition policy. Political economists typically thought that law would provide all the answers to policy questions about how much competition is enough. Lawyers typically thought that such questions presented a problem in political economy. But each group had a great and growing faith that something called "competition" was a good thing, and that the State should encourage more of it.

Although classicists were concerned to preserve "competition," they did not understand that term as we understand it today. In both classical law and classical economics, "competition" carried a very different meaning. Competition was not a theory about cost/price relationships, as it came to be in neoclassical economics. Nor was it a theory about the "struggle for survival," as it was for some legal policy makers during the Gilded Age. Rather, competition was a belief about the role of individual self-determination in directing the allocation of resources, and a theory about the limits of State power to give privileges to one person or class at the expense of others.

The law of competition was classicism's mechanism for keeping politics out of state decision making about the allocation of resource—particularly the allocation of entrepreneurial opportunities. Classicism purported to give the same opportunity to all. It abhorred special privileges. In this sense, classicism was the preeminent device for separating politics and state policy.

With the rise of neoclassicism in the 1870's, political economy became less credible as a device for keeping law and politics distinct. The great British neoclassicist Alfred Marshall and his wife made perhaps the most valiant attempt to preserve the separation when they argued that the classical name "political economy" should be replaced by "economics."[6] . . . For [the Marshalls], "economics" had to be separated from "politics." The first dealt with the welfare of society as a whole; the second merely with the welfare of interest groups.

But the inevitable result of the Marshallian revolution—signalled by Alfred's great synthesis published the same year as the Sherman Act[7]—was that the science of economics became more technical and less approachable by the nonspecialist. Neoclassicism became preoccupied first with marginal utility theory, then with price-cost relationships, the geometry of the marginal cost and marginal revenue curves, and the relationship between consumers' surplus and monopoly. Subjectively, economics became increasingly concerned with technique, preoccupied with theory, and less concerned about issues of state policy. . . .

Just as the neoclassical revolution was turning the political economist into an expert, American lawyers were doing the same thing. Legal formalism instructed lawyers searching for the law not to look outside their case reporters. Many of America's elite lawyers came to believe that the law was a closed system, just as mathematics. Law had its own techniques, and these were different than the techniques of economics or philosophy. These attitudes greatly impoverished the law, and in the process created the illusion that law and political economy really never had very much to do with each other.

Nonetheless, even during the heyday of legal formalism people doing economics and people doing law were in one sense engaged in the same enterprise. Political economists applied their increasingly sophisticated tools to the understanding of markets. Lawyers and judges surely tried to understand them too, if only to regulate them. Not coincidentally, political economists and lawyers continued to describe markets in the same way, particularly as long as they used the same language. Only when the modern theory of "perfect competition" began to emerge in the 1920's and 1930's, attended by technical notation and the mathematics of marginalism, did economics and law begin speaking about competition in completely different languages. The Babel that resulted was in many ways the worse for both economics and law.

B. "Public Policy," Economics, and the Common Law

Classical political economists were expressly concerned with public policy, much more than their neoclassical followers. For many nineteenth century lawyers, however, the common law was purely "private," expressing little or no concern about the sovereign's economic policy. This distinction between classical political economy's expressly "public" and the common law's "private" character was an important part of classical political theory. The public purpose of classical political economy was to show that the State ought to stay out of most legal disputes, except in its role as mediator. The law purported to follow the rules that classical political economy discovered.

Forceful arguments have been made that the American common law in the nineteenth century was heavily concerned with developmental policy.[8] That is undoubtedly true. Nonetheless, most of the common law rhetoric was distinctly private, expressly eschewing "public policy" concerns unless these had been articulated in a statute. Policy making was for the legislature, not the courts. . . .

An important exception to this bias against public policy was the common law of contracts in restraint of trade—i.e., contracts in which a person promised not to engage in a particular business, usually for the benefit of some competitor.[9] When legal scholar Charles F. Beach identified why such contracts were void he cited, not a statute, but rather the "general principle" that "it is the duty of the law-making power to secure to every citizen the right to pursue his ordinary avocation and dispose of his labor, or of the product thereof, without restraint, and to protect the public from the evil consequences of an agreement under which it would be deprived of the benefits of competition in skilled labor."[10] The law of contracts and combinations in restraint of trade was one of the few areas where the courts expressly accommodated the nineteenth century state's economy policy.

The explicit articulation of public policy in the law of contracts in restraint of trade was an open door for economic doctrine. When economic theory changed, the legal rules followed quickly. The result was a law that was not formalist at all, but quite responsive to ideological change. In this case the law responded quickly to three, nearly simultaneous revolutions. One was a revolution in economic theory, another in the forms of business organization and the rise of the modern business corporation, and a third in technology.

A pressing item on the Gilded Age policy maker's agenda was the formation of a new legal model for the regulation of competition. The eighteenth century common law of contracts in restraint of trade seemed quite irrelevant to the perceived evils of big business. The classical law of monopolies, which viewed them as exclusive grants from the sovereign, had little to do with the modern, emerging *de facto* monopoly. How the state could regulate enterprise while yet preserving the distinction between public and private law, and the essentially private nature of voluntary business transactions, became a vexing problem.

C. Classical and Neoclassical Competition

Within the modern neoclassical model "perfect competition" describes a state of affairs in which price is driven to marginal cost and firms are forced to minimize their costs through innovation and growth to the optimal size. But classicism knew nothing of marginal cost, in fact, very little of the difference between fixed and variable costs.[11] American classicists wrote little about competition, and wrote about monopoly chiefly to attack exclusive privileges given by the government. But for them as well as the

English classicists, competition meant both rivalry and freedom from constraints such as the exclusive privileges so common in the Mercantilist period.

The first generation of economists who might be called neoclassical talked about competition, but even for many of them "competition" referred to a theory about liberty and free choice, not to a description of price-cost relationships. As late as 1888 M.I.T.'s Francis Walker defined competition as "the operation of individual self-interest, among the buyers and the sellers of any article in any market. It implies that each man is acting for himself solely, by himself solely, in exchange, to get the most he can from others, and to give the least he must himself."[12] Under this definition buyers and sellers were in "competition" with each other, just as sellers competed among themselves. Further, anticompetitive conduct was identified as a restraint on individual freedom, rather than a relationship between prices and costs.

Within a decade, however, "competition" had acquired a much more technical meaning. In Yale political economist Arthur Twining Hadley's 1896 *Economics*,[13] which had the benefit of Alfred Marshall's great *Principles*, competition was something that existed only among the buyers within a single market, or only among the sellers. Hadley relied on a theory of marginal utility which he borrowed from English political economist W. Stanley Jevons and the influential Austrian school of political economists[14] to explain why demand curves slope downward, and to illustrate that under competition output would increase to the point that the demand curve intersected the cost curve. In 1899, John Bates Clark's *Distribution of Wealth*, likewise relying heavily on the Austrians, developed an even more sophisticated model of "perfect competition," illustrating that social welfare was maximized when "marginal social gain" and "marginal social sacrifice" were equated.[15]

The law actually kept close step with these changes in the conception of "competition," gradually lessening its concern about the restraints on individual freedom that contracts in restraint of trade entailed, and becoming increasingly concerned about arrangements, such as price fixing, that were anticompetitive in the neoclassical sense.

The historical concern of the common law of contracts in restraint of trade was coercion, or the elimination of noncontracting parties' freedom to act. Although completely voluntary agreements to eliminate competition, such as by price-fixing, were not generally enforceable in court, neither were they indictable offenses or even challengeable by third parties in civil actions. The law stepped in only when entrepreneurs combined to force the recalcitrant to cooperate or adhere to their terms. Thus concerted refusals to deal, or boycotts, were generally condemned. . . .

This concern with contract and freedom from coercion rather than price cost relationships explains why the classical model made little distinction between "horizontal" and "vertical" arrangements in restraint of trade. When M.I.T. economist Francis Walker and jurist Oliver Wendell Holmes, Jr., spoke of "competition," they both referred to the rivalry that existed between buyers and sellers as well as that which existed among buyers. Sellers were free to charge whatever price they pleased. They were free to do so unilaterally, and generally they were free to act in concert, provided that their agreements were purely voluntary—i.e., that no one was coerced to join the cartel. . . . Cartels did not jolt the classical lawyer's economic conscience because no one's freedom was being denied. Sellers were free to set their price, and buyers were equally free to say no. Neoclassicism greatly broadened this concept of "coercion" to include what might be called "market coercion," or the deprivation of opportunities that the competitive market itself could be expected to provide.

The concern with liberty in the classical conception of competition likewise explains the common law's obsession with consideration in cases challenging agreements in restraint of trade. Early on, courts stressed that promises not to compete would be enforced only if supported by adequate consideration. The theory appeared to be that the court had to satisfy itself that the person who had promised not to compete would not become a charge on the community. The court did this by determining that the promisor had received the market value of his promise.[16] . . . American courts sometimes noted the earlier English rule inquiring into adequacy of the consideration in cases involving contracts in restraint of trade. . . . But as early as 1811 American courts had held that nominal consideration could support a contract in restraint.[17] Some courts held much later that contracts given under seal, which needed no consideration to be binding under the general common law of contracts, nevertheless required consideration if they were contracts in restraint of trade.[18]

By the 1880's most courts held that the doctrine of consideration respecting contracts in restraint of trade was identical with the doctrine of consideration in contracts cases generally.[19] The courts would not inquire into the adequacy of the consideration; however, they would ensure that consideration had been given. . . .

The rationale of the consideration requirement was certainly not that the amount of competition interfered with depended on the presence of consideration. The point was that the doctrine of competition was part of the doctrine of liberty of contract. One could be forced to give up his freedom to make free market choices only if he had been adequately bound by contract, and contracts required consideration. Consideration tended to establish that a refusal to engage in business was voluntary and not coerced.

D. Contracts and Combinations in Restraint of Trade

Until the rise of the trusts in the 1870's and 1880's, American competition policy was located principally in two bodies of law. First was the law of corporate charters, and the questions about when they implied monopoly rights or when explicit monopoly rights would be recognized. Second was the law of contracts in restraint of trade. . . .

. . .

During most of the nineteenth century the law of cartels and mergers was not part of the law of contracts in restraint of trade. Few American decisions before 1870 dealt with price-fixing[20] and even fewer dealt directly with the competitive consequences of mergers.[21] . . . The law of contracts in restraint of trade and boycotts expressed the classical meaning of "competition," with its emphasis on liberty and freedom from coercion. But a voluntary price-fixing agreement was not "anticompetitive" in the sense that anyone's freedom to act was artificially restrained. At common law they might be unenforceable, but they were almost never actionable by nonparticipants. But beginning in the 1890's the law of cartels and mergers became the quintessential expression of neoclassical price theory, particularly of its emerging theory of competition.

This common law distinction between contracts in restraint of trade and price-fixing agreements accounts for some of the confusion concerning the meaning to be given to § 1 of the Sherman Act, which condemned "every contract, combination in the form of trust or otherwise, or conspiracy in restraint of trade." Section One was only rarely applied to covenants not to compete in the classical sense, and they were generally upheld. It quickly became, for all practical purposes, a price-fixing and antimerger statute.

One might argue that § 1 of the Sherman Act condemned both "contracts" and "combinations," and that while the first covered covenants not to compete the second covered combinations such as cartels and mergers to monopoly. But the most careful scholars of the common law, such as Justice Holmes, knew that the common law itself made no such distinction. Concern with the voluntary elimination of competition between producers simply had not played much of a part in common law adjudication. Justice Holmes's large lexicon of dissenting opinions in antitrust cases includes the following, rather startling proposition:

> The court below argues as if maintaining competition were the expressed object of the [Sherman] act. The act says nothing about competition.[22]

. . .

Holmes explained at some length why the two things forbidden by the Sherman Act, contracts or combinations "in restraint of trade" in Section One, and "monopolization" in Section Two, really had nothing to do with competition, and thus did not condemn this particular merger. "Contracts in restraint of trade" were defined by the common law as "contracts with a stranger to the contractor's business . . . , which wholly or partially restrict the freedom of the contractor in carrying on that business as otherwise he would," and "the trade restrained was the contractor's own."

"Combinations or conspiracies in restraint of trade," Holmes continued, "were combinations to keep strangers to the agreement out of the business." The objection to them was not "to their effect upon the parties making the contract" but rather "to their intended effect upon strangers to the firm and their supposed consequent effect upon the public at large." As such, they "were regarded as contrary to public policy because they monopolized, or attempted to monopolize, some portion of the trade or commerce of the realm." Labor boycotts were the most widely cited example of combinations or conspiracies in restraint of trade.

Holmes argued that the Sherman Act's words "in the form of trust or otherwise," referred not to price fixing agreements, but rather to "exclusionary practices" directed by the large combination against its competitors. Congress' concern

> was not the union of former competitors, but the sinister power exercised or supposed to be exercised by the combination in keeping rivals out of the business and ruining those who already were in. It was the ferocious extreme of competition with others, not the cessation of competition among the partners, that was the evil feared.[23]

Holmes's *Northern Securities* dissent adopted the classical position that the Sherman Act, like the common law, must be concerned with artificial restrictions placed on the individual's freedom to act. It should not care about purely voluntary arrangements, such as cartels or mergers, that simply had the effect of raising price. . . .

. . .

Holmes was correct about the historical meaning of the common law. The classical doctrine of contracts in restraint of trade had little or nothing to do with the emerging neoclassical doctrine of competition. Arthur J. Eddy observed in his treatise on combinations (1901) that "the law governing contracts in restraint of trade has no direct connection with the law governing combinations." Nevertheless, "nearly every decision against a combination assigns as one of the reasons for its illegality that it is 'in restraint of trade.' " This "involves a misapprehension and misapplication of the law governing contracts in restraint of trade."[24] A cartel agreement, for example, "is in no sense a contract in restraint of trade, unless it directly seeks to prohibit some one from again embarking in business."[25]

Frederick H. Cooke, whose appreciation of the neoclassical revolution was far greater than Eddy's, made the same observations in his important treatise on Combinations, Monopolies, and Labor

Unions (1898),[26] emphasizing even more forcefully the common law's lack of concern about "competition." The law of contracts in restraint of trade was irrational, he argued, if it were viewed as being concerned with preserving competition. . . .

. . .

That restraints doctrine was not designed to preserve competition is obvious from the way courts employed the doctrine. Under English law a restraint was "general" if it applied to all of England, or "partial" if it applied to anything less.[27] Likewise, under the American common law, restraints were ordinarily characterized as general if they applied to the entire state, or partial if they applied only to a smaller part. As one court explained this rule in 1901, it had nothing to do with competition, but rather with the fact that each state regulates its own internal affairs, "supports those who become public charges, and is interested in the industries of its citizens."[28] It did not matter that markets might encompass either much more or much less than a single state. . . .

Some of the earliest Sherman Act decisions read the common law approach into the Act. They followed Holmes, and refused to condemn cartels or mergers unless the defendants had also made contracts that were in restraint of trade at common law. . . .

But the inevitable direction of both common law and Sherman Act jurisprudence was toward more sanguinity about common law contracts in restraint of trade as a substantial public threat, and more concern about purely voluntary agreements among competitors who collectively dominated some market. The law gradually accommodated a new, more neoclassical concept of "competition," within which few contracts in restraint of trade were perceived as anticompetitive. Most of them were nothing more than noncompetition agreements attending the sale of businesses in competitively structured industries. These simply did not create the opportunity to monopolize a market.

. . .

Under this developing model even general restraints, or contracts unlimited as to time or place, could be reasonable. The rule of reason announced in the English case of *Mitchel v. Reynolds*[29] considered time and space restrictions an important attribute of reasonableness, and many later decisions held that unlimited restraints were inherently unreasonable. In *Nordenfelt* (1894),[30] however, the House of Lords held that limitations as to time and space were only elements to be considered in determining reasonableness. If the restraint covered only a small part of the market, "competition," neoclassically defined, was not injured. . . .

Coupled with classicism's traditional harshness toward contracts in restraint of trade was a surprising casualness about cartels. Within the classical model, the simple price-fixing conspiracy, with no exclusionary practices directed at nonparticipants, was not particularly offensive. Nevertheless, to say that the classical law of cartels was not concerned with competition is not quite accurate. Classicism's emphasis on liberty, coupled with the complete absence of any notion of barriers to entry, yielded a complete theory of competition. Within the classical paradigm monopoly prices could never be earned in any industry unless people were artificially restrained from entering. Such restraints could take two forms. First, they might be a grant of exclusive privileges from the sovereign, which classicism abhorred and classicist jurists repeatedly condemned. Second, the restraint could take the form of a privately-created restriction on entry, either by a contract including the restricted person as a willing participant, or else by a combination directed at other people as targets. A mere agreement among several sellers to fix prices was of little concern, provided that neither the price fixers or the State forbade others from entering the field. If the cartel members sought to charge monopoly prices, new competition would immediately frustrate their attempt. Classical cases that did condemn cartel agreements generally emphasized the defendants' efforts to exclude or coerce nonparticipants. The mere fact that customers were required to pay a higher price was not a kind of "coercion" that classicism recognized, because the customers were free to walk away and purchase elsewhere. . . .

The emerging neoclassical model of competition began to change the presumptions, however. As Frederick Cooke noted, there should be little concern for competition when one business person out of a thousand obligated himself not to practice his trade. The other nine hundred ninety-nine would continue to compete with each other. Competition would be maintained even if the one withdrew from the trade everywhere and for the rest of his life.

On the other hand, if all of those competing in a certain area should limit production or fix their prices, then the competitive injury could be substantial, even if their agreement covered only a finite geographical area and was for a finite length of time.

One of the consequences of the revolution in economic theory was a change in the legal definition of "coercion" to encompass the collective refusal to deal, and eventually to include even the loss of market opportunities that competition would have afforded. When the neoclassical revolution was complete, even the customer forced to pay a high price because of cartelization or monopolization was legally "coerced." The Sherman Act itself reflected this emergent neoclassicism. Not only did the new statute federalize the perceived common law, it also changed the status of contracts, combinations, and conspiracies in restraint of trade from merely unenforceable to affirmatively illegal. The government or even private parties forced to pay higher prices for monopolized goods had an action under the Sherman Act. . . . Section Seven of the Sherman Act gave a cause of action to any private person "injured in his business or property" by a violation. . . .

. . . The importance of this change has often been underestimated. Writers have often suggested that the Sherman Act "adopted" the common law, with the relatively minor distinction that arrangements that had been unenforceable at common law became positively illegal—that is, actionable by third parties or the state. But this change itself was revolutionary. To put it simply, there was no effective law against price fixing in the United States before the antitrust movement. The common law sometimes made price fixing agreements unenforceable—but this merely told price fixers that their cartels had to be enforced by other means than judicial action. We have no way of knowing how many cartels existed in nineteenth century America. Undoubtedly, however, in the great majority of cases they survived or thrived free from the legal challenges of customers or, in most cases, competitors injured by concerted refusals to deal. In small, isolated markets containing only a few sellers—and nineteenth century America was full of these—cartels were likely widespread and highly profitable. Recalcitrant members or newcomers could be dealt with through exclusive dealing contracts, or other more subtle forms of discipline. For all practical purposes, the perceived judicial hostility toward price-fixing agreements was not enough to become even a minimal state "policy." . . .

. . .

In the 1890's the rule of reason began to disappear from state law price-fixing cases. Almost uniformly up to that time the courts that refused to enforce price fixing agreements stressed the un-reasonableness of the defendants' conduct, their control of the market, or their exclusionary acts directed at others. In the 1890's, however, American state courts began holding for the first time that price fixing was illegal without regard to the reasonableness of the prices fixed or the market position of the defendants.[31] The framers of the Sherman Act could not have had these cases in mind, for none had yet been decided in 1890. In his famous *Addyston Pipe* decision, . . . Judge Taft cited them for the proposition that American courts had always condemned "naked" restraints without inquiry into their reasonableness, and that this per se rule had been enacted into the Sherman Act. In fact, in 1890 American courts had done no such thing.

By the turn of the century, then, the common law's theory of competition had changed completely. The rhetoric had changed relatively less, however, and some courts continued to use the language of contracts in restraint of trade in condemning price fixing and even mergers. The result was a great confusion about what the common law of trade restraints had been, and what the Sherman Act was designed to do.

. . .

E. Competition and Liberty

The doctrine of liberty of contract, drawn largely from classical political economy, held that people had a right to contract for what they pleased. During the Gilded Age, state and federal courts constitutionalized that economic doctrine. As a result, the public policy concerns articulated by the common law of contracts in restraint of trade danced dangerously near the edge of the Constitution. Did people have a liberty of contract that entitled them to eliminate competition among themselves? Both the Supreme Court and state courts eventually held that states had the general power to prohibit contracts in restraint of trade, liberty of contract notwithstanding. . . . A few state antitrust statutes were struck down under the Fourteenth Amendment, and the opinions striking them down contain some liberty of contract language. However, the statutes that were condemned impermissibly attempted to govern out-of-state transactions or exempt certain industries from their coverage.[32] State restraint-on-trade legislation or common law rules were struck down on liberty of contract grounds only rarely, although state courts frequently cited liberty of contract as a consideration in declaring a particular restraint legal.

According to classical political economy, competition itself was a form of liberty. People should be unrestrained in their decisions about what calling to pursue, what price to charge, or with whom to deal. But just as one could give up some liberty by entering into a contract, so also one could bargain away his right to compete. . . .

1. Coercion and its Meaning

The rise of neoclassicism in economics and law effected a subtle but substantial change in the meaning of "coercion." Classicism tended to view coercion as contractual and its existence as an either-or proposition. One was either coerced or he was not, and the absence of a binding contract or a concerted refusal to deal suggested that there was no coercion. Someone who was merely asked to pay a high price for a particular commodity was not coerced, for he could always walk away. . . .

But neoclassicists viewed the problem of free choice and restraint in a more subtle way. Coercion was something that could exist in degrees, and the market itself could coerce. . . .

From 1890 until around 1920 courts engaged in considerable debate over the distinction between "competition" and "coercion" in trade restraints. Most everyone agreed that certain kinds of agreements were "coercive" and ought to be condemned, but determining where the line should be drawn between competitive and coercive activities proved to be very difficult. The debate was complicated by the fact that it became a focal point of an even larger debate over the role of subjective intent in common law adjudication. . . .

For the time being, the debate over objectivism appeared to leave the problem of identifying anticompetitive restraints untouched. Courts deciding antitrust cases would continue to use subjective criteria for a long time. But one important consequence of the debate was increased attention to objective criteria in determining the plausibility of anticompetitive consequences. For example, in the 1890's and after courts looked increasingly to the economic power or size of the defendants in relation to some "market" in order to determine whether their restraint might be anticompetitive. . . .

But another important consequence of the rise of neoclassical legal theory was a shift in the meaning of "coercion." . . .

. . .

Within the classical notion of competition and liberty of contract the mere fact that a combination was designed to raise prices was insufficient to justify a legal attack by a nonparticipant. Customers as well as competitors were free to make their own market choices. They were equally in "competition" with sellers, and if the price of a commodity was raised too high, they would respond by refusing to buy. . . .

The classical American doctrine of contracts in restraint of trade thus recognized and permitted two kinds of "coercion" as consistent with the individual's liberty of contract. First, individuals could bind *themselves* contractually. Reasonable contracts in restraint of trade, were generally enforceable among the parties. Secondly, individuals agreeing with each other could coerce third parties provided that the coercion was expressed in the market and nowhere else. In that case, "competition" would protect the coerced parties. Today we have little difficulty regarding cartelization as a form of coercion directed at customers—but in the classical model the customers were free to walk away, just as sellers were free to set their prices. . . .

Classical political economy took nearly a century to develop a model of competition in which certain kinds of business conduct were "coercive" simply because they altered the structure and character of the market. During the last quarter of the nineteenth century judges and political economists simultaneously developed the theory that when a firm or a group of firms acting together comes to dominate a particular market, then their price increases or refusals to deal may be *inherently* coercive—because the buyers in the market do not have adequate alternatives. Through the second half of the century the "rule of reason" used by courts to determine whether to enforce contracts in restraint of trade gradually became a rule that looked principally at the defendants' position in the market. If the defendants collectively controlled the entire market, their combination was more likely to be enforced in court. But if they controlled less than the whole market, then the court was more likely to see competitive alternatives and commensurately less likely to condemn the arrangement. . . .

Market dominance became the test of illegality in other areas of the law as well. In some cases the departure from the traditional common law was remarkable. For example, the common law trust device and the asset acquisition became important vehicles for corporate mergers in the 1870's and 1880's. They were designed to evade restrictions in the corporation acts of every state ᵗhat forbad ownership by one corporation of the shares of another corporation (holding companies) and corporations that engaged in a wider variety of business than was authorized in the original charter. When states attorneys general brought *quo warranto* proceedings against these corporations the directors seemed to be quite literally in compliance with their charters. Nevertheless, state courts quickly developed the rule that corporate mergers creating market dominance were illegal simply because corporations were not authorized by their charters to monopolize their markets. . . . At common law a combination yielding a monopoly may sometimes have been an agreement unenforceable as between the parties. But the new challenges had been brought by the state against completely voluntary mergers.

As noted earlier, the Sherman Act represented an important structural departure from the common law in that it permitted state or third party challenges to agreements that never would have been challenged successfully at common law. . . . So the court was *necessarily* writing on a clean slate when it determined the standard for illegality. There could not have been a common law standard. . . .

2. The Classical Exception: Articles of
Prime Necessity

Classicism recognized one important exception to its position that combinations and cartels did not coerce customers. Customers were not free to walk away if the restraint covered the market for an article of "prime necessity"—something that no one could do without. Restraints involving the necessities of life, were treated more harshly than those involving goods about which buyers had discretion. This rule of heightened scrutiny applied to both classical contracts in restraint of trade and to price-fixing agreements.

. . .

By 1890 neoclassicism had begun to develop a model of competition in which the concept of "prime necessity" was all but irrelevant. Alfred Marshall's 1890 *Principles* generalized about the difference between the amount that a customer was willing to pay and the price that a competitive market should yield. There was almost always a difference, although it might be larger for articles of prime necessity. But even a cartel covering the most frivolous luxury might raise price above the competitive level. More importantly, questions about the "necessity" of an article were far less important in the new competition model than questions about how easily it could be produced, and how quickly new producers could enter the field. . . .

As noted earlier, the judiciary responded to the emergence of the neoclassical model of competition with an increased hostility toward price fixing. Initially, the hostility was directed at cartels of articles of prime necessity. In 1889 even the United State Supreme Court took the position that price fixing with respect to an article of "public necessity," in this case illuminating gas, should be illegal even though price fixing in ordinary items might be protected by liberty of contract:

> Hence, while it is justly urged that those rules which say that a given contract is against public policy, should not be arbitrarily extended so as to interfere with the freedom of contract, yet, in the instance of business of such character that it presumably cannot be restrained to any extent whatever without prejudice to the public interest, courts decline to enforce or sustain contracts imposing such restraint, however partial, because in contravention of public policy.[33]

The hostility toward price fixing and other anticompetitive agreements quickly became much more generalized, and the focus on articles of prime necessity began to fall away. . . . In the principal Sherman Act price-fixing cases, *Trans-Missouri* (1897), *Joint Traffic* (1898), and *Addyston Pipe* (1898), the courts found it absolutely irrelevant that the price-fixed products were not articles of prime necessity. . . . From that point on the collusion rule became generalized to all goods and services. . . .

3. The Sherman Act and Liberty of Contract

Classicism's concern to protect liberty of contract accounts for a great deal of its reluctance to interfere with contracts in restraint of trade. This antinomy between liberty of contract and competition quickly spilled over into judicial interpretation of the Sherman Act. Few people believed the Sherman Act should be declared unconstitutional for interfering with the constitutional liberty of contract that the Supreme Court had found in the Fifth and Fourteenth Amendments. Much more important was the economic issue of how broadly the words "contract, combination . . . or conspiracy in restraint of trade" should be defined, given liberty of contract. . . .

In his dissent in *Trans-Missouri* (1897) Justice (later Chief Justice) White expressed the belief that the Sherman Act would violate the constitutional liberty of contract if it deviated from the common law rule of reason and condemned certain restraints as illegal per se:

> The plain intention of the law was to protect the liberty of contract and the freedom of trade. Will this intention not be frustrated by a construction which, if it does not destroy, at least gravely impairs both the liberty of the individual to contract and the freedom of trade? If the rule of reason no longer determines the right of the individual to contract, or secures the validity of contracts upon which trade depends and results, what becomes of the liberty of the citizen or of the freedom of trade? Secured no longer by the law of reason all these rights become subject, when questioned, to the mere caprice of judicial authority. Thus, a law in favor of freedom of contract, it seems to me, is so interpreted as to gravely impair that freedom.[34]

The defendants in the *Joint Traffic*, *Addyston Pipe* and *Northern Securities* cases all argued that price fixing agreements or mergers among voluntary participants were protected by liberty of contract, for they were not unreasonable restraints of trade at common law. ... But Justice Peckham, although one of the Court's great champions of liberty of contract, adopted the narrow position that railroads were "public franchises" operating under corporate charters and with the state's permission. One could not presume that the franchises entitled the railroads to behave anticompetitively.[35]

This argument suggested implicitly that unincorporated businesses might have the constitutional right to fix prices. But in its *Addyston Pipe* affirmance a year later, the Supreme Court clarified itself, Justice Peckham once again writing the opinion. Although liberty of contract was protected by the Constitution, the power of Congress to regulate interstate commerce was also protected by the Constitution. In a remarkable departure from traditional principles of federalism, Peckham then held that the commerce clause was not only a division of regulatory power between the federal government and the states, [but] it also divided regulatory power between the federal government and private parties. The doctrine of liberty of contract "has never been ... held" to include "the right of an individual to enter into private contracts [which] would, if performed, result in the regulation of interstate commerce and in the violation of an act of Congress upon that subject."[36]

This turned out to be a brilliant solution to the problem. ... It completely disassociated the classical concern with liberty of contract from the Sherman Act's concern about elimination of competition. If a restraint was within Congress' power to regulate interstate commerce, and thus within the jurisdiction of the Sherman Act, then liberty of contract did not apply. This rationalization effectively paved the way for a much more neoclassical federal antitrust policy.

· · ·

Conclusion

Ever since the Sherman Act was passed jurists have ascribed to it a "constitutional" quality. The Supreme Court concluded in 1933 that the Act had "a generality and adaptability comparable to that found to be desirable in constitutional provisions."[37] This is simply another way of saying that the antitrust laws are a tool of economic policy making. As such, they are eternally wedded to prevailing economic doctrine and forced to change when economic ideology changes.

The result is a statute whose meaning has changed over the years, and which certainly is less predictable than some would like it to be. But such instability is a small price to pay, considering the alternatives. The worst alternative is a statute frozen in time, applying an economic ideology of a past era simply because that ideology prevailed at some particular moment.

One cannot escape the Sherman Act's dependence on economic ideology by interpreting it to follow a set of common law rules, unless one naively believes that the common law is somehow exempt from economic ideology in a way that the federal legislation is not. The common law experienced its own evolution, which closely tracked changes in economic doctrine. The nineteenth century judge applying the common law of trade restraints implicitly applied an economic ideology just as certainly as the federal judge deciding an antitrust case in 1892, 1960 or 1988. For that reason, the Sherman Act is "constitutional" in exactly the same way that the common law was "constitutional." Escaping ideology is never easy. When economic policy is concerned, it is always impossible.

*A longer version of this essay is printed in the Iowa Law Review (1989).

Part II

POSTMODERN ANTITRUST

Part I of this volume demonstrates that the political economy of the Sherman Act is rich and varied. One can hardly read these essays and come away with the impression that antitrust is one dimensional. Diversity and pluralism of thought informed the early debates of the Sherman Act; they continue to do so today. Does this mean that antitrust is ephemeral, without form or substance? A linear history of antitrust suggests that its form and substance are cyclical. Antitrust is bound by its cultural experience, political institutions, corporate climate, political movements, and philosophical agendas. What period, then, is represented by today's antitrust? Are we likely to see new directions for antitrust?

The essays in Part II address the contemporary debates that surround the Sherman Act. As in other academic disciplines, such as art and architecture, antitrust movements can be identified and characterized. In antitrust jurisprudence, a discernible intellectual period began some fifteen years ago. Modernism in antitrust ("The New Learning"), though growing in the academic literature and some lower court opinions in the 1960s and early 1970s, did not reach the Supreme Court until around 1974 with the decision in the *General Dynamics*[1] case. Modernism in antitrust, as a definable period, corresponds roughly with the latter part of the modern period in art and architecture in the 1970s and 1980s. If the question is asked whether there are identifiable characteristics among these otherwise divergent disciplines, the answer seems in the affirmative and, indeed, the postmodern era seems similar as well.

Modernism in antitrust is the period when courts began to reinterpret the policy and goals of the Sherman Act. This reinterpretation is described and analyzed by the articles in this section by Posner, Rule, and Meyer. Their views demonstrate a countercurrent to the more traditional antitrust paradigms. Up to the 1970s, antitrust convention was comfortable with a multivalued approach to antitrust policy, as represented by the industrial organization approach of the 1940s to 1970s.[2] That view is explored in Professors Kaysen and Turner's essay. Modernism, however, ushered in an entirely different paradigm. Consequently, the antitrust canvas was significantly altered.

Neoclassical economics forms the core of the modern analysis. Marginal utility and price theory dominate the constructs. The geometry of the language speaks of demand and supply curves. Rational behavior in the market is defined in terms of profit motivation. The technical terms reference allocative efficiency as the central analysis. The style is characterized by reference to the sovereignty of the market; there is little concern for market failures and negative externalities. Perfect competition and the state of market equilibrium serve as the intellectual baselines. Competition, in turn, is defined as conduct that maximizes economic efficiency without regard to distributive consequences. The political economy of antitrust has not been important to the development of the modern period. The question asked, rather, is whether a certain allocation of resources is efficient. The distributional consequences of the allocation are irrelevant.

Modernism in antitrust, as in art and architecture, has a predictable, monolithic style.[3] There is strength in its purity, logic, and procedural formalism. Its logic and form are straight lined and direct. Its style is preformed but static. Its substance and content are shaped by ideology. In practice, as well as in theory, there is a certain minimalist, if not austere, approach in application.

Antitrust in the modern era forces self-examination of our whole antitrust regulatory policy toward American business. In the process, antitrust is polarized. One could claim that antitrust modernism has produced what Thomas Kuhn, when writing about the history of science, observed as a "paradigm crisis: a moment in history when the accepted belief system becomes inadequate and the possibility of a new belief system is only vaguely perceived."[4] Modernism has rejected substantial portions of the legislative history of the Sherman Act. The distributive goals of entrepreneurial independence, equal access to markets, dispersion of economic power, and balance of power among competitors are discarded in favor of a simple calculus that promises quantitative results. And, in this case, the formula selected often preordains the outcome.

At its extreme, the "efficient market theory" of the modern era posits that if the conduct is inefficient the market will correct it; thus there is no need for government intervention. As a concession, the proponents of the efficiency model now recognize that horizontal cartels and horizontal mergers that result in high market shares can lead to output restrictions and higher prices that warrant antitrust correction. But even here, the enforcement range is substantially narrower than that permitted by the traditional period of antitrust as described in this part by Kaysen and Turner. Contradictions abound between the broad-based interventionist viewpoint of traditionalists and the regulatory minimalism espoused by the proponents of the modern school of antitrust economics.

The articles by Kaplow, Fox, and Flynn that follow demonstrate, in contrast to those by Posner, Rule, and Meyer, that antitrust has been polarized, that there is little consensus among the antitrust scholarly community.[5] Indeed, one might ask, as Rule and Meyer do, whether we are on the verge of an antitrust counterrevolution, or at least a "paradigm crisis." If so, what alternatives are there that can be faithful to the legislative history and at the same time accommodate the important contributions that the modern school of antitrust has given us? In short, can the new learning in antitrust, ushered in during the modern era, be replaced with a new discourse, a new era? The essays by Flynn, Kaplow, and Fox suggest the answer to this question is in the affirmative. But we must inquire what synthesis can be made from this counterattack.

The past can still illuminate the future. Postmodern antitrust, like its counterparts in art and architecture, should return to more traditional, classical origins. The weight of the historical record, as this volume demonstrates, is that certain important values articulated during the Sherman Act debate, during the common law and during the traditional period of antitrust, have been lost during the modern era. A return to a more traditional interpretation of "competition" would be more faithful to the legislative history and the original intention of the Sherman Act. In order to return antitrust policy to an interpretation more anchored in its historical foundations, we need not discard the important concept of economic efficiency. Rather we need to reaffirm that the *raison d'être* for antitrust is the promotion of competition.

Importantly, however, competition has been defined in various ways since 1890. To be sure, if anything is certain about the history and political economy of antitrust it is that antitrust is cyclical in nature. Patterns develop and reemerge as economic and political theories change.[6] As this study of the Sherman Act indicates, we have gone through at least four periods where the theory of competition has changed: The classical period (1880 to the 1920s); the neoclassical period (1920 to the 1940s); the industrial organization period (1940 to the 1970s); and the modern era ("The New Learning") (1970 to the present). And now, perhaps, we are on the verge of a new era that once again will transform our understanding of competition. Postmodern antitrust can borrow from much of the early learning as we consider a new, or rearticulated theory of competition.

The classical definition of competition and the modern era's emphasis on efficiency need not be considered at odds. Between these two theories, balance and proportion can be reached in harmonizing the cycles of antitrust. For example, in the classical era of antitrust, competition was defined as a market process—the process of rivalry between large and small competitors in markets that were open and accessible. There was no bias toward small firms, no prejudice against large firms. The ideal envisioned that the process of rivalrous competition would result in efficient outcomes: producers would supply goods desired by consumers at competitive prices with the least amount of resources being expended in the production and distribution of the product to the consumer.

The market in the classical sense was dynamic and robust. Competitive and competing strategies were the norm.[7] The "process" of competing strategies was central to the vitality of the market. Plainly, the market theory was, as Henry Carter Adams observed, to open the door of opportunity wide and to trust the results.[8] This dynamic process shaped the definition of competition in the classical period.

Many classicists were opposed to antitrust reform and government intervention in the market. They believed that the idea of competition as a process of rivalry would achieve efficient outcomes even if firms grew to monopoly proportions. Large scales were thought to produce certain economies in production and distribution. Not all classicists, however, shared the view that government intervention was unnecessary. Henry Carter Adams and Allyn Young both advocated a role for market intervention when a firm's size unleashed monopoly power.[9] For them, competition and monopoly power were not synonymous.

> There is a substantial difference between competing and 'attempting to monopolize' [and] . . . [t]here can be little doubt but that the public policy which the [Sherman] Act was intended to embody is that competition should be maintained, artificial monopoly destroyed, and its growth prevented.[10]

Thus, even in the classical period, limited government intervention was contemplated. If rivalry as a process is to be encouraged, then the enforcement objectives of antitrust are clear: markets must be open and free so that competitors (both suppliers and consumers) can enter and exit without trade being restrained. Government must assure that barriers to entry and exit are not artificially erected to injure competition, that differential barriers between incumbents and potential competitors are eliminated, that market opportunities are encouraged, that market independence and interaction are sanctioned, and that market power that results in predation or exclusion is enjoined. Only in a regime where these objectives are protected can consumer welfare be enhanced. Rivalrous competition can succeed only when diverse interaction and individualism dominate the culture of the market and when government is prepared to fashion a remedy when market imperfections occur.[11]

If classicism was, in the main, the protector of "entrepreneurial opportunities" and liberty of contracts,[12] how can state intervention in the market find limited acceptance beyond the concern over market power by a few? What learning can we take from classicism? Does classicism inform the role that the Sherman Act should play today, for example, in vertical contracts?

Classicism did offer a public policy against contracts in restraint of trade. If individual freedom was restrained, the conduct was characterized as anticompetitive;[13] hence the contract was unenforceable in court. Coercion in contracting was abhorred, as were concerted refusals to deal. Voluntary agreements were sanctioned, but involuntary or coerced agreements were contrary to the classical model of competition. If buyers were not free to set contract terms, their freedom was restrained, trade was impaired, and rivalry was affected between both producers and buyers and among buyers.[14]

The Sherman Act incorporated this theory of the law of contracts in restraint of trade and concerted refusals to deal. It took what at common law was merely an unenforceable contract and created a public offense when liberty and freedom were violated through coercion or when combinations attempted to monopolize through exclusion. Thus, artificial restrictions on one's freedom to act, which coerce or exclude others, form the core of the classical concerns and the early Sherman Act interpretations.[15] But, under the modern era, a new learning, one informed by neoclassical thinking, has become entrenched. Competition is not defined in terms of rivalry but rather economic efficiency. In the name of the advancement of efficiency, freedom of contract and liberty have been lost in certain instances.

Given the change in interpretation of the Sherman Act under both the neoclassical and modern eras, the concern for coercion and lack of freedom in contracting, particularly in the more permissive area of vertical contracting, is an important insight or rediscovery of the roots of the Sherman Act. It suggests a greater role for government enforcement and broader liability for suppliers of products who coerce retailers into numerous unwanted and costly contract terms.

In a broader sense, the lack of liberty among all suppliers and buyers in the market belies a market characterized by rivalrous competition. The legislative history of the Sherman Act that was debated during this classical era strongly demonstrates that any contemporary meaning of competition should be inclusive. The idea of competition should not be defined narrowly with the result that important historical meanings are lost. An inclusive meaning of competition embraces the idea of competition "as a process," not as an end result or conclusion that a certain transaction is efficient and thus lawful. Moreover, an inclusive meaning should sweep in the idea that market strategies that coerce, exclude, or predate are illegal.[16] As first recognized during the neoclassical era, cartelization and monopolization can legally and practically coerce, exclude, and predate.[17] Antitrust policy, then, should contemplate a more activist enforcement role from both the public and private sectors. As the reaction to the modern era becomes more thoughtful, an austere antitrust landscape and a minimalist enforcement approach are unlikely to advance further in the postmodern era.

This postmodern antitrust synthesis draws on and is suggested by the articles set forth in Part I and those that follow in this part. The evolution of antitrust has been gradual and fluid. Each of the following essays invites our attention and invokes our thoughts. Collectively, they portend a new period of antitrust—a postmodern era; individually, they suggest that a solid consensus has not yet emerged. What is clear, however, is that antitrust has not been nor should it be one dimensional;[18] viewed in historical perspective, it is multidimensional. *Ex post* rationalization for conduct can not replace an *ex ante* deliberative process.[19] Nor should antitrust be dominated by economic cliches.[20]

The essays in this part of the volume begin with the industrial organization view of antitrust policy. Professors Carl Kaysen and Donald Turner awoke the antitrust debate in the 1960s with the publication of their book, *Antitrust Policy: An Economic and Legal Analysis*. It represents the position of the industrial organization period that lasted from the 1940s to the middle 1970s. With nearly seventy years of Sherman Act experience at the time of this publication, *Antitrust Policy* urged a fresh look at the relationship between market structure and business behavior, particularly the economic problems resulting from oligopoly.

Market structure and economic performance were not seen in isolation but rather as a concomitant paradigm that could bring greater clarity to the issue of competition as affected by market power. Maintaining competition became the objective of antitrust as the chief means of ensuring efficient use of resources; efficiency itself as the goal of antitrust was rejected. Competition analysis at its core centered on the market structure, conduct, and performance and the resulting effect on market power.

Kaysen and Turner, in short, refocused the antitrust debate on the "reciprocal relation between market power and business conduct." Clearly, their antitrust examination was both descriptive and normative, both microeconomic and macroeconomic in orientation. Their viewpoint included the welfare of society as well as the efficiency of a particular transaction between a supplier and buyer in a single market. They embraced certain noneconomic goals for antitrust as well as economic maximums, including: a limitation on the power of big business; performance, including both efficiency and progressiveness; fair dealing; and protection of the process of competition through a restraint on market power.

As we see in their writing, Kaysen and Turner's call for antitrust reexamination urges more government intervention to correct market failures attributed to excessive market power. Thus their conduct-performance-structure paradigm admits more antitrust liability. This analysis, at bottom, became the core of the government enforcement efforts in the 1960s and 1970s and, in turn, was embraced by the Supreme Court antitrust jurisprudence of the time. At its simplest, it condemns market power and barriers to entry, unrelated to economies of scale, as unfair trade conditions warranting antitrust correction. But the authors do qualify their thrust.

> . . . insofar as reduction of market power is incompatible with efficiency and progressiveness, we subordinate [the reduction of market power to efficiency and progressiveness]. If, for example, the efficient scale of operation in a particular market is so large in relation to the size of the market that efficient firms are so few in number as to make their possession of market power likely, and the reduction of market power cannot be achieved except at the cost of a substantial loss in efficiency, our policy would call for no action against the power itself.[21]

And, the other two goals—promoting fair business conduct and the redistribution of social power between small and large business—are lower in the hierarchy of policy.

Plainly, however, Kaysen and Turner view "the achievement and maintenance" of the process of competition as crucial. "Competition is seen as an end in itself rather than as a means to achieve desirable economic results."[22] Functionally, competition is linked to "the desirability of limiting business power,"[23] and instrumentally it is the foundation on which Kaysen and Turner advance the theme of "fair dealing among business firms."[24] Finally, competition as a process of rivalry is seen not only as a constraint on business decision making but, in economic terms, "it forces businesses to move closer to a policy of long-run profit maximization."[25]

In "The Chicago School of Antitrust Analysis," Judge Richard Posner describes the early origin of the "Chicago" approach to antitrust. He identifies its genesis in neoclassicism. The central themes of marginal utility and price theory first emerged around 1890 when Alfred Marshall's now classic text was published. The modern version of neoclassicism appeared at the University of Chicago in the 1950s. It is from this point that modern antitrust, with its price theory focus, has developed into a rich, though controversial, philosophy of antitrust. The Chicago School gained ascendance in the 1970s; in the 1980s it reached its pinnacle of influence. Numerous antitrust scholars as well as courts have, at various times, embraced the Chicago philosophy of antitrust. The period of modernism in antitrust, which includes approximately the last fifteen years, is the era of the Chicago School neoclassical approach.

As the essays in Part II of this volume reveal, the Chicago viewpoint accepts only permissive regulatory intervention; great faith is placed in the market to correct market failures and externalities. Unilateral action by a monopolist is not a concern. Government intervention or private enforcement of the Sherman Act under a traditional industrial organization approach is condemned. Minimal enforcement and market sovereignty reign supreme in the modern period of antitrust. Judge Posner, like Judge Bork before him, explains why the modern, neoclassical approach has captured the attention of the American courts the last fifteen years.

The first principle of antitrust, according to the Chicago

School, is that firms "cannot in general obtain or enhance monopoly power by unilateral action unless, of course, they are irrationally willing to trade profits for position." Given this premise, antitrust enforcement should be directed only at cartels and horizontal mergers that have the potential to create monopolies or drastically reduce the number of sellers. This theory comes from neoclassical price theory. Assumptions rest on the premises that all businesses are rational profit maximizers, that demand curves slope downward, and that resources gravitate toward areas where they will earn higher profits and returns.

Unlike the traditional industrial organization school of antitrust that generally studies specific industries, Posner credits the Chicago School with developing a general theory that explains economic behavior across a range of industries. He chides traditionalists with building economic theories only after empirical data are gathered from specific industries rather than beginning with a general economic theory that explains all economic behavior across industries. He applauds the work of Aaron Director in not studying specific antitrust practices "but by looking for an explanation for them that squared with basic economic theory." For example, tying arrangements were once thought of as facilitating devices where a monopolist could use its monopoly in one product as a leverage into another product market. Barriers to entry were thought to prevent new competitors from entering markets even when the monopolist was pricing well above marginal costs. Neither idea, Posner asserts, was well founded.

Today the wealth maximization theory claims that tie-ins are merely a method of price discrimination that may reduce "the misallocative effects of monopoly." The original theory of barriers to entry has come under attack for its overinclusiveness. Existing firms usually face the same cost structure as new entrants. Thus the law should not recognize the theory of barriers to entry unless the costs to the new entrant exceed those that the incumbent competitor bears. It is only a differential effect that should warrant antitrust scrutiny, Posner and Stigler claim.

Posner recognizes that the Chicago School has undergone certain revisions since the early period in the 1950s. Cartels were considered too unstable to require enforcement attention. Collusion was not considered an antitrust issue, since it could not last because it would be futile absent real barriers to entry. Only later, beginning around 1969, did theorists of the Chicago School grudgingly concede that antitrust concerns include explicit price fixing agreements and horizontal mergers that created monopolies. Posner concludes, however, with the observation that "changes of mind" within both the Chicago School and its principal rivals have produced a steady trend toward convergence. He posits that vertical integration, once considered a serious problem, is no longer, that advertising once considered a barrier to entry is now seen as actually helping consumers, and that predatory pricing is seen by many as irrational and impractical.

Posner's attempt to make the intellectual differences seem minimal is an effort to cast the Chicago position as a broad-based, widely entrenched philosophy. For many courts, it has become just that as the efficiency analysis has become accepted in many antitrust contexts. Many antitrust scholars, however, would disagree with Posner's assessment, as the remaining articles in this volume attest. A new era or cycle of antitrust may be emerging. Postmodern antitrust awaits us.

Charles Rule and David Meyer challenge the scholarly attacks on the Chicago School's economic approach. Their essay represents a clear statement of Reaganesque ideology. Their introduction even suggests that they would favor a business autonomy rule over Sherman Act coverage of economic activity. But their textual tone moderates when they defend an antitrust policy grounded in the goal of wealth maximization. Their thesis, however, incorporates the idea that efficiency does not mean the lowest possible price to the consumer. Rather, the supplier's business judgment to expend money to innovate, to advertise, to promote, and to make the product as desirable as possible should be respected and without legal challenge.

The Sherman Act, in their opinion, should be interpreted to maximize both producer and consumer surplus, thus increasing the total surplus of society. Wealth distribution concerns are irrelevant, at least if one is attempting to protect consumer surplus at the expense of producer surplus. The fact that a monopolist fails to pass cost savings on to consumers through lower prices should not trigger the Sherman Act, the authors opine, because eventually an equilibrium will be achieved. The social cost of monopoly power is less relevant than the benefits that can be achieved through increases in producer surplus. When the authors balance the trade-off effects of producer and consumer surplus, they favor the protection of producer surplus to the detriment of, at least, short-run consumer surplus.

A canvass of the Supreme Court treatment of the Sherman Act leads Rule and Meyer to observe that the "Supreme Court has more or less consistently adhered to an efficiency-based rationale." Their canvass from 1890 to 1974, however, includes but one small paragraph and fails to explain scores of the leading cases, including the famous admonition in *Trans-Missouri* that the Sherman Act should aid "small dealers and worthy men." At best, their review of Supreme Court antitrust jurisprudence is selective and limited. The cases they do cite, moreover, do not provide meaning or content to the theme of the authors' article: consumer welfare as the goal of the Sherman Act. Few would disagree that consumer welfare is at the core of the Sherman Act. The debate is how that term is defined in the legislative history and how it is or should be applied today through the antitrust laws.

Professor John Flynn offers a jurisprudential attack on the neoclassical model of antitrust advanced by Posner, Rule, and Meyer. He condemns the application of one school of thought as the exclusive means for interpreting antitrust policy. Flynn rejects the Chicago claim that its economic model is neutral and objective. That claim, he observes, is intellectually arrogant and is similar in application to the rise a century ago of legal positivism. Flynn denounces both approaches in their "belief that law could be reduced to fixed rules capable of mechanical and repetitious application divorced from the deeper moral values that law reflects."

Flynn, as does Fox in her subsequent essay, views the antitrust goals established by Congress as multivalued. "Every competent and objective study of the legislative history of the antitrust laws indicated that they were passed with a series of qualitative political, social and economic goals or values in mind to guide their implementation." He elaborates by undercutting the deductive logic inherent in the Chicago School's approach.

Flynn believes that the analytical process of antitrust should include a component of inductive logic where the relevant facts and "moral objectives" underlying the law, together with the history and experience of the law, inform the resolution. A deductive analytical regime that assumes a model of perfect competition and rational, profit-centered buyers and sellers is labeled "abstract and unexamined." The discourse is normatively anchored, he laments. Utilitarianism and libertarianism are both philosophies that support the neoclassical paradigm. In either case, a political and philosophical agenda drives the decision-making model. Neutral, objective criteria mask the reality of the real analysis which, at bottom, centers on monetary value and materialism. Flynn, too, concludes that our antitrust regime must be broader and richer; it must be examined through a transaction-oriented lens that focuses on the process of the competition, not on a quantitative concept grounded only in the rigid deductive science of economics.

In "Antitrust, Law and Economics and the Court," Professor Louis Kaplow opens his discussion with a broad based attack on the Chicago School's economic analysis. He pointedly notes that the use of economic theory did not begin with the Chicagoans' new law and economics perspective. Reliance on economic theory in antitrust decision making goes back at least to the 1940s. But this antitrust jurisprudence was not grounded in the geometry of marginal utility or price theory. Instead, the industrial organization concepts of structure, conduct, and performance were the lens through which antitrust conduct was viewed. For example, the Warren Court era heavily used the economic analysis of industrial organization in its antitrust cases, although the approach differed markedly from the Chicago style employed by the Burger Court. As such, Kaplow does not believe that there has been a substantial increase in the use of economic analysis in decision making. Only the nature of the economic theories has changed.

Kaplow's thesis is that the Chicago School of antitrust does not represent "the best and most current economic wisdom to the economic questions posed by antitrust law." While he concedes that price theory has utility as a starting point in the analysis, it is nevertheless underinclusive in scope. Case studies of particular industries provide important empirical data that are, in large measure, ignored by theorists of the Chicago School. He faults the Chicago approach for too heavy reliance on the 1890 formulation of price theory, to the exclusion of theoretical advances in microeconomics that suggest that the analysis is far more dynamic than the static model used by the profit maximization school of economists. Still further, the Chicago School, he opines, has been slow to appreciate the growing literature that has emerged on the role strategic behavior can play in the market and injuries to rivals that can follow from it.

Kaplow also questions several basic premises of the modern school of economic analysis. First, it operates from the premise that markets are largely self-correcting.

It assumes a perfectly functioning market. If practices within the market are restrictive, they are presumed to produce efficiencies. Hence there is no need for antitrust enforcement. A regime of antitrust, on the other hand, proceeds from the premise that intervention in the market through enforcement can better compensate and deter restrictive practices then can the market. Antitrust can respond to restrictive practices in dynamic markets, while static models of price theory are really nonresponsive. Moreover, Chicagoans do not address seriously enough the obvious question in their perfect market assumptions: How long it takes to weed out inefficient practices before the market self-corrects. Time delays can produce significant injuries to rivals and consumers. Temporal limitations are not part of the market evolution theory.

The rule of reason analysis invoked by the new law and economics era is questioned by Kaplow. Chicago advocates are fond of employing the rule-of-reason decision-making style to the exclusion of the traditional per se test of illegality. This formulation is applied to almost all restrictive practices except simple horizontal price fixing. Kaplow raises the question whether this legal rule is a disguise to remove restrictive practice from antitrust scrutiny. Is antitrust deregulation the aim of modern antitrust analysis?

Other concerns raised by Kaplow include the modern preference for proof of market power as a precondition to any liability, and hostility to the relevance that intent evidence may play in an antitrust regime. Kaplow notes that it is not obvious that economists can tell us or have anything to say about how much market power is too much before antitrust should intervene. Moreover, is not intent evidence highly relevant on the questions, for example, of whether a proposed joint venture is actually a cover for price fixing or whether a firm actually wanted to price below cost and recoup the cost later after the rival is forced to exit the market? Antitrust has always inferred effects from intent. And, after all, the modern school assumes firms will know the effects of their planned conduct better than a court. Kaplow asks whether it follows, then, that intent evidence should be given great weight. But Chicagoans are only interested in economic effects.

After making his point that the use of economic analysis by the Supreme Court has not increased significantly over the years, Kaplow addressed the remaining question: Are politics and ideology the driving forces behind the court's shift in antitrust? His review of the Supreme Court cases indicates that the earlier cases plainly made "explicit references to broader purposes" beyond economic efficiency as the sole objective of antitrust. This is true, he finds, from the earliest case of *Trans-Missouri* in 1897 through the Warren Court era. He debunks the notion that the Supreme Court has adopted in whole the Chicago economic model of how markets work. He sees precedent not cited in some instances and taken out of context in others, and a patchwork of ideas from Chicago that only inconsistently has found its way into the Court's opinions.

Finally, Kaplow concludes that the modern interpretation of the legislative history of the Sherman Act is "so farfetched that it is hard to take . . . seriously." It is "virtually impossible that the Sherman Act could have been crafted with only economic efficiency in mind." This is so because the legislators "gave little attention" to economists; and economists at the time were hostile to any antitrust movement. Moreover, the concept of allocative inefficiency with its implications for welfare loss advanced by Judges Bork and Posner was not understood by economists at the time the Sherman Act passed. Thus we cannot expect that the legislatures understood it or codified it into law. At bottom, Kaplow sees the modern era of antitrust with its static price theory as merely an

activist recreation of antitrust rather than . . . an attempt to return to the statutes or their original meaning. Overall, recent changes in antitrust—actual or advocated—are in large respect a function of politics, even though the position advocated is defined in terms of economics.[26]

In the final article, Professor Eleanor Fox takes issue with the modern antitrust focus on efficiency. In her article, "The Modernization of Antitrust: A New Equilibrium," she contrasts modernization with the more traditional era of antitrust that reflected a philosophy rooted in a competition equality model. Dispersion of economic power and access to markets were benchmarks that characterized antitrust jurisprudence through the 1960s. She finds antitrust's goals to be complementary, not exclusionary.

Efficiency as the sole or main goal of antitrust is as popular today, Fox asserts, because it is a normative judgment driven by a conservative political philosophy and agenda. A conservative philosophy advocates less government intervention in the market and more individual freedom. Fear over government regulation is greater than fear over aggregate power held by big business. Faith in the ability of the individual is strong, and any attempt to "equalize opportunity" in the market will only interfere with meritocracy. "If the job of antitrust . . . is only to prohibit transactions that impair efficiency, then government interference with private business transactions is minimized and the values of a free society are preserved."

Liberal philosophy, in contrast, fears concentrated power and wealth, favors government intervention to correct market failures, and views business as unequal in opportunity. "The liberal view is compatible" with a competition equality paradigm where government, through antitrust, can regulate business and provide equal access and opportunity to small business that may have equal abilities but not equal access or opportunity. Fox equates liberal philosophy with the multivalued goals of antitrust.

She recognizes that virtually all antitrust scholars and judges today agree that antitrust should attempt to facilitate a system that increases the "responsiveness of producers to consumer's wants." She identifies three models for evaluating efficiency within this context. The first is centered on an output restriction analysis, or allocative efficiency. Welfare economics is used to determine whether certain practices enhance or retard social welfare. The second approach begins with the idea that business is efficient, that it is a rational profit maximizer, and that business freedom and autonomy should be maximized. Government intervention in the market should be minimized. This model contemplates the narrowest role for antitrust. It is the most extreme or libertarian view of government authority to regulate.

The third model is one that defines competition not in technical economic terms but rather simply as a process of rivalry. Through an environment that fosters numerous competitors in rivalrous competition, efficiency will emerge and consumer welfare will increase. A dynamic market characterized by diversity, where competitors are in competition to satisfy consumer desires, is the optimum goal of this approach.

For this approach to work, the antitrust regime must assure that entry barriers remain low, opportunities for entry into markets are high, and market power is checked. The model, therefore, assumes that government vigilance of markets will remain strong and the process of competition is the central value. From this state, the most efficient market in terms of allocative as well as productive efficiency will emerge.

It is this last model that Fox advances as the most consistent philosophy of antitrust and one that is faithful to the history and tradition of the Sherman Act. While it is based on an efficiency outcome, it is the one paradigm that can be harmonized with the many nonefficiency objectives of antitrust, including dispersion of economic power, opportunity for entrepreneurial access to markets, and promotion of consumer interests. In sum, freedom of choice, both for the supplier and consumer, is maximized when a society chooses to define competition as the dynamic process of rivalry.

In short, if we return to a competition definition that embraces a modified nineteenth century, classical concept of competition as a "process of rivalry," antitrust will more likely promote consumer interest in the long run. The classical inquiry centers on whether the transaction is voluntary or coercive and views interference with individual business decisions through monopoly power as contrary to law. If modified to condemn price fixing and use of monopoly power, as the Sherman Act Congress directed, a competition policy centered on a process of rivalry will promote business autonomy, market individualism, diversity and flexibility, economic efficiency, business choice, and output expansion. Antitrust in the postmodern era will have come full circle. The law, as a matter of public policy, will not glorify either large firms at the expense of small firms or stifle entrepreneurial efforts at innovation. A correction or tilt away from the modern era's favoritism of large firms for their own sake will occur if competition is viewed as a process that promotes opportunities for rivalry among all competitors. As opportunities for rivalrous competition are maximized, efficient outcomes will follow. In the end, consumers will determine which firms are efficient and worthy of their purchase decisions.

These essays have raised the thoughtful question of when government can serve as a positive instrument in promoting market forces and economic advancement. The failure of government to intervene in the market in limited ways in the face of market imperfections gives the market enterprise a bad name and, ultimately, could lead to more pervasive intervention or even an industrial policy.

Antitrust Policy: An Economic and Legal Analysis

CARL KAYSEN AND DONALD F. TURNER

The Aims of Antitrust Policy

Antitrust policy may serve a variety of ultimate aims: . . . the attainment of desirable economic performance by individual firms and ultimately by the economy as a whole; the achievement and maintenance of competitive processes in the market-regulated sector of the economy as an end in itself; the prescription of a standard of business conduct, a code of fair competition; and the prevention of an undue growth of big business, viewed broadly in terms of the distribution of power in the society at large.

A. Desirable Economic Results

The desirable economic results which we seek refer ultimately to the whole economy. At this level we wish to see: (1) efficiency in the use of resources—the achievement of the largest bundle of desired outputs from the available bundle of resources; (2) progress—growth of total output and of output per head and development of new cheaper production methods and new improved products; (3) stability in output and employment—growth at a relatively stable rate, rather than with large fluctuations; and (4) an equitable distribution of income. Not all of this quartet of virtues are connected to the functioning of markets in an equally intimate way. Efficiency is most closely dependent on the operation of markets. While the existence and character of market competition is one of the forces influencing the pace of innovation, it is only one; and others, including the supply and training of technical personnel, the expenditures by government on industrial research, the attitude of consumers toward new products and of managements and workers toward new methods of production, are in the aggregate of greater importance. To the extent that an equitable distribution of income implies the passing along of the fruits of efficiency and progress to consumers, it is related to the functioning of markets. To the important extent that ideas of equity involve judgments that some income receivers should receive more and some less than they could get from the market—no matter how competitive—equity must be sought by policies (such as taxation) other than those which affect the operation of markets. Finally, fluctuations in output and employment are primarily responses to fluctuation in aggregate demand rather than to events in particular markets, and again, policies designed to promote stability find their primary means outside the sphere of market organization. Thus, to the extent that we conceive of antitrust policy as designed to promote certain desirable economic ends, we should measure its impact in the areas of economic efficiency and progress. The particular contribution to equity in income distribution which is made by the promotion of competitive markets is the bringing down of prices to costs. . . .

Efficiency is ideally a distributive or relational concept, which embraces the whole economy. Essentially, it is a state in which no rearrangement of outputs among products and no redistribution of inputs among firms could increase consumer satisfaction. We make the usual assumption that even though economy-wide efficiency is impossible to achieve, because of the existence of natural monopolies, government monopolies, and areas exempted from the requirements of competition for other reasons, it is desirable to make as close an approach to the conditions of economic efficiency in as many sectors of economy as possible. On this basis, we can apply the concept of efficiency to individual industries and firms. Its elements are the efficient relations between prices and costs, capacities and outputs, demands and capacities; and production at efficient scale in efficient locations. The characteristic results of the competitive model define efficiency. In technical terms, prices should equal both long-run average costs (including normal profits) and marginal costs for each product as well as for the enterprise as a whole; capacity should be fully utilized in periods of high demand (excluding obsolete stand-by capacity) and, where capacity is not fully utilized, firms should not be earning positive profits; increases or decreases in the level of demand should call forth corresponding changes in capacity (with an allowance for lags due to uncertainty, and for the slowness with which declines in fixed capital take place); output should be produced at minimum costs, in plants of efficient scale; plants should be at efficient locations. . . .

In defining progressiveness as an aspect of desirable economic performance which it might be the goal of antitrust policy to promote, we can add little to what we have said. Progress consists in increasing output, in increasing output per unit of input by the development of new techniques, and in producing new and better final products. These results are achievable in part and are observable at the level of the firm and the industry, as well as aggregatively for the economy as a whole. . . .

To sum up, efficiency and progressiveness are the most important economic results whose achievement can be substantially influenced by antitrust policy. Thus they furnish the criteria by which antitrust policy aimed at producing desirable economic results must be judged.

B. Promoting Competitive Processes

The achievement and maintenance of competitive processes in the market-controlled sector of the economy is the second goal that antitrust policy can serve. In this sense, competition is seen as an end in itself rather than as a means to achieve desirable economic results. An effort to extend as far as possible the market-controlled area and to limit sharply the government-controlled one is directly complementary to this goal; its relation to the goal of achieving desirable economic performance is less clear. Competition as an end in itself draws its justification from the desirability of limiting business power.... This can be achieved either by superimposing control by politically responsible authority or by the internal limitation provided by the competitive market; we have assumed the latter is the preferable alternative. Business power can be viewed either narrowly in terms of economic power, or broadly in terms of power in the society at large. The two aspects are, to be sure, interconnected, but for the purposes of the present topic we focus on the economic power and leave the latter aspect to further discussion below. Again, we can view the economic power of business in relation to the community at large, both consumers and suppliers of labor, or more narrowly in relation to the power of some firms vis-a-vis others in interbusiness transactions. The demand for limiting business power springs more often from those who feel themselves at a disadvantage in interbusiness transactions than it does from households either as consumers or as suppliers of labor. Competition in this context is desirable because it substitutes an impersonal market control for the personal control of powerful business executives, or for the personal control of government bureaucrats. The impersonality of market regulation makes it fair in the eyes of those subject to it; the sense of fairness is greater when the same restriction on conduct is imposed by the market than when it is viewed as the result of a personal decision by a powerful individual. This same attribute of the competitive market is seen in another aspect for all who deal in the market as the existence of effective alternatives; no one source of supply, no one outlet, confronts buyer or seller with terms that must be met because no alternative exists. The buyer who gets no copper because excessive demand has pushed price to an unprofitably high level does not experience the same sense of unfair treatment as he would if the copper were denied him by the allocation decision of a single supplier. In this sense, competition is a code of fair dealing among business firms.

From the perspective of the whole society, this same impersonality appears as the compulsion that the competitive market exercises upon the transactors in it. Rather than having scope to choose more or less desirable patterns of conduct, the firms in the competitive market are compelled along the only economically feasible line of conduct by the constraints of the market.

Logically, constraints and impersonality derive from the model of a profit-maximizing enterprise in a perfectly competitive market. The markets of experience deviate in many ways from the competitive model, and the enterprises of experience likewise deviate from rigorous devotion to maximizing the present value of an unambiguously defined flow of profits. Even in the most competitive of real markets, enterprises retain some scope for discretion in behavior: markets are less than perfect and less than purely competitive; firms must be thought of as maximizing some utility index, in which profits have an important weight, but into which desires for security, growth, and avoidance of various kinds of "trouble" also enter. However, the less competitive the market, the wider the scope of this discretion. The firm with a good monopoly position may well have profits which are both high and stable; a firm in a more competitive market will have little room for choosing between smaller and more secure profits and larger though more fluctuating ones, though it will not be entirely without some discretion in this matter. Competition not only constrains business decisions in general; it forces businesses to move closer to a policy of long-run profit maximization than they would necessarily be under other market conditions.

C. "Fair Conduct"

Although competitive processes provide one standard by which fair business conduct can be defined, it is not necessarily the only one. One possible goal of antitrust policy is the maintenance of a standard of business conduct which is considered fair. A policy oriented toward this goal would concern itself with judgments on the way business power was used rather than with whether or not such power existed. The content of fairness is vague once its identification with competitive market processes is abandoned. In general, fairness entails some concept of equal treatment of those in similar situations; but this achieves specific content only if the principles of classification, which determine who are in the same situation, can be stated. Unless there is fairly general social agreement on the relevant classificatory variable—as for instance income and family status in deciding on income tax rates—fairness tends to mean equal treatment for everybody. In practice, in the context of a market, this may mean equal treatment for firms now operating in the market, rather than equal treatment for existing firms and potential entrants, since the realities of administering equal treatment, whether by private or public administrators, can be met only by dealing with existing rather than with potential claimants. Fairness also has the content of fair play or sporting behavior, which in the market context may be translated as not using market power where it exists, and in general seeking reasonable rather than maximum returns. Both "equal treatment" and "reasonable returns" may lead to the rule of preventing any changes in a given situation which are disadvantageous to any participants therein; or which are more disadvantageous to some than to others. It is out of this type of fairness that "grandfather rules" arise, whether expressed in legislation or in business practices of serving old customers in times of shortages. . . .

Forbidding the use of unfair tactics as a means of acquiring monopoly power has of course been an important element in antitrust policy. Nevertheless, this description of the problem is to some extent superficial. If a firm can coerce rivals, suppliers, or customers, there must be some reservoir of force on which it draws that accounts for the acquiescence of the coerced party in a situation that, by definition, is not the result of mutually free bargaining. There are three possible kinds of force which a firm can resort to: violence (or the threat of it), deception, or market power. While the first two are not unknown in the records of antitrust cases, they are illegal in themselves and hardly need be considered in defining the goals of antitrust policy. Typically, then, coercion consists in the ability of a firm with market power to impose terms in a bargain which the other party would refuse, were there an alternative transactor with whom he could deal more advantageously. The normal instruments of business bargaining, delays, refusals to deal, representations which fall short of complete candor . . . can be turned uniformly to the advantage of the powerful bargainer, because his partner in the transaction would be even worse off if he did not accept the terms imposed. This is not to say that the use of unfair tactics in this sense in order to increase or maintain a position of power is without significance in particular markets. Rather it is to argue that this meaning of unfairness must be viewed as an aspect of market power, and that if the prevention of unfair conduct is a distinct policy aim, it must refer to the kind of characteristics of transactions discussed above in terms of equal treatment of those similarly situated.

D. *Limiting Big Business*

The last broad class of goals to which antitrust policy can be directed is the creation of a desirable distribution of social power among business units by changing the relative positions of "large" and "small" firms in the economy. This goal is broader than that of limiting the market power of firms, since it aims at what we have called social power broadly defined, rather than economic power in particular markets. Power in this sense has some relation to economic power in particular markets, but it transcends it and includes political power and general social leadership.

The goal of a "proper" distribution of power between large and small business is rationalized in terms of certain Jeffersonian symbols of wide political appeal and great persistence in American life: business units are politically irresponsible, and therefore large powerful business units are dangerous. The political and social power of the independent proprietor is the foundation of democracy; therefore his power as against that of the corporate bureaucrat must be maintained or re-established. The power of absentee ownership and management in relation to the local community and local and state governments must be diminished, lest the failure of state and local control provoke an increase in federal intervention in both business and local community life, and a corresponding increase in federal power. These doctrines, often in inchoate form, undoubtedly provide an important emotional substratum on which political support for antitrust policy of some kind rests.

Public policy directed to reducing big business power can move along three lines. First, it can reduce the size and relative importance of large business firms directly in one way or another. Second, it can place limitations on the conduct of large businesses, especially on conduct viewed as having a competitive impact on small businesses. Third, it can provide direct subsidies to small businesses. The first two of these fall within, the third falls without, the usual scope of antitrust policy.

Aims of Past and Present Antitrust Policy

The four possible aims of antitrust policy that we have examined—promoting desirable economic performance, limiting market power, enforcing a standard of fair conduct in business, and reducing the social power of large and promoting that of small business—are in part competitive and in part complementary. An assessment of the extent to which the pursuit of each reinforces or interferes with the achievement of the others is prerequisite to any antitrust policy proposal that purports to rest on an articulated statement of aims. . . . At this point, we wish to describe briefly what the approach and purposes of American antitrust policy seem to have been up to now, with an eye toward what the weaknesses and difficulties might be.

Present antitrust policy is the product of a long evolution, influenced by the views of a succession of Assistant Attorneys General and a more slowly moving succession of Supreme Court majorities, and punctuated only twice, in 1914 and 1936, by major legislative pronouncements. If there has been any persistent policy and approach, it has been that of protecting competitive processes by preventing unfair, unreasonable, or coercive conduct, but this is a faulty generalization at best.

It is obvious that in passing the Sherman Act, "Congress was dealing with competition, which it sought to protect, and monopoly, which it sought to prevent."[1] The legislators were well aware of the common law on restraints of trade, and of the power of monopolists to hurt the public by raising price, deteriorating product, and restricting production. At the same time, there was at least equal concern with the fate of small producers driven out of business, or deprived of the opportunity to enter it, by "all-powerful aggregations of capital." There was no obvious inconsistency in these two interests. One could readily have identified free access and large numbers of comparatively small producers with competitive processes, and in turn have identified competitive processes derived from such market structures with beneficial economic results for the public at large. Or, to short circuit the proposition, one could have equated beneficial economic results with the protection of large numbers of small independent producers.

We think it reasonable to suppose that those legislators who dwelt on the matter proceeded on such a premise. Nevertheless, it seems probably that they also desired to protect equal opportunity and equal access for small business for noneconomic reasons: concentration of resources in the hands of a few was viewed as a social and political catastrophe as well. Indeed, if Congress had decided to prohibit "monopoly in the concrete," it might have been reasonable to conclude that dispersion of power was the Sherman Act's primary goal. But this was not done, or so the courts have interpreted the act, unless *Alcoa*[2] means otherwise, which we do not think it does. The Act was deemed by its sponsors not to be applicable to one "who merely by superior skill and intelligence . . . got the whole business because nobody could do it as well."[3] Perhaps it was believed or hoped that the exception would never be of any significance, that few if any positions of monopoly power could be gotten and held so long as anticompetitive behavior was proscribed—a belief akin to the suggestion that beneficial economic results may be equated with competitive market structure. But whatever the premise for it, the exception was an indication that power obtained or maintained by the kind of behavior that competition is thought to foster, if not compel, was immune even though businesses and business opportunities were destroyed in the process. In short, in the event of conflict in goals, protection of incentives to competitive behavior would prevail over dispersion of market power.

Several factors prevented realization of the hope that regulation of conduct would prevent significant growth and persistence of undue market power, and prevent attenuation of opportunities for "small" businesses in many important areas. Economies of size, in the absolute if not in the relative sense, assumed an importance not foreseen when the Sherman Act was passed. Patent monopolies contributed more to the concentration than to the dispersion of economic power, though a priori there might have been reason to suspect that such would not be the case. Moreover, the courts, in enforcing the Sherman Act, did not sweep into the category of illegal conduct all that could or should have been put there. Unreasonable conduct tended to be confined to behavior, such as price-fixing, which had traditionally come to be thought of as illegal restraints, and to behavior of a predatory or abusive nature that had been or could be readily described as unfair. For some periods at least, the courts were unduly lenient with cooperative trade association activities, with restrictive practices by patentees, and perhaps most important with the growth of market power by peaceful combination. . . .

During these periods of what we advisedly call weak enforcement, when fair conduct was apparently the predominant policy goal, it might be said that a concept of desirable economic performance played a part, but that the role of monopoly (or market) power was in practice an extremely attenuated one. The courts appeared to assume, more than the facts would justify, that efficiency and progressiveness went hand in hand with large size. This assumption at least contributed to decisions in cases where large combinations were either absolved of antitrust charges or protected against dissolution. Market power, on the other hand, rarely appeared to have independent significance as a test of illegality; generally speaking, it was found when unfair conduct was found, and found absent in the absence of abuse.

In the past fifteen or twenty years, some notable changes have been made. The law has been tightened on such conduct as tying arrangements, requirements contracts, collective refusals to deal, patent licensing restrictions, and (presumably) on mergers. Moreover, it is clear that in the *New Tobacco, Alcoa, United Shoe,* and *Cellophane* cases, in the remedy in *Paramount*, and in the opinions on remedy in *National Lead* and *Alcoa*, market elements were given new emphasis in antitrust policy.[4] In one way or another, market structure and market behavior either influenced the court's evaluation of conduct not in itself wrongful under old cases, or led the court to propose or reject a remedy for reasons other than deprivation of wrongfully acquired gains. *Tobacco, Aluminum, United Shoe,* and *Cellophane* involved determinations of liability resting to a larger or smaller degree on an evaluation of market structure (and to some extent market behavior) which supported the conclusion that defendant firms possessed or did not possess monopoly power (in the judges' language) or market power (in ours). *Paramount* showed the rejection by the Supreme Court of one proposed remedy (competitive bidding) and the suggestion of another (dissolution) largely on the ground that the former would not change the market structure sufficiently to produce the desired degree of competition. *National Lead* and the *Alcoa* remedy opinions both involved rejection of a request for dissolution in part on performance grounds: the former as promising no improvement in performance; the latter for the reason that defendant's performance had been good and the proposed remedy threatened to make it worse. Nevertheless, whatever advances have been made, we do not believe that the law on monopoly has reached the point of covering, or could be fairly construed to cover, the case where monopoly power is effectively exercised, wholly without agreed-upon courses of action, by a small group of sellers in an oligopoly market.

But this has not meant that market power, even though legitimate in itself, goes untrammeled. This was the key issue in *United Shoe*, and one that is part of a pervasive, yet still unsettled, problem of antitrust policy. In essence, the decision in *United Shoe* was that a monopolist, though his power was legally acquired, could not indulge in practices, though otherwise legal, that unnecessarily raised the barriers to growth or entry of competitors. As we indicated above, the Sherman Act has been interpreted—and properly, we think—to leave room for legal monopolies, that is, for monopolies acquired solely by competitive merit (within which patents should be included). Nevertheless, a decision that monopoly power is legal does not compel the acceptance as legal of everything the monopolist does. It may be desirable to curb the uses to which monopoly power is put, particularly in light of the aim of antitrust policy to protect competition. The reward for successful competitive endeavor should not be destroyed, but it may be lowered by restrictions on the use of power without noticeably diminishing the efforts to achieve power. If so, the clear benefits to be derived from such curbs are a net economic gain; even if there were some losses in incentive, the gains might still outweigh them.

In any event, the courts have proceeded, albeit erratically, on the premise that an accommodation must be made between the economic interests of those possessing legitimately acquired power, and the economic interests of others. The legality of many practices—tying arrangements, lease-only arrangements, requirements contracts, and the like—has at one time or another turned on the existence of monopoly power in the hands of the practitioner.

It is in this connection that the second historic aim of antitrust policy—that of preserving the opportunities of smaller businesses competing with, buying from, or selling to the "monopolist"—has retained continuing vitality, and a vitality that has been renewed from time to time by legislative enactment. . . .

The Chicago School of Antitrust Analysis

RICHARD A. POSNER

The use of the term "Chicago" to describe a body of antitrust views to which I, among others, am thought to subscribe is very common. I shall argue in this paper that although there was a time when the "Chicago" school stood for a distinctive approach to antitrust policy, especially in regard to economic questions, and when other schools, particularly a "Harvard" school, could be discerned and contrasted with it, the distinctions between these schools have greatly diminished. This has occurred largely as a result of the maturing of economics as a social science, and, as a corollary thereto, the waning of the sort of industrial organization that provided the intellectual foundations of the Harvard school. More generally, this change can be attributed to the fact that the diversity in fundamental premises among economists studying antitrust questions has substantially diminished. No longer is it such a simple thing to identify a Harvard or a Chicago position on issues of antitrust policy. Partly this is a matter of growing consensus; partly of a shift from disagreement over basic premises, methodology, and ideology toward technical disagreements of the sort that would be found even in a totally nonideological field.

. . .

Reprinted from 127 U. Pa. L. Rev. 925 (1979).

1. The Chicago and Harvard Schools:
The Foundations

The basic features of the Chicago school of antitrust analysis are attributable to the work of Aaron Director in the 1950's. Director formulated the key ideas of the school,[1] which were then elaborated on by students and colleagues such as Bowman, Bork, McGee, and Telser.[2] These ideas did not, I believe, emerge from a full-blown philosophy of antitrust. Rather, they were the product of pondering specific questions raised by antitrust cases, and only in retrospect did it become clear that they constituted the basis of a general theory of the proper scope of antitrust policy. . . . [T]he key ideas may be stated as follows:

1. A tie-in (*i.e.*, requiring a buyer to buy a second product as the condition of buying the first) is not a rational method of obtaining a second source of monopoly profits, because an increase in the price charged for the tied product will, as a first approximation, reduce the price that the purchaser is willing to pay for the tying product. A tie-in makes sense only as a method of price discrimination, based on the fact that the amount of the tied product bought can be used to separate purchasers into more or less elastic demanders of the tying product. There is no need to worry about price discrimination, however, because it does not aggravate the monopoly problem. On the contrary, price discrimination is a device by which the monopolist in effect seeks to serve additional consumers, i.e., those having the more elastic demands, who might be deterred by the single monopoly price that would be charged in the absence of discrimination. Thus, price discrimination brings the monopolist's output closer to that of a competitive market and reduces the misallocative effects of monopoly.

2. From the standpoint of the manufacturer imposing it, resale price maintenance is not a rational method of distribution if its effect is to give dealers monopoly profits. Yet manufacturers, if permitted, often will impose it. The explanation is that, by preventing price competition among dealers, resale price maintenance encourages dealers to offer consumers presale services (such as point of sale advertising, inventory, showroom display, and knowledgeable sales personnel) up to the point at which the cost of these

services at the margin just equals the price fixed by the manufacturer. Such services, which enhance the value of the manufacturer's product to consumers and hence the price he can charge the dealers, might—because of "free-rider"[3] problems—not be provided if price competition among dealers were permitted.

3. Selling below cost in order to drive out a competitor is unprofitable even in the long run, except in the unlikely case in which the intended victim lacks equal access to capital to finance a price war. The predator loses money during the period of predation and, if he tries to recoup it later by raising his price, new entrants will be attracted, the price will be bid down to the competitive level, and the attempt at recoupment will fail.[4] Most alleged instances of below-cost pricing must, therefore, be attributable to factors other than a desire to eliminate competition.

These ideas generated others. The tie-in analysis, for instance, was extended to vertical integration in general. To illustrate, it makes no sense for a monopoly producer to take over distribution in order to earn monopoly profits at the distribution as well as the manufacturing level. The product and its distribution are complements, and an increase in the price of distribution will reduce the demand for the product.[5] Assuming that the product and its distribution are sold in fixed proportions, and thus that the price discrimination analysis is inapplicable, the conclusion is reached that vertical integration must be motivated by a desire for efficiency rather than for monopoly.

The analysis of resale price maintenance generalized readily to other restrictions on distribution, such as exclusive territories and exclusive outlets. The predatory-pricing analysis generalized to other methods by which firms were thought to hurt others by hurting themselves—for example, by demanding that purchasers sign longer-term contracts than they desire, in order to deny a market to competing sellers: a rational purchaser would demand compensation for accepting such a disadvantageous term.

From these various analyses, a conclusion of great significance for antitrust policy emerges: firms cannot in general obtain or enhance monopoly power by unilateral action[6] unless, of course, they are irrationally willing to trade profits for position. Consequently, the focus of the antitrust laws should not be on unilateral action; it should instead be on: (1) cartels and (2) horizontal mergers large enough either to create monopoly directly, as in the classic trust cases,[7] or to facilitate cartelization by drastically reducing the number of significant sellers in the market. Since unilateral action ... had been the cutting edge of antitrust policy for a great many years, to place it beyond the reach of antitrust law ... implied a breathtaking contraction in the scope of antitrust policy.

What was the source of Director's heterodox thinking? Because of Director's close personal and professional associations with Milton Friedman, it is common to think that Director's antitrust analysis was the product of conservative (which is to say, "liberal" in the nineteenth-century sense of the term) antipathy to government intervention in the economy. I question this view. I believe Director's conclusions resulted simply from viewing antitrust policy through the lens of price theory. Each of his ideas was deducible from the assumption that businessmen are rational profit-maximizers, the deduction proceeding in accordance with the tenets of simple price theory, i.e., that demand curves slope downward, that an increase in the price of a product will reduce the demand for its complement, that resources gravitate to the areas where they will earn the highest return, etc. "Simple" and "easy" are not the same thing, however. Although the analytic tools used by Director were simple, the insights they yielded were extremely subtle. Certainly they were resisted for many years.

Yet it is still fair to ask why the application of price theory to antitrust should have been a novelty. The answer ... is that in the 1950's and early 1960's, industrial organization, the field of economics that studies monopoly questions, tended to be untheoretical, descriptive, "institutional," and even metaphorical.[8] Causal observation of business behavior, colorful characterizations (such as the term "barrier to entry"), eclectic forays into sociology and psychology, descriptive statistics, and verification by plausibility took the place of the careful definitions and parsimonious logical structure of economic theory. The result was that industrial organization regularly advanced propositions that contradicted economic theory.

An example is the "leverage" theory of tie-ins that Donald Turner, a Harvard economist in the Edward Mason and Joe Bain tradition, espoused shortly after Director had developed his price-discrimination theory of tie-ins.[9] The leverage theory held that if a seller had a monopoly of one product, he could and would monopolize its indispensable complements as well, so as to get additional monopoly profits. Thus, if he had a patented mimeograph machine, he would lease the machine at a monopoly price and also require his lessees to buy the ink used in the machine from him and charge them a monopoly price for the ink. This procedure, however, makes no sense as a matter of economic theory. The purchaser is buying a service, mimeographing. The pricing of its components is a mere detail; it is, rather, the total price of the service that he cares about. If the seller raises the price of one component, the ink, the purchaser will treat this as an increase in the price of the service. If the machine is already being priced at the optimal monopoly level, an increase in the price of the ink above the competitive level will raise the total price of the service to the consumer above the optimal monopoly level and will thereby reduce the monopolist's profits.

There was a similar confusion in the concept of a "barrier to entry," a concept that played—and still plays—a large role in thinking about competition. Suppose that it costs $10,000,000 to build the smallest efficient plant to serve some market; then, it was argued, there was a $10,000,000 "barrier to entry," a hurdle a new entrant would have to overcome to serve the market at no disadvantage vis-a-vis existing firms.[10] But is there really a hurdle? If the $10,000,000 plant has a useful life of, for example, ten years, the annual cost to the new entrant is only $1,000,000. Existing firms bear the same annual cost, assuming that they plan to replace their plants. The new entrant, therefore, is not at any cost disadvantage after all.

. . .

A clue to the nature of the Harvard School of industrial organization is that its practitioners were so fond of doing studies of competition in particular industries—airlines, tin cans, aluminum, rayon, Douglas firs, etc. These studies exemplified the particularistic and non-theoretical character of the field. The powerful simplifications of economic theory—rationality, profit maximization, the downward-sloping demand curve—were discarded, or at least downplayed, in favor of microscopic examination of the idiosyncrasies of particular markets.

The "kinked demand curve," "workable competition," "cutthroat competition," "leverage," "administered prices," and the other characteristic concepts of the industrial organization of this period had this in common: they were not derived from and were often inconsistent with economic theory, and in particular with the premises of rational profit maximization. They were derived from observation, unsystematic and often superficial, of business behavior. Director's approach was the opposite. He explained tie-ins, resale price maintenance, and other business behavior described in antitrust cases not by studying the practices but by looking for an explanation for them that squared with basic economic theory. When they first began to emerge in the articles written by his colleagues, students, and disciples, Director's ideas made little impact either on scholarly opinion or on policy. In some quarters the Chicago school was regarded as little better than a lunatic fringe. Kaysen and Turner's *Antitrust Policy*, the classic statement of the Harvard school, published in 1959, contains virtually no trace of any influence of the Chicago school.

Twenty years later, the position is dramatically changed. Partly as a result of George Stigler's attacks on the intellectual foundations of traditional industrial organization[11] and partly as a result of the growing sophistication of economic analysis, the traditional industrial organization is becoming discredited in academic circles. The Chicago school has largely prevailed with respect to its basic point: that the proper lens for viewing antitrust problems is price theory. At the same time, some of the specific ideas first advanced by Aaron Director have been questioned, modified, and refined, resulting in the emergency of a new animal: the "diehard Chicagoan" (such as Bork and Bowman) who has not accepted any of the suggested refinements of or modifications in Director's original ideas.

The work of Director and his followers focused on the question when, if ever, a firm can unilaterally obtain or maintain monopoly power. The question when a firm can obtain such power by collaboration with its competitors received less attention. Partly, perhaps, for tactical reasons (not to seem to reject antitrust policy in its entirety), the members of the Chicago school would sometimes denounce price fixing. But it is unlikely that they regarded even price fixing, let alone oligopoly, as a serious problem. In the classical economic tradition running from Smith to Marshall, the tradition in which the Chicago school operates, a clear recognition of the propensity of sellers to attempt collusion was conjoined with a general indifference to, and sometimes an explicit rejection of, the desirability of imposing legal sanctions on collusion. This complacency (if one can call it that) rested on the belief that cartels were, first, highly unstable because of the propensity of members to cheat (so long as the cartel was not legally enforceable), and, second, in the long run futile in the absence of substantial barriers to entry. Collusion might still be attempted frequently if attempting it was cheap, but it would rarely succeed and its overall misallocative effects would be too slight to warrant inevitably costly public proceedings.

Given this tradition, given the Chicago school's rejection of the expansive notion of "barriers to entry," given the lack of any clear theoretical basis for oligopoly theory, . . . given Harberger's tiny estimate of the welfare costs of monopoly,[12] given the atheoretical, ad hoc, and unsupported character of the efforts to avoid the implications of Harberger's analysis by ascribing to oligopolists failures of innovation or cost control, it was not to be expected that the Chicago school would attach great importance to vigorous prosecution of colluders. But such enforcement activity, in contrast to that directed against unilateral monopolizing acts, was not deplored.

. . .

By 1969, then, an orthodox Chicago position (well represented in the writings of Robert Bork) had crystallized: only explicit price fixing and very large horizontal mergers (mergers to monopoly) were worthy of serious concern.

2. The Growing Convergence of the Two Schools

The basic tenet of the Chicago school, that problems of competition and monopoly should be analyzed using the tools of general economic theory rather than those of traditional industrial organization, has triumphed. The concepts and methods of traditional industrial organization are increasingly discredited in economics as practiced in the leading universities and this change is beginning

to be reflected in the application of economics to antitrust law. . . .
At the same time, the application of price theory to antitrust law
has not left the pioneering work of Director and his followers
untouched.

Let us consider now how the passage of years has affected some
of the specific controversies between the Chicago and Harvard
schools.

1. Tie-ins

The leverage theory of tie-ins early gave way in Harvard thinking
to a barriers-to-entry theory.[13] A tie-in was said to complicate entry
because the new entrant would have to produce the tied as well
as the tying product. When the motive for tying is price discrimination, however, the producer of the tying product need not assume control over any part of the production of the tied product,
let alone produce it all. Instead, all that is required is that he act
as an intermediary between the producer and the ultimate consumer so that he can reprice it in accordance with his discriminatory
scheme. A new entrant will be able to obtain the tied product from
the same source that the existing firm obtains it from.

One element (and an important one) of the Chicago analysis is,
however, subject to criticism: the assumption that price discrimination is on the whole socially beneficial because it moves the
monopolist's output closer to the competitive level and hence reduces the misallocative effects of monopoly. As Joan Robinson
pointed out long ago, if price discrimination is not perfect (and it
never is), it may lead to a smaller, rather than a larger, output
than single-price monopoly. . . . [14]

In the light of . . . criticism, the original Chicago analysis of the
effects of tie-ins now seems a little oversimple. Nevertheless, the
conclusion that tie-ins should not be forbidden seems both correct
and increasingly influential on academic opinion.

2. Vertical Integration

Here too the leverage theory was eventually replaced by a barriers-
to-entry theory (the economic analysis of vertical integration being,
as I have indicated, symmetrical with that of tie-ins).[15] The thinking
was that if, for example, supplier A acquires all of his retail outlets,

B, in order to compete, will have to open his own chain of outlets. This, in turn, will make B's entry more costly. The steps in this analysis are illogical, however, and evidence of monopolization by such means scant or nonexistent.[16] A will find it very costly to buy more outlets than he needs. B, on the other hand, will not have to open his own outlets to enter; if his entry is anticipated, the outlets will be there to greet him. Moreover, even if B did have to open his own retail outlets, the higher capital cost of his entry would still be no greater than the (also higher) capital cost to A of being a retailer as well as a manufacturer. The analysis does not depend on whether retail outlets are cheap or expensive to build or acquire or on whether the integration in question is forward into distribution or backward into raw-material, or other, supply. The essential point is that the cost to the monopolist of integrating is prima facie the same as the cost to the new entrant of having to integrate.[17] The validity of this analysis is not affected even if the result of integration is completely to deny the new entrant access to some essential input except by dealing with the existing firms in the market. The cost to the existing firms is still the same as to the new entrant, although now it is in the form of an opportunity cost. Suppose, for example, that kryptonite is an indispensable input in the manufacture of widgets. A owns all the kryptonite in the universe and also manufactures widgets. He could, of course, refuse to sell kryptonite to B, a prospective entrant into widget production. The cost to A of this refusal is the price B would have been willing to pay. Stated differently, by his control of kryptonite A can extract any monopoly rents available in the widget industry without denying a place in widget manufacture to others' firms. If there is a proper antitrust objection, it is to the kryptonite monopoly rather than to vertical integration.

Yet, despite the force of these arguments, it is incorrect to dismiss entirely the possibility of monopolistic consequences from vertical arrangements. The above arguments assume that, as in the case of the manufacturer-retailer, the relevant inputs, e.g., the manufactured product and its distribution, are combined in fixed proportions to produce the final output (the sale at retail). Suppose, however, that some input is used in variable proportions with other inputs to produce the final output, e.g., uranium and enrichment services in the production of nuclear fuel. If one of the inputs is monopolized, causing its price to rise in relation to those of other inputs, the output manufacturer will seek to reduce the proportion in which he uses this input and, instead, use more of the other inputs. The possibility of such substitution acts as a partial check on the monopoly power of the input monopolist. Assume, however, that the input producer buys the input user. This will eliminate the threat of substitution and so reduce the elasticity of demand for the input in question.[18] Even so, it does not follow that the merger should be prohibited, for one of its effects is that the inputs will now be used in the proportions that minimize the true social costs of manufacturing the output. But it cannot be said that such a merger, merely because it is vertical, cannot possibly increase monopoly. So saying, I do not mean to suggest that such an equivocal and perhaps remote danger warrants reversing the growing support at least in academic circles for a permissive policy toward vertical mergers and vertical integration generally.

The change in thinking that has been brought about by the Chicago school is nowhere more evident than in the area of vertical integration. Kaysen and Turner, writing in 1959, advocated forbidding any vertical merger in which the acquiring firm had twenty percent or more of its market.[19] Areeda and Turner, writing in 1978, express very little concern with anticompetitive effects from vertical integration. In fact, as between a rule of per se illegality for vertical integration by monopolists and a rule of per se legality, their preference is for the latter.

3. Restricted Distribution

As noted above, the Harvard reply to the Chicago analysis of resale price maintenance was that the benefit that the manufacturer sought to obtain by restricting competition among his distributors, i.e., presale services, was actually a social evil, because these services resulted in "product differentiation," a barrier to entry. Facing no close substitutes for his brand because it was differentiated in the consumer's eyes from competing brands,[20] the producer could charge a monopoly price. If the case of fraudulent advertising is put to one side, the conclusion that advertising and related promotional methods create monopoly power, at least in any sense relevant to antitrust policy, cannot be derived from the premises of economic theory. Consumers will not pay more for one brand than for another unless the first is cheaper or better. Advertising can make an advertised brand cheaper by reducing the consumer's search costs by an amount greater than the difference in nominal price between that brand and nonadvertised brands of the same product. The same point can be made with respect to the other presale services, e.g., display, that are encouraged by restricted distribution.

The new industrial organization, which relates advertising to the costs of search, has transformed advertising from a social evil into a social benefit. . . . Although inter-school differences relating to the welfare effects of advertising remain, the position of the Chicago school on restricted distribution has become the orthodox academic position. The decision in *Continental T.V., Inc. v. GTE Sylvania Inc.*,[21] suggests that it is well on its way to becoming the legal position as well.

4. Predatory Pricing

McGee's famous article on the Standard Oil Trust combined the startling empirical finding that the trust, contrary to popular and academic belief, had not engaged in predatory pricing, with theoretical arguments for doubting the rationality of the practice. One of McGee's major arguments—that the trust would not have used predatory pricing because it is cheaper to buy a competitor than to sell below cost—was vulnerable to the criticism of being irrelevant to present-day circumstances, since acquiring a major competitor is clearly and unconcealably unlawful whereas predatory pricing may be difficult to detect. There is, however, a deeper problem with the McGee argument: it neglects strategic considerations. Assume that it is lawful to buy a rival. It does not follow that a firm will never resort to predatory pricing. After all, it wants to minimize the price at which it buys its rivals, and that price will be lower if it can convince them of its willingness to drive them out of business unless they sell out on its terms. One way to convince them of this is to engage in predatory pricing from time to time.

Since classical (or, one might add, modern) economics contains no generally accepted theory of strategic behavior, it is not surprising that the Chicago school should not have been particularly concerned with predatory pricing. Eliminate strategic considerations, and it becomes impossible to construct a rational motivation for predatory pricing without assuming (very uncongenially to a Chicagoan) asymmetric access to the capital markets for financing a period of below-cost selling. But to ignore strategic considerations is not satisfactory. Even without having a well-developed theory of strategic behavior, one can easily imagine circumstances in which predatory pricing, at least in the absence of legal prohibition, would be a plausible policy for a profit-maximizing seller to follow. Suppose that he sells in many markets, and his rivals sell in only one or a few markets each. If he sells below cost in one market, his losses there are an investment that will be recouped with interest in his other markets in the form of more timid competition from the rivals in those markets. Knowing that the multimarket seller can obtain substantial gains from a demonstrated willingness to sell below cost for an extended period of time in one market, the local victim may not think it worthwhile to try to outlast him.

To be sure, the administrative and error costs of trying to prevent this sort of thing may outweigh its dangers to the competitive process. That, however, is a different point. My point is that predatory pricing is not irrational. It is not in the same category with, for example, attempting to get a second monopoly through tying. Bork is able to place predatory pricing in the irrational category only by failing to mention the possibility of strategic behavior.

Additional evidence for the decline of "schools" of antitrust economics is the position that Areeda and Turner (both of the Harvard Law School) have taken on predatory pricing. Their influential article on the subject (and the amplification of the article in their new treatise) is an essay in price theory.[22] Strategic considerations, the sort of thing the traditional industrial organization embraced eagerly, e.g., in oligopoly theory, are not mentioned, and skepticism of the likelihood of predatory pricing is registered. Using the basic premises of classical price theory, Areeda and Turner argue that the only price that should be condemned as predatory is one below short-run marginal cost. Any higher price implies an opportunity to utilize scarce resources more fully by lowering price and expanding output. This is pure textbook price theory unadorned by any of the concepts of traditional industrial organization.

It is not surprising that Professor Scherer, a leading adherent of traditional industrial organization thinking, launched a sweeping attack on the Areeda-Turner article,[23] or that Professor Williamson criticized Areeda and Turner for ignoring strategic considerations in designing a rule against predatory pricing.[24] What is, perhaps, surprising is that I attacked Areeda and Turner as unduly permissive. Unfortunately, my attack bogged down in a terminological dispute. I said that the proper criterion of predatory pricing was selling below long-run rather than short-run marginal cost with intent to destroy an equally or more efficient rival *and* that short-run marginal cost is lower than long-run marginal cost even when the firm is operating at its full (optimal) capacity, because some elements of long-run marginal cost are fixed in the short run. Areeda and Turner pounced on the assertion that short-run marginal cost is below long-run marginal cost at full capacity. They pointed out that it would be costlier for a firm already operating at full capacity to expand in the short run than in the long run, for only in the long run could the firm make the adjustments in plant scale, etc., necessary to optimize production at a higher level. I accept this criticism. Although I continue to be troubled by cases, potentially significant in the predatory-pricing context, in which long-run marginal cost might be *thought* to exceed short-run marginal cost even without excess capacity, these cases can be dealt with by careful definition of the relevant terms.

But this is a side issue that only obscures the serious problems of the short-run marginal cost standard. The lesser problem is that the standard gives the would-be predator an incentive to maintain excess capacity and thereby reduce his short-run marginal costs, an incentive the predator might have anyway in order to make his threat to sell below cost more credible.[25] The greater problem is that the administrative difficulties of basing the legal rule on the concept of short-run marginal cost are so acute as to have led Areeda and Turner themselves to reject short-run marginal cost as the operational standard and instead substitute average variable cost. Yet they continue to defend that standard by reference to the arguments, such as they are, for allowing firms to cut price to

short-run marginal cost. Average variable cost could be much below short-run marginal cost. A standard of average variable cost
should be defended on its own merits, rather than by reference to
a different standard for which it is the crudest possible proxy. But
Areeda and Turner do not attempt to defend an average variable
cost standard, save as a proxy for short-run marginal cost.

What is the point of having such a low price floor? It would be
unusual for a firm that wanted to engage in predatory pricing to
set a price equal to or only slightly above zero. It would set a price
designed to make its competitors' business unprofitable at minimum cost to itself. Any firm that sells at a price equal to its average
variable costs, a price that doesn't cover any of its fixed costs (let
alone generate any return on investment), will be unprofitable.
Therefore, even if the competitor is somewhat more efficient than
the predator, a price equal to the predator's variable costs, and
hence close to the competitor's variable costs, should be an effective predatory price.

. . .

. . . In any event, if there is sufficient danger of predatory pricing
to warrant having a legal rule, as Areeda and Turner for whatever
reason believe, that danger is triggered when a firm that is less
efficient than its rivals cuts its price to its variable costs in order
to make it unprofitable for those rivals to enter or remain in the
market. Indeed, to repeat an earlier point, it is hard to see why a
predator would ever have to price below that level in order to
discourage rivals.

Whoever is correct in the debate over predatory pricing, one
thing is clear: the debate is no longer one between schools that
employ consistently different and ideologically tinged premises to
reach predictably opposite results.

3. Remaining Differences

There is one very important area in which traces of the traditional
differences between Chicago price theorists and Harvard industrial
organizationists persist: the two schools continue to disagree over
the significance of concentration and the wisdom of a policy of

deconcentration. Williamson and many other lawyers and economists continue to believe that persistently high concentration in an industry warrants breaking up the leading firms. Brozen, Demsetz, Stigler, Baxter, and others disagree (the last two names, it should be noted, are defectors from the ranks of the deconcentrators). Areeda and Turner, as will be seen, appear to take an intermediate position.

The heart of the difference is not over the strength of the positive correlation, found in many studies, between concentration and profitability but over the explanation for it. The Harvard school, still identifiable as such on this issue, contends that the correlation is explained by the fact that the leading firms in highly concentrated industries employ "conscious parallelism" to avoid price competition and thereby earn abnormal profits. The Chicago school does not deny that concentration is a factor that facilitates collusion of a sort difficult to detect, although it attaches less significance to concentration per se than do the oligopoly theorists. It asks, rather, how it is that excessive profitability can persist without attracting new entry that will cause prices to fall to the competitive level. The Harvard school, after all, wants to restructure only the persistently concentrated industries. If the leading firms in such industries are able, by virtue of concentration, to obtain supracompetitive profits, these profits should act as a magnet to other firms in the economy and their entry will deconcentrate the industry. That is what happened to the steel industry in the years following the formation of U.S. Steel Corporation in 1901. Persistent concentration implies either that the market in question simply does not have room for many firms (economies of scale) or that some firms are able persistently to obtain abnormal profits by cost reductions or production improvements that competitors and new entrants are unable to duplicate. Neither case is an attractive one for public intervention designed to change the market structure.

The Harvard reply is that there is an alternative explanation for persistent concentration in particular industries: barriers to entry. Because Stigler's definition of a barrier to entry, as a cost that differentially affects new entrants compared to firms already in the market, is now generally accepted, the search is for costs having this characteristic. The most sophisticated quester, Oliver Williamson, has found one: the uncertainty of the new entrant's prospects may force him to pay a higher risk premium to obtain capital than existing firms must pay.[26] This is a legitimate point. But it is difficult to believe that such a difference in the cost of capital would be enough to prevent entry if the firms in a market were charging prices substantially above their costs. The risk premium is unlikely to be a large fraction of the new entrant's costs. Interest and profit are rarely more than ten percent of a manufacturing firm's sales price and often they are a much smaller percentage. Thus, even if a new entrant had to pay a ten percent higher interest rate and (expected) return to shareholders to attract the necessary capital, its total costs would be only about one percent higher than those of the firms already in the market. There is no doubt that the differential risk premium is smaller if the new entrant is a well-established firm in other markets, as will typically be the case, and, to the extent that the risk is diversifiable, the risk premium will be still smaller or even disappear entirely. Another important source of new entry, viewing the term functionally rather than lexicographically, is the expansion of the existing small firms in the market. In response to supracompetitive pricing, a fringe of small firms in a market may be able to expand output moderately without incurring significantly higher capital costs than those borne by the larger firms in the market. All in all, it seems far-fetched to base a policy of deconcentration on the allegedly higher borrowing costs of new entrants in concentrated markets.

Williamson has also argued that if a firm once grows big, for whatever reason, there is no reason to expect it to decline as a result of the random shocks to which it and other market participants will be subjected over time.[27] But he neglects a crucial factor. The firm is by hypothesis charging a supracompetitive price as a result of the interdependence or collusion fostered by the concentrated market structure in which it finds itself. That price will attract new firms (or, what amounts to the same thing, expansion by the smaller firms in the market) and the oligopolist will either have to cut price or surrender market share. In the former case, profits will fall and in the latter, concentration will decrease. The persistence of high concentration *together with* excess profitability remains to be accounted for.

Deconcentration policy, then, is critically dependent upon belief in the existence of substantial barriers to entry in many industries. Once "barrier to entry" was redefined as a differentially higher cost borne by the new entrant, the plausibility of supposing that barriers to entry are common, or commonly substantial, diminished sharply. The deconcentrators are thus arguing from an abandoned premise.[28] ... The important point, however, is that, believing barriers to entry to be numerous and prevalent, [one has] a rational basis for wanting to deconcentrate concentrated markets. . . .

Conclusion

Although this paper has not attempted an exhaustive canvass of rival theories of antitrust analysis, it has, I hope, said enough to persuade the reader that the oldest and most persistent stereotype in antitrust economics, that of the Chicago school, bears little relationship to the current state of academic thinking. Changes of mind within both the Chicago school and its principal rival, which I have called the Harvard school, have produced a steady trend toward convergence. Differences remain, but increasingly they are technical rather than ideological.

An Antitrust Enforcement Policy to Maximize the Economic Wealth of All Consumers

CHARLES F. RULE AND DAVID L. MEYER

Some commentators have suggested that a movement, a sort of "counterrevolution," is under way in the halls of academia, in the offices of state attorneys general, in the courts, and even in Congress to reverse the advances in antitrust policy that have been made over the past several years. That would be unfortunate, for the revolutionary developments of the past 10–15 years . . . have brought antitrust law and enforcement into line with its proper aim of maximizing the welfare of American consumers. Whether well-intentioned or not, any return to the policies of the past—so-called "counterrevolution"—would harm consumers and hurt America's competitiveness in the increasingly global economy.

Before turning to the benefits of current antitrust policy, a few observations about the hoped-for "counterrevolution" and its advocates will help clarify the nature of the choices facing any future antitrust policy maker. First, those who assert that recent changes in antitrust policy ought to be rolled back in order to save the American consumer from some perceived evil must be questioned closely on their facts and assumptions. All too often the critics of the economic analysis that the Supreme Court and this adminis-

Reprinted from 82 Antitrust Bulletin 677 (1988).

tration have applied to antitrust law substitute demagoguery for any coherent alternative mode of analysis, and platitudes for objectively verifiable facts. The attacks of these critics on current policy are based on a "straw man" that is a barely recognizable caricature of the actual policy it purports to represent.

Second, one should go behind the sloganeering and inspect the premises upon which the critics base their attacks on current policy. The vision of our society and its economy that is embodied by those premises is not one shared by most Americans. It appears, moreover, that despite their self-anointed status as "consumer advocates," many of these critics actually disdain the common consumer because he or she has a nasty habit of exhibiting preferences that are at odds with the critics' own. For example, many critics refuse to acknowledge that the manufacturer of a product rather than law makers in Washington might actually know best how to make his product most attractive to consumers. Some critics appear to harbor contempt for consumers foolish enough not to shop at discount stores,[1] ignoring the possibility that some consumers might rationally prefer expert salespersons and reliable post-sale service to the lowest possible price. The critics all too often prefer that marketing techniques be dictated by legislation or court decision rather than by the marketplace, even when there is clearly no risk of impeding interbrand competition.

But one cannot be sure whether the critics distrust the free choices of American consumers or merely misunderstand the strength and resilience of the American free market system. Because their arguments are often phrased in undefined and subjective terms, it is not possible to predict with any degree of certainty the implications of the policies the critics advocate. One thing is clear, however: their policies would greatly increase government interference in the marketplace and thus substantially raise the cost of legitimate private market transactions.

In an age characterized by the increasing importance of foreign competition to the American economy and by a concern for the competitiveness of American firms, antitrust must evolve rather than calcify. What is needed is an intelligent antitrust policy that does not stifle the efficiency and innovation generated by private initiative. The policy should promote dynamic markets. It should protect consumers from private restraints on output but not prevent American businesses from competing successfully in global markets by interjecting governmental regulation of the competitive process. In short, what is needed is an antitrust policy that is focused on economic concerns, that takes account of a restraint's impact on efficiency, and that has as its overriding goal the protection of the well-being of consumers. And what is needed—a "consumer welfare" approach—is precisely what the antitrust "revolution" of the last 10 years has been about.

Maximizing Consumer Welfare

Whether the critics like it or not, consumer welfare is today the guiding principle of antitrust law and policy. At their core, the antitrust laws represent this nation's commitment to a free market economy—an economy unimpeded by either private or governmental restraints. The law is based on America's capitalist traditions, which rely on the "invisible hand" of impersonal market forces to allocate resources efficiently and, thus, to maximize the economic welfare of society.

The welfare of all consumers is maximized when two conditions hold: First, goods and services should be produced, distributed, and marketed using just enough of society's scarce resources to ensure that those goods and services are as desirable as possible to consumers. This does not necessarily mean that a given product—for example, a color television set—must be manufactured, shipped, and sold as cheaply as is theoretically possible. Certainly economic efficiency encompasses such pure cost savings. But efficiency also requires that consumers get the product they desire most. Thus, just because a TV set can be sold at the lowest possible price if consumers buy it in the box out of a warehouse—saving the resources necessary to build and operate an expensive showroom—it does not follow that selling it that way is more efficient. Consumers may prefer a showroom in which they can view the picture, compare the set with similar models made by other manufacturers, and consult electronics experts. Or they may wish to place trust in the seller's long-standing reputation, which required significant expenditures to develop and retain. These aspects of the "product" are as much a part of the consumer's demand for the TV set as is his or her desire to watch a favorite program once the set is home and unpacked. Economic efficiency, then, requires not only that goods and services be produced and distributed using no more of society's resources than necessary, but also that the goods and services that are produced and distributed be as desirable as possible.

Second, maximum consumer welfare requires that those goods and services be sold at prices that are as close as possible to the cost of the last, or marginal, unit sold. At that price, the resources (i.e., dollars, which are the monetary returns to the consumer's investments, including those in human capital) expended by the consumer to purchase the product or service reflect the value of society's resources (i.e., ore, timber, grain, labor, investment in reputation, or any other input) that went into producing it. Under these conditions, resources are neither wasted nor underutilized, but are used in ways that society values most. In short, the objective of a consumer welfare standard is to maximize the well-being of society by stretching its resources to the maximum extent possible.

. . . [T]he consumer welfare standard seeks to maximize total surplus. Total surplus can be defined as the difference between the value society places on the resources used to make each additional unit of the product—the marginal cost—and the value society places on each additional unit that is sold. The latter is measured by the price each consumer would be willing to pay for the product (i.e., the reservation prices of the consumers who buy the product) and is represented by the demand curve. . . . Maximizing total surplus assures that society reaps the most gain from the use of its resources.

It can easily be seen that maximizing only a component of total surplus would not yield the best uses of society's resources. Total surplus is made up of consumer surplus and producer surplus. Consumer surplus describes the difference between what a particular product is worth to consumers—i.e., the "reservation prices" that they would have been willing to pay to buy the product—and the price consumers actually pay. Producer surplus describes the difference between the price at which that product is sold and its marginal cost—the values of society's resources that went into producing each unit. Producer surplus can roughly be described as profits. Maximizing either of these alone would simply ignore a fundamental factor in the calculation of whether society is getting the most value or utility from its resources.

. . .

Thus, contrary to what some critics have argued, current enforcement policy does not seek to maximize producer surplus at the expense of consumers. For example, collusive conduct that increases the parties' control over price (their market power) without producing economic efficiencies that outweigh the increase in market power will not be tolerated. . . . Although such practices increase producer surplus, they do so merely by transferring surplus away from consumers. Their effect on total surplus and on the economic well-being of society is negative, because they artificially restrict output and raise price.

On the other hand, enforcement policy does not blindly seek to maximize consumer surplus without regard to the impact on economic efficiency and total surplus. Even if a practice does not immediately pass on its efficiency savings to consumers in the form of lower prices, it still increases consumer welfare (i.e., total surplus) as long as the efficiency gains outweigh the increase in market power.[2]

Consumers are better off when goods or services are produced, distributed, and marketed as efficiently as possible. This is obvious when competition drives prices down to the lower cost—and consumers and producers share the increase in total surplus. It is also true even when the greater efficiency results in no shortrun price decrease in the market where the efficiency is obtained but in an increase in producer profits. This is because greater efficiency frees resources to produce additional goods and services in other sectors of the economy. As resources are freed for other uses, other products will be cheaper to produce, and consumers will ultimately share in the gains to the economy as a whole.

Moreover, the prospect of the profits generated by producer surplus provides the incentive for risk-taking, innovation, and other fixed investments that are necessary to bring to consumers all the benefits of a dynamic, productive economy. This country's patent laws and other intellectual property laws formally recognize and seek to capitalize on the relationship between risk-taking and investment on the one hand and, on the other hand, the prospect of producer surplus when that risk-taking is successful. The claims to producer surplus protected by intellectual property rights have achieved remarkable success in enabling this country to maintain world technological leadership for almost a century.

In addition, it is not necessarily clear whether the consumer or the producer is more worthy of the surplus generated by a particular transaction. It is not clear, for example, that policy should be skewed toward consumers of luxury items such as Cadillacs and against "producers" of the product, who may, in the final analysis, be the proverbial widows and orphans whose only source of income is the dividends from the "producers'" stock. In a very real sense, then, it is impossible to generalize that "producers" are individuals who are less deserving of a share in the direct gains from improvements in economic welfare.

Therefore, for example, a business arrangement that increased profits by generating significant efficiencies in production should not be challenged even if the cost savings were not passed on to its immediate customers. To challenge such an arrangement just because the benefits to the consumer could not be measured tangibly, in the form of actual lower prices for the affected products, would be shortsighted and counterproductive to a healthy American economy. In time, all American consumers would feel the pinch as society's resources were squandered on inferior uses.

Some have argued that consumer surplus, rather than total surplus, is the appropriate focus of antitrust policy because the profits earned by anticompetitive behavior are inevitably converted into social costs, as the opportunity to gain a monopoly profit attracts resources by sellers to monopolize and by consumers to avoid being charged monopoly prices.[3] To the extent that profits from the exercise of market power (i.e., increases in producer surplus) are dissipated into socially valueless efforts to attain and retain those profits, of course, the effect of such a practice on the well-being of all consumers (i.e., consumer welfare) would be equivalent to its effect on consumer surplus alone.

The fact that some dissipation of producer surplus might occur, however, does not mean that producer surplus ought to be ignored in assessing net consumer welfare effects, and thus in guiding antitrust policy. First, as the proponents of the rent dis-

sipation theory acknowledge, expenditures on monopolizing
(i.e., dissipation of surplus) will probably never be truly valueless.[4] In some cases such expenditures will have little or no
value, such as the efforts spent on policing adherence to the
agreed-upon prices of a price-fixing conspiracy and concealing
the conspiracy from law enforcement authorities. In other cases
the dissipation might take the form of activities, such as providing excessive levels of service or quality, that create consumer
benefits that are substantial, although not as great as the resources expended in undertaking those activities. Nevertheless,
it is also possible that the expenditures on monopolization will
produce social benefits that equal or exceed the funds spent on
monopolizing. For example, producer surplus may be spent on
research that yields an important patented invention, the social
value of which actually exceeds the funds spent on research. Indeed, probably the most common means of competing to retain
market power is by reducing price, thus transferring producer
surplus directly to consumers of the product by passing on efficiencies. Consequently, even if some funds are spent on competing to attain or retain market power, those expenditures
clearly do not eliminate the social welfare benefits of increases
in producer surplus.

Second, in the instances where a socially valueless dissipation
of producer surplus is most likely, such dissipation is likely to be
prevented by a total surplus standard. Because no welfare trade-
off is necessary to conclude that naked horizontal agreements such
as price fixing and bid rigging hurt consumers, it does not matter
that resources are wasted to organize, police, and conceal these
activities. These practices by definition produce no significant efficiencies, and thus yield increased profits merely by restricting
output and raising price and in turn creating a dead-weight loss to
the economy. Thus, whether or not dissipation occurs in these
circumstances, the practices are unlawful and are vigorously challenged by antitrust enforcers.

The consumer welfare standard of the antitrust laws therefore
looks to the total size of the economic pie, adjusted if necessary
for resources wasted to achieve market power, not merely to the
size of the individual pieces. As long as a business arrangement
does not shrink the size of the consumer's share more than it

increases total wealth, consumers as a whole will be better off. Thus, a consumer welfare—or total surplus—standard is the policy that best ensures that a vigorous American economy will provide maximum benefits to all consumers.

. . .

Court Interpretation

At least for antitrust practitioners, it is the courts—to which the Executive Branch is bound to look to "say what the law is"[5]—that provide the most important exposition of the antitrust laws' objectives. In making the basic interpretive decisions regarding the scope of the Sherman Act, the Supreme Court has more or less consistently adhered to an efficiency-based rationale. Early on, for example, it concluded that price fixing would not be sanctioned even when it was necessary in order to overcome economic distress or "ruinous" competition in an industry[6] and that size alone was no offense.[7] As early as 1958, the Court explicitly stated that economic efficiency was Congress' aim, with the protection of other noneconomic interests being merely a welcome collateral benefit.[8]

More emphatically, during the last 15 years the courts have consistently recognized efficiency and consumer welfare as the basis for sound antitrust enforcement. In cases like *General Dynamics*,[9] *GTE Sylvania*,[10] *Monsanto*,[11] *Matsushita*,[12] and *Sharp*,[13] the Supreme Court has recognized that behavior previously viewed with suspicion, and sometimes even condemned as per se unlawful, often benefits consumers by achieving economic efficiency. In *GTE Sylvania*, the Court expressly recognized that antitrust rules must be based on "demonstrable economic effect[s]."[14] And, most clearly on point, the Supreme Court in 1979, in the course of reviewing the legislative history of the Sherman Act, stated that that history "suggest[s] that Congress designed the Sherman Act as a 'consumer welfare prescription.' "[15] The days when the courts occasionally viewed the Sherman Act . . . as a compendium of all good values—from a desire to aid the "small dealers and worthy men"[16] to a desire to avoid "great aggregations of capital" that produced a "helplessness of the individual before them"[17]—are long gone. . . .

Consumer Welfare Is the Most Effective Standard

The antitrust laws, their legislative history, and the courts' interpretations of them all provide a strong case that enforcement of
the laws should be focused on consumer welfare, economically
defined. Fortunately, such a focus is also the most effective and
easiest to implement. . . . [I]f the framers were choosing anew the
appropriate standard to govern enforcement of the antitrust laws,
consumer welfare would be the superior choice.

Consistency of a Consumer Welfare Approach

Any more diffuse standard that incorporated amorphous social
and political concerns in addition to generalized economic ones
would be at best extremely difficult to administer and at worst no
standard at all. Employing a consumer welfare focus involves a
single, coherent, and objectively verifiable standard. Moreover,
consumer welfare offers a single standard of measurement that can
be calibrated in dollars. The trade-off that matters to the antitrust
laws—that between allocative efficiency on the one hand and productive efficiency on the other—can be objectively based, measured, and compared on that single common standard. In other
words, the measurement and evaluation of the trade-off in principle does not depend on the subjective predilections of the person
performing the analysis.

The fact that consumer welfare involves a comparison of "apples
with apples" has several benefits. First, it means that the costs of
administering the standard are likely to be low relative to those
of administering any standard that incorporates several diverse
concerns not directly comparable. Thus, an antitrust enforcement
policy based solely on economic values can develop cost-saving
mechanisms for determining whether or not a practice is harmful
to consumer welfare. For example, the law condemns as per se
unlawful certain clearly harmful "naked" agreements that have
few or no potential economic benefits—such as price fixing and
bid rigging—without the need to inquire into the actual economic

effect in a given case.[18] Were other, noneconomic values relevant, however, antitrust enforcers and courts would not be able to stop with such a limited inquiry. Rather, they would have to engage in an inherently costly and unpredictable ad hoc examination of a practice's impact on the "social" or "political" interests sought to be served by the antitrust laws.[19]

Second, it is far easier to assess the success of a competition policy—or of any policy, for that matter—when it focuses on a single economic goal. Attempting to compare the political gains achieved by some antitrust doctrine or particular enforcement action under the law with the economic costs of that doctrine or action is objectively impossible. The law, of course, is silent not only as to the noneconomic values that should be served, but even more as to how such values would be compared with economic efficiency. Indeed, a competition policy that is other than economic simply is incapable of providing objective criteria by which law makers, enforcement authorities, or the public can judge when the law is, on balance and in the objective sense, successful and when it is not. The outcome of the trade-offs will therefore depend largely, if not exclusively, on the subjective values of the particular person making the decisions, and society will never know whether it would have been better off had a different balance been chosen.

Of course, even under a consumer welfare analysis an analysis of trade-offs can be difficult. For example, it is rarely possible to calculate demand and supply elasticities or marginal costs precisely. This difficulty is often remarked upon by the critics. Nevertheless, the simple fact that the trade-off analysis under a consumer welfare standard is rarely capable of precise quantification does not undercut the conclusion that it is superior to the next-best alternative. Moreover, and more importantly, for the consumer welfare analysis to be effective in practice, it is often sufficient for it to be able to compare the costs and benefits on the basis of orders of magnitude. It will often be clear, for example, that the anticompetitive threat (that is, the impact on allocative efficiency) of a particular practice is nonexistent, or at least negligible. In such a case no enforcement action is necessary, regardless of the ability to identify and quantify efficiencies. Only rarely will the trade-offs be so close that the limitations on the ability of courts and enforcers to quantify the costs and benefits will as a practical matter interfere with the successful administration of a consumer welfare standard under the antitrust laws.

Relative Costs

At the very least, the proponents of an antitrust standard that attempts explicitly to incorporate noneconomic goals must acknowledge that such a standard will have substantial economic costs that may or may not outweigh the benefits, depending, of course, on a person's point of view. Any approach that elevates other values—however laudable they may be—over economic welfare may often frustrate economic efficiency and lead to higher prices, poorer quality, and slower innovation for American consumers; and in turn render American firms less competitive in world markets. The costs will be not only in terms of dollars for consumers, but in terms of jobs and technological progress. Restricting firms to some arbitrary maximum size, for example, would sacrifice the economies of scale and scope that are necessary for firms to compete in increasingly global economies, without achieving any countervailing economic benefits. Such a policy would likely penalize the very firms that were most successful, discouraging others from striving for success. America as a nation can choose smallness and decentralization of economic units for their own sake or it can choose the size dictated by the marketplace. But it is clear that no antitrust policy can accomplish both, and only the marketplace choice will result in the use of this nation's scarce resources—labor, energy, etc.—that best maximizes the needs, desires, and overall well-being of all America's consumers (and *everyone* is a consumer).

Moreover, it is likely that the apples-with-oranges comparisons required by any incoherent, multifaceted, and inherently subjective standard would lead in the long run to counterproductive results even with respect to the noneconomic goals that such a standard purported to serve. For example, rules aimed at protecting small businesses must, to be successful, make it more difficult for other firms to compete effectively against those small businesses. Such a policy will surely benefit the small businesses already in the market. Over time, however, such protection will discourage new entry and will ultimately hurt the very class of upstart small entrepreneurs (those who have not yet entered the market) that ostensibly the policy was meant to protect. The reality is that free markets are dynamic, and artificial protections for any one group merely protect those fortunate few who are members today while harming or discouraging those who are not yet members of the favored group. As the American experience demonstrates, the best way to protect diversity, plentiful economic opportunity, and prosperity for all groups is to avoid attempting to protect a class or classes of competitors at the expense of some others.

Finally, an enforcement policy focused on consumer welfare is most consistent with traditions of personal liberty. Any competition law will to some extent constrain the ability of individuals to direct their own economic affairs. However, a claim to government interference with economic freedom on the basis of ambiguous and subjective political goals represents a serious and, to many, intolerable threat to personal liberty. Truly the greatest threat to individual liberty is not private power, economic or otherwise; it is government's power to coerce. And the greatest protection for individual liberties is a limited government. An interpretation of the antitrust laws that is not founded on the objective criterion of consumer welfare embodied in the statutory language, but that calls for government intervention in the market to achieve ill-defined, subjective "values," is a prescription for tyranny. It is nothing more than central planning by lawyers.

Moreover, the fact that the antitrust laws focus on consumer welfare does not mean that society's desire to promote social and political values cannot be met. As this discussion should suggest, a consumer welfare standard is generally consistent with the most fundamental social and political concerns in this country. A consumer welfare standard protects dynamic markets and removes the threat that government antitrust enforcers will arbitrarily punish economic success. It constrains the discretion of government enforcers. And it promotes the expansion of society's economic pie, creating wealth that can, at least in part, be devoted to solving social problems.

More importantly, a focus on consumer welfare does not oversell antitrust. It can be argued, for example, that antitrust is simply unsuited to addressing and balancing the social and political concerns affected by the effort of the Department of Justice and the court to regulate this country's telecommunications industry in the aftermath of the breakup of AT&T. It is far preferable to leave those decisions to the legislative branches of government. The tax laws and state welfare programs can be used to redistribute income, small business and other set-asides may be used to benefit discrete classes of businesses, and other laws can be specifically devised to deal with the myriad other legitimate social concerns. Antitrust can then focus on the task to which it is best suited—promoting and protecting consumer welfare.

Implications

Application of the consumer welfare standard has important implications for antitrust policy. Ideally, antitrust enforcement would prevent all business activity that on balance reduces total efficiency, while tolerating all other conduct. Unfortunately, the world is not ideal, the detailed and complex information necessary for such accurate forecasts is unavailable, and the acquisition of available information is expensive. There are essentially three costs associated with government enforcement that must be minimized in order to implement effectively the consumer welfare goals of antitrust:

> First, of course, there is a cost associated with failing to prevent conduct that on balance reduces economic efficiency and harms the welfare of consumers. In effect, this is the cost of inadequate enforcement or of nonenforcement.
>
> Second, there is the cost of mistakenly stopping conduct that in reality is not, on balance, anticompetitive, but may even be procompetitive and efficiency-enhancing. Because enforcers must operate on imperfect information and try to predict the future effect of conduct, such mistakes are a serious concern.
>
> Third, there are administrative costs to any enforcement program. These include the resources expended by businesses and individuals in complying with the law as well as the government resources—lawyers,

economists, judges, etc.—expended to enforce the rules. Among the most substantial administrative costs are those incurred by firms that avoid innovative, potentially procompetitive behavior because they fear the litigation costs associated with defending an antitrust enforcement action. This chilling of procompetitive activity will, of course, be the greater the more uncertain and ambiguous are the rules of antitrust liability and enforcement.

In order to maximize consumer welfare, then, an enforcement program must minimize *all* of these costs, not just the costs associated with failing to prevent anticompetitive business practices. Accomplishing this aim, however, is not easy. The clearest possible rule that thereby reduces administrative costs might be one that prohibits everything, or nothing, but such a rule surely would entail very high costs by allowing anticompetitive conduct or by preventing procompetitive conduct. Similarly, the most accurate set of rules is likely to require the kinds of enforcement discretion and careful analysis that preclude certainty and entail significant administrative costs.[20] Therefore, in its zeal to rid the economy of unreasonable private restraints on free markets, antitrust enforcement must be careful neither to overreach nor to create uncertainty, for to do either will sacrifice the procompetitive and competitively neutral activities that are the hallmarks of free markets and the very purpose of the antitrust laws.

The resilience of free markets in correcting competitive problems offers some guidance in setting up an optimal enforcement policy that minimizes these costs. Market forces are usually quite effective at overcoming private restraints on competition. Anticompetitive price increases trigger new entry into the market and development by other firms of substitutes to which consumers may switch. Thus, even when antitrust law fails to prevent an anticompetitive practice, the market will eventually overcome its restraining effect. . . . Of course, government intervention in the market in the form of antitrust enforcement will often correct private restraints on competition more quickly. Nevertheless, in considering how best to minimize the costs of enforcement, one must keep in mind the self-correcting tendency of the markets, which naturally ameliorate—if not eliminate—the costs of mistakenly failing to condemn anticompetitive conduct.

On the other hand, when the government mistakenly creates

a rule that condemns procompetitive conduct, there is no self-correcting mechanism in government that tends to rectify the mistake; indeed, explicit doctrines like *stare decisis* and implicit ones like bureaucratic infallibility deliberately frustrate such self-correction. Consequently, parties will be deterred by the fear that they too will be penalized. The danger to the welfare of consumers posed by a policy that prohibits too much may therefore be significantly greater than that posed by one that prohibits too little.

Criminal Deterrence

. . . Price fixing, bid rigging, and naked territorial allocation are among the classes of naked horizontal agreements that produce no significant efficiencies, yet invariably restrict output, raise prices above cost, and unambiguously harm consumer welfare. However, because such conduct typically is covert, it is not always detected. Thus, in order to deter the conduct successfully, the penalties imposed when a scheme is detected and prosecuted must be well in excess of the actual harm caused in that individual case. If the penalties were equal only to the harm caused by the conduct (or even to the benefit gained, which will be *smaller* than the harm caused because of the transactions costs of entering and maintaining an illegal agreement), then businesspeople considering whether to engage in the conduct will find it economically profitable. This is because the benefits (the expected profits) will virtually always be greater than the expected costs (the penalty that will be imposed if caught, *discounted* by the probability that it will be imposed).[21] In many instances, only the fines and jail terms available under the criminal law provide a deterrent penalty adequate to render this conduct unprofitable *ex ante* . . . .[22]

. . .

Impact On Small Businesses

Some critics have argued that current antitrust policies hurt small businesses. It is certainly true that this administration's policies have not consciously *favored* small business, just as they have not favored big business or any other discrete class of economic interests. But it is simply inaccurate to say that those policies hurt small businesses. In fact, by unshackling the competitive vigor of America's entrepreneurs in order to maximize consumer welfare, current policy has been the best friend small business ever had.

Small businesses traditionally have played an important role in America's economy by bringing innovative new products and services to the market and by identifying and exploiting important new product "niches." They provide vigorous competition that lowers prices and enables this country to participate fully in world markets. It is creative individuals, through the medium of small business, that make the U.S. economy unique and dynamic.

A free market economy, unfettered by unnecessary government intervention, is the best environment for small businesses. Because the market is always evolving, new opportunities and market niches are always being created for entrepreneurs to exploit. Any enforcement policy that stifles the dynamism of the market serves to entrench existing dominant players. Government regulation, including intervention in the form of antitrust enforcement, has all too often penalized innovative small firms and protected larger firms against unsettling competition. In the past, the antitrust laws in fact were at times used to challenge innovative arrangements adopted by small firms to compete with their larger rivals. *Topco*[23] and *GTE Sylvania*[24] provide two examples of such conduct that was challenged—in one case successfully. . . .

The Supreme Court recognized in *GTE Sylvania*[25] and again in *Sharp*[26] that nonprice vertical restraints, such as exclusive territories, more often than not enhance competition and should therefore be analyzed under a rule of reason. [The present enforcement policy] incorporates that analysis and acknowledges the possible procompetitive benefits of such vertical business arrangements, while recognizing the limited circumstances under which a nonprice vertical restraint actually can harm consumer welfare.

The rule-of-reason approach to nonprice vertical restraints has provided small businesses with greater flexibility to market their goods and services in the most efficient way possible and so to compete effectively against larger rivals. Small manufacturers now have an alternative to complete and total vertical integration—

often too costly—by which to control distribution of their products and services. Instead, small businesses are generally free to deal through independent wholesalers and retailers—themselves usually small businesses—by imposing the kinds of contractual restrictions that ensure that their products are made as attractive as possible to consumers.

As a result, the options available to American consumers—both in terms of products and services and in terms of distribution channels—have grown exponentially. Without the freedom afforded by *Sylvania*, some manufacturers would have been practically forestalled from successfully introducing new products and services. And some distributors would have been unwilling, or unable, to obtain established products or services to sell to the public. Moreover, these benefits to small businesses have not come at the expense of large discount retailing chains, which have thrived in recent years. . . .

Conclusion

As the decade of the 1990s approaches, it is indeed an appropriate time to assess the correctness of our antitrust policies. This appraisal should not be conducted in a vacuum, but in the context of a world marketplace in which, perhaps more than ever, this country cannot tolerate policies that hamper innovation and efficiency. It is a good time to ask: Do we want markets in which inefficient businesses are protected from competition and innovation is stifled? Or do we want a dynamic marketplace in which the most efficient practices and competitors succeed, in which American consumers are given the widest choice of the most innovative and lowest-cost products and services, and in which American businesses are able to compete effectively? To most concerned parties—even the counterrevolutionaries—the answer should be clear.

Legal Reasoning, Antitrust Policy, and the Social "Science" of Economics

JOHN J. FLYNN

. . . In the clash of law with the "Chicago" or Neo-Classical School of Economics there is turbulence because the assumptions (moral and factual) and the methodology or reasoning process of the one do not conform with those of the other. . . . [T]he unthinking blend of law and social sciences can contaminate the rhetoric and methodology of both disciplines, and the resulting turbulence can obscure rather than advance our understanding of reality and search for the truth.

. . . [N]eoclassical thought is incompatible with the reality facing antitrust, the substantive goals of antitrust policy, and the demands of legal reasoning and the institutional constraints placed upon it. While law is dependent upon a number of disciplines (including economics) for insights and for understanding the reality that the rules are intended to regulate, the current attempt to make one school of economic thought the exclusive means for determining the relevance, meaning and application of both the rules and the facts of legal disputes is a serious mistake.

There is a deeper statement underlying my criticism. It is an epistemological statement rejecting the claim that the only know-

Reprinted from 62 Antitrust Bulletin 713 (1988).

able source of standards for legal decision making is one that can be objectively verified by testing pursuant to a model that purports to quantify reality objectively—whether it be a political, economic, social, legal or other fixed model of the *is* to determine the *ought*. Scientific models—from Newton's laws of gravity to phrenology to economic models—are, like all broad aesthetic statements, premised upon assumptions; moral or *ought* assumptions that define what will and what will not be permitted to be "reality" for purposes of the analysis and what will and what will not be permitted to be the values given weight in the analysis. An empirical investigation unaware of its own assumptions and values is neither empirical nor an investigation. It is an exercise in confirming one's fixed and unchallengeable ideological beliefs.

. . .

Part of the problem is caused by the tendency of the legal process to resist a liberation of its thinking from reified rules and rigid concepts applied mechanically without regard for the values and history that underlie the law, and that change reality and generate new insights into old problems. Lawyers and judges develop vested interests characterized by minds fixed in known rules ordering a known reality. It is easier and less threatening to apply the known than to reexamine assumptions and the comfortable reality we arrogantly think we know. The connotation and denotation of concepts underlying the language of law are, however, obliterated by the mindless mechanical application of rules to an unseen but changing reality. Because of this, law and legal analysis are for the intellectually arrogant; persons convinced that only they and their reified views possess truth, beauty and justice. . . . [T]hey are intolerant of insights behind their particular sun. Legal disputes and their involvement with the *is* in light of the *ought* should, however, constantly remind us of what we are about while illuminating what we are becoming in the context of what we have been.

The proponents of neoclassical thought view economics as a "science" in the 19th-century meaning of that term; a science producing unyielding and eternal truths and fixed assumptions for measuring reality.[1] They assume that models can produce quantifiable data for reduction to "truth" through the "neutral" tools of language, mathematics, statistics and simplistic deductive logic.[2] For some economists and other social scientists, political science, economics, psychology, and sociology became hard "sciences" through the seemingly objective methodology of mathematics, abandoning "soft" humanism.[3] Similar afflictions stultified American law a century ago with the rise of legal positivism and the belief that law could be reduced to fixed rules capable of mechanical and repetitious application divorced from the deeper moral values that law reflects and the evolutions in reality and our understanding of it. . . .

The tragedy may begin to be minimized by changing the category of economics from a "social science" back to a subdivision of moral philosophy—where Adam Smith began—and by adopting a more humble and skeptical attitude with regard to the dependability of the 19th-century methodologies of science relied upon without abandoning their use altogether. Indeed, one might even hope that economists, judges and lawyers afflicted by 19th-century positivism might begin to see themselves as engaged in a calling requiring them to practice their craft on the higher plane of being an art: the art of moral philosophy. The use of moral philosophy in economics should produce insights into the human condition through inductive and deductive reasoning about the economy and through an awareness of the normative assumptions underlying the analysis and the insights of history, political science, psychology and sociology. . . .

Substance and Form

. . .

On the substantive side, it is clear that the Congressional goals for antitrust policy were and continue to be far broader than the narrow and technical concept of "efficiency" dictated by the factual assumptions and normative values underlying neoclassical price theory. Every competent and objective study of the legislative history of the antitrust laws indicates that they were passed with a series of qualitative political, social and economic goals or values in mind to guide their implementation.[4] The overall goal is that a "competitive process," not the quantitative concept of "competition," be the rule of trade for big and small. . . . [5]

The suggestion that these qualitative values are unknowable, too vague, or in mutual conflict and are therefore incapable of providing guidance for the law, and that only the quantitative guidance provided by Chicago School economic modeling can provide knowable standards for decision, is . . . unfathomable. It is a quaint return, dressed in the garments of scientism, to the disastrous legal positivism of the last century.[6] The legal process is constantly confronted with reconciling competing and conflicting moral values underlying its rules in light of the specific realities of individual disputes, role definitions, and the consequences of the decision. Indeed, this function is central to the legal process, and the art with which it is carried out distinguishes the great jurists from the mediocre. . . .

. . .

Neoclassical Economic Methodology and the Demands of Legal Reasoning

The methodology relied upon . . . is that of a simplistic form of deductive logic. A syllogism is established, whose major premise forecloses consideration of the normative and factual issues that legal analysis and the antitrust laws require to be investigated by those charged with enforcing and administering the law. A minor premise consisting of only those "facts" the major premise permits to be "facts" is then put forward without regard to the facts of the dispute and the circumstances of the case before the court.[7] The only conclusion permitted by the model of Rules × Facts = Decision is then mechanically derived by the decision maker. The rigid deductive logic followed displaces the complex inductive and deductive logic required in legal analysis, where the facts determine which rules are relevant, what those rules mean, and how they should apply; while the rules determine which facts are relevant, what they mean, and how they contribute to the consequences that "ought" to be mandated. Inductive logic, the facts of the dispute, and insights from relevant disciplines play a significant role in determining which rules are relevant and in pouring meaning into the rules found relevant. Inductive logic and the rules found relevant also play a significant role in defining which facts are relevant to the major premise and what weight they should have in the minor premise. One breaks into this otherwise closed system by understanding the moral objectives underlying the area of law involved and its interrelationship with other areas of law and the social sciences, the history and experience that caused those values to be captured in law by Congress, and the factual and institutional framework in which those moral values are given effect.

The analytical process of neoclassical thought goes through none of these steps. It begins with a series of abstract and unexamined factual and normative assumptions and definitions about the affairs of the real world. Although the language used in neoclassical thought has a praiseworthy meaning in popular thought, one should be forewarned that the central concepts are technical definitions with specific meanings and consequences not related to the more amorphous and general popular meaning of the terms. Indeed, often the technical meaning of a term is used interchangeably with other technical meanings, and sometimes is even used in its more general popular sense. A central concept of the model is the neoclassical concept of "efficiency." The neoclassical concept of "efficiency"[8] is a narrow and technical concept derived from a series of assumptions about a model of an unreal world of perfect competition[9] and a tautological definition of "rational" individual and collective conduct. . . . It has . . . been suggested that "law and economics advocates further claim that economists have no concern for the wisdom or morality of choices made by businessmen and consumers, that theirs is but an accounting function of toting up the choices made." It should be noted that the definition of what is "rational" is circular, since rational is whatever is chosen and whatever is chosen is rational—a definition that underlies a philosophy of extreme utilitarianism and can be made the basis for a philosophy of radical libertarianism. Why the discipline of economics "ought" to adopt such a circular and meaningless definition of *rational* and measure the choices made only in terms of what people are willing to pay for their choices is not explained by advocates of the Chicago School. Speculation about the "ought" underlying these definitions might include a moral preference in favor of socially unimpeded individual freedom and materialism without reference to the complexities of how one goes about adjusting those values to the apparent need to have an organized

society, lest individual freedom be sacrificed to anarchy. Or speculation might suggest that we as a society ought to revive a 19th-
century absolutist view of property and contract rights and the
unrealistic view of reality that accompanied them, despite a modern reality dictating otherwise. Or it might reflect a choice to favor
the political agenda of extreme libertarianism despite the absence
of any debate among "rational maximizers" in the political process
as to whether that type of anarchy is the basic political value we
wish to rely upon to govern economic rights and relationships in
society—if one could believe there could be a society guided by
such a theory. The simple fact is that we are never told what
objective is behind the adoption of a simplistic and circular definition or rationale to determine what the law ought to mean.
Perhaps the objective is to allow this system of analysis to have
the appearance of being a closed system of analysis like geometry,
capable of always producing truth and being beyond normative
criticism, so long as one does not examine its closed system of
reasoning and the assumptions upon which the definition of *rational*
is based.

Moreover, the definition excludes from consideration everything
that cannot be materialistically quantified by the measure of pay-
ment the definition permits (willingness to pay), and it excludes
from consideration the inaction of those unable to express their
choices because they lack the things of "value" (as defined by the
model) to exchange for the choices they wish to make. Other forms
of efficiencies, like innovation and production efficiencies, are ignored by the calculus. . . . A hidden "ought" assumption is being
made when the unexplained assumption is used to define and measure the choices observed in terms of willingness to pay (without
regard for the factual circumstances, the existing distribution of
wealth, and the ability to pay). That assumption is that materialism
and self-gratification are the only factors motivating human conduct and that they are the only factors that the legal system ought
to value. There is a multiplicity of explanations for human behavior
available from other disciplines that make a considered study of
human behavior and motivation and the consequences of curbing
or not curbing some forms of behavior, instead of beginning with
a tautological definition of the problem the proponent of this form
of reasoning is called upon to study. . . .

From this circular definition of pseudo-rationality is derived the neoclassical definition of *efficiency*, a definition premised upon the unstated normative assumptions underlying the definition of rationality: "Efficiency is a technical term: it means exploiting economic resources in such a way that human satisfaction as measured by aggregate consumer willingness to pay for goods and services is maximized. Value too is defined by willingness to pay."[10] This definition is further subdivided into definitions for the concepts of "allocative efficiency" and "productive efficiency." Judge Bork has defined them as follows: "Allocative efficiency, as used here, refers to the placement of resources in the economy, the question of whether resources are employed in tasks where consumers value their input most. Productive efficiency refers to the effective use of resources by particular firms."[11] And, Bork asserts, "The whole task of antitrust can be summed up as the effort to improve allocative efficiency without impairing productive efficiency so greatly as to produce either no gain or a net loss in consumer welfare."[12] While the distinction may be useful for abstract theorizing, and the values represented by these technical definitions of efficiency are worthy of consideration, the distinction falls to pieces when confronted with the complexities of reality and the normative question underlying all antitrust litigation: what ought to be the scope of the state-created property and contract rights of the proponent of the restraint in light of the social, political and economic normative goals for antitrust policy set forth by the lawgiver (Congress)? The methodology of logical positivism causes one to answer this question by ignoring it in one's major premise and by ignoring the reality of the dispute being analyzed. Although logical, it is hardly a rational form of decision making. It is a simplistic form of deductive reasoning reaffirming the theological postulates underlying the model without regard for the reality under investigation or the moral ends of the law in question and the moral consequences those ends dictate.

Moving up the inverted pyramid of tightly interwoven definitions and assumptions, "consumer welfare," in turn, as defined by neoclassical price theory, means "behavior whose net effect is output restricting and hence detrimental"—detrimental in terms of the normative and factual assumptions underlying neoclassical price theory and in light of the strict deductive logic employed by the theory to determine which values will be permitted to be considered and which facts are "facts" for purposes of the analysis.

The analysis is attractive because of its underlying and exclusive concern with maximizing human freedom and its emphasis upon the value of allocative efficiency. "The analysis is also seductive, not the least for its clever use of language with a laudable popular meaning (rational, efficiency, consumer welfare) to describe what are normatively loaded and technical concepts which can only be understood in light of the tautological definitions and hidden normative assumptions underlying the model."[13] The analysis is also seductive because of its rigid use of deductive logic and the self-proclaimed aura of being a science in the sense of a system of thought capable of producing objective truth without reference to other disciplines, requirements of the legal process like the division of judge and jury functions, the moral goals of the law involved, and the normative consequences of the choices made. Further, "the analysis taps into the simplistic fear of discretion afflicting logical positivists by claiming that reliance upon the model in the legal analysis of antitrust disputes ends the risk of the 'irrationality' of discretion."[14] Discretion is considered irrational, rather than inescapable, because discretion undermines a knowable analytical framework to control the arbitrary exercise of judicial power that would otherwise impinge upon the unstated normative libertarian ideological values of absolute property and contract rights or upon the utilitarian objective of maximizing short-term majority desires and providing the point upon which the entire inverted pyramid rests. From the viewpoint of developing a sensible role for antitrust policy in defining the scope of legally enforceable property and contract rights in light of contemporary reality and historical experience, the goals of antitrust policy and constraints upon the legal process, reliance upon the mechanical and deductive application of the model results in the abolition of the antitrust laws. From the viewpoint of modern jurisprudence and a reflective and empirically based discipline of economics, this covert rebirth of rigid positivism[15] is as startling as it is intellectually indefensible. From the viewpoint of the complex nature of legal reasoning, reliance upon this methodology of naive positivism in the academy and by the courts in this day and age is inexplicable. From the viewpoint of faithfully enforcing the laws that government officials have sworn to uphold and defend, reliance upon this methodology of logical positivism and the values underlying the model results in a denial of their oath of office.

Conclusion

Two conclusions should *not* be drawn from all that I have said and all that could be said about the present exclusive reliance upon neoclassical economic theorizing in legal analysis in general and in the enforcement and interpretation of the antitrust laws in particular. The first incorrect conclusion would be that I am suggesting there is no role for insights from the social sciences—particularly economics—in legal analysis generally and in antitrust analysis in particular. Both the meaning and application of law and our understanding of reality are dependent upon insights from other disciplines, as is an appreciation for the subtleties of legal reasoning and the moral obligations of law. There is a desperate need for creative and constructive social science research aware of its own assumptions and the normative values underlying the law and the institutional constraints upon the law's administration. The values of allocative, productive and innovative efficiencies are clearly concerns of relevance to the administration and interpretation of the antitrust laws. They are, however, factors that must be evaluated in the light of history, experience, modern realities, the realities of particular cases and the complex of other normative goals Congress has mandated for the antitrust laws. In the antitrust field we need to study the impact of institutional size upon individuality, invention and creativity; the impact of exalting individual greed upon the long-term interests of community; the effect of mergers on local communities, the labor force, economic concentration, political and social liberty and the long-term evolution of specific industries; case studies on the effects of pricing practices within the context of specific industries; studies of the effect of specific industry structure on pricing, innovation and political power; the emergence of an interdependent world economy; motivational studies of management and the behavior of firms from other nations; and on and on. What we do *not* need are further ideological tracts detached from reality and the Congressional goals for antitrust policy; tracts useful only for confirming the moral and political presuppositions of the theologians writing the tract.

The second conclusion that should not be drawn from what I have said is that law and the legal analysis of antitrust policy are an open-ended and meaningless exercise destined to reflect the whim of the person making the analysis. There are boundaries to the scope of the law's relevance, meaning and application in the interpretation and enforcement of the antitrust laws. They are to be found in the language used in the law, its history, the facts to which it is expected to be applied, the role definitions of those expected to apply it, and—most importantly—the underlying normative values (including but not limited to economic values) that the law is expected to foster and implement. Elsewhere I have identified a knowable and workable framework for the analysis of antitrust policy and disputes.[16] It is one that relies upon the insights of a number of the social sciences—including a more reflective and skeptical form of economic analysis—one not ensnared in the trap of tautological and meaningless definitions and unrealistic and unexamined moral and factual assumptions. It is one that relies upon devices of legal analysis like evidentiary presumptions and shifting burdens of proof to enable the analysis to take account of the reality unique to the dispute under investigation, while also blending skillfully the complex of normative goals underlying the law and unavoidably impacted by the controversy. And it is one capable of taking account of the social, political and economic goals of antitrust policy—the goals Congress mandated antitrust policy account for in the administration and enforcement of the law.

Some of the proponents of an exclusive reliance upon neoclassical theory to dictate antitrust policy would undoubtedly characterize what I advocate as a form of poetry; poetry in the sense of sentimental or meaningless guidelines incapable of surviving analytical rigor or of providing consistent application. Every legal decision, however, is unavoidably a moral decision; an "ought" determination in light of our understanding of the "is"—and vice versa. For those of us of Irish descent and concerned with the nature of legal reasoning and the underlying moral content of law and related disciplines like economics, it is a fine compliment to label as poetry what we understand intellectual inquiry to be—the exploration of the "good" behind the shadows in Plato's cave and the sun that creates them, if you like. For us, poetry is truth dwelling in beauty.

Antitrust, Law and Economics, and the Courts

LOUIS KAPLOW

1. Introduction

In the past decade, a new picture of the antitrust landscape has begun to emerge. The dominant emphasis of the ever more popular view concerns the ascendance of economics in antitrust decision-making and doctrine, particularly in Supreme Court adjudication, which is leading the way for the lower courts. Moreover, it is not just economic analysis in the abstract that supposedly has come to the forefront but the strand of economic argument associated with the Chicago School. The new insight thought to be contained in this brand of economic analysis is allegedly responsible for the doctrinal shifts that generally have narrowed the scope of antitrust liability.

. . .

   Simply observing a broader context [of Supreme Court decisionmaking where parallel shifts are taking place]—which is virtually never to be seen even in the footnotes of most recent commentary concerning these developments in antitrust—is sufficient to cast serious doubt on the explanation based on the Supreme Court's recent learning of economics, Chicago style. Nor can the simple story be rescued through a broader claim suggesting

Reprinted from 50/4 Law & Contemp. Probs. 181 (1987).

that the law and economics perspective generally was responsible for all the recent shifts in Burger Court jurisprudence. Although law and economics has been applied to virtually all areas of law, and although some parallel developments do reflect more of an economic approach, it would be extremely difficult to make the case that the broad changes in Supreme Court doctrine are primarily or even substantially explained by these phenomena.

· · ·

2. Has There Been a Significant Change in the Degree to Which Economic Analysis Is Used to Address Economic Issues?

Statements that the new law and economics has come to dominate the Supreme Court's antitrust decisionmaking typically encompass some combination of three subsidiary claims: Economic analysis is used more frequently in addressing economic issues; economic analysis has come to yield different answers to economic questions; and economic questions have come to be more important in deciding antitrust cases. . . .

The proposition that economics has long been accepted in antitrust, although contrary to much of current commentary, is really quite familiar. After all, the most prominent works in the 1950's took a decidedly economic approach,[1] even if one omits the work of the Chicago School.[2] It has been contemplated for decades, if not from the beginning, that economics would play an important role in analyzing antitrust issues. In fact, the law and economics movement of the past few decades is often thought of as involving the application of economics to all aspects of law *except* antitrust, regulation, and a few other fields—those in which the use of economics has long been taken for granted.

The most notable antitrust opinions over this time period rather uniformly display the application of economic analysis, whatever one thinks of the quality or content of the analysis in particular opinions. Consider first the earlier decades. In his recent analysis, Frederick Rowe argues that the strong connection between economics and antitrust doctrine was established in the 1940's.[3] That the heavy use of economics in leading antitrust decisions dates back at least this far is amply supported by a consideration of the most salient cases of the period. Learned Hand's opinion in *Alcoa*[4]—one frequently and heavily criticized in the new law and economics of antitrust—is well-known for its extensive discussion of market definition and its relation to market power, one that greatly surpassed most of what had come before (and much of what has come after) in economic sophistication.[5] *United Shoe*,[6] another of the leading monopolization opinions of the earlier era that has been heavily criticized by the new law and economics of antitrust, is particularly known for its heavy use of economic analysis. The Supreme Court's *Cellophane* opinion,[7] which contains one of the most prominent and extensive discussions of market definition of the period, relies heavily on economic concepts, such as the cross-elasticity of demand. In the merger area, *Brown Shoe*[8] is the most criticized opinion. Yet it is also known for reading the rather ambiguous language of the 1950 amendment to the Clayton Act—"in any line of commerce in any section of the country"[9]— as referring to product and geographic markets in the sense economists mean by those terms. Although the examples could be multiplied, it suffices for the purposes of this argument to have established the prevalence of economic analysis in a number of the most prominent opinions of the era, and in particular those now most heavily criticized by the new law and economics of antitrust.

Given this history, it would be rather difficult to imagine that antitrust decisions of the most recent fifteen years could reflect a substantially greater use of economics in addressing economic questions than was employed in these earlier times. In fact, the more recent cases best known for signaling the new direction of the Supreme Court exhibit a similar level of reliance on economic analysis. Although widely heralded as indicating a new direction for the Supreme Court in the merger area, analysis of the decision in *General Dynamics*[10] reveals surprisingly little change of any kind. That opinion is most known for looking beyond simple market share statistics. The Court's primary observation was that past market share was a poor predictor of the future in this unique market. Companies with significant past sales of coal, such as one of the merger partners in the case, might be of little competitive significance in the future if they were almost out of reserves.

This point hardly reflects the application of new or particularly sophisticated economic analysis. Moreover, the Court explicitly quoted *Brown Shoe*—that earlier and allegedly anti-economic analysis opinion—in support of its claim that it was appropriate to look beyond simple market share statistics. In addition, the reasoning behind this departure from market share statistics is rather limited.

Nor did the dissent, consisting of the Warren Court holdovers, disagree in principle with the majority's willingness to move beyond market share statistics based on past sales to consider reserves. Instead it argued that reserves should have been considered at the time of the merger, when the nondepleted company did in fact possess substantial reserves. Furthermore, the dissent suggested that the company's deep-mine reserves, although not currently being mined, should be included because the company had previous deep-mining experience. Whatever one thinks of the merits of this dispute, the dissent's position is hardly one that can be characterized as opposition in principle to the application of economic analysis. *General Dynamics* therefore involved no revolution in the use of economics in antitrust decisionmaking.

The most-cited decision in discussions of the rise of economics in antitrust is *Sylvania*.[11] In at least one important sense, this case did involve a substantial departure from the past: It reversed part of the Court's decision in *Schwinn*.[12] Much of the Court's criticism of *Schwinn* was directed to its formalism. This criticism had been emphasized previously by numerous commentators, who did not base their arguments particularly on economic analysis. Of course, an important part of the Court's basis for permitting territorial restrictions was economic arguments that had come to receive wider attention. Such reliance, however, is hardly a characteristic unique to this opinion or to antitrust decisions generally. Furthermore, the Court's acceptance of the economic arguments was limited.

Some of the other more prominent antitrust opinions of the past decade reflect the use of economic analysis while others show less evidence. In any event, it is clearly not the case that there has occurred a fundamental change in the view of courts concerning whether economic analysis provides a useful and important source of wisdom concerning antitrust law. Economics was well received by courts and commentators alike long before the recent emergence of the new law and economics of antitrust. If changes are to be identified, therefore, it must be either in the content of the economic analysis, which is explored in the next part of this article, or elsewhere.

3. Has There Been a Significant Change in What Economic Analysis Says About the Economic Issues in Antitrust Cases?

The question whether there has been a substantial increase in the use of economics to analyze economic questions could be answered simply and in the negative. The question addressed in this part of the article, concerning the content of the economic analysis, is more complex. . . .

A. Changes in Economists' Analyses

At one level, the claim that there has been a significant change in antitrust scholars' economic analyses of restrictive practices is undeniable. This shift can readily be seen in the leverage context, which involves the alleged extension of monopoly power from one market to another. Previous simplistic views concerning the possibility of leverage have been strongly critiqued by the Chicago School, often with little effective reply. It seems fair to say that, in its simplest form, the original leverage analysis has largely vanished. Although the Chicago School position has been the subject of much criticism, the debate has hardly been resolved.

More generally, despite the new law and economics criticism of many traditional views, it is not the case that the Chicago School of antitrust simply reflects application of the best and most current economic wisdom to the economic questions posed by antitrust law. Quite the contrary, the "price theory" widely hailed by the Chicago School as its heart and soul, although a useful starting point, is in fact the earliest and simplest form of economic analysis of industry. Much of the Chicago School commentary fails to appreciate that divergent work by economists was a response to the shortcomings of the simple price theory that Chicagoans hawk in competition with these other economic approaches.

One dimension of the change in economic analysis concerns the work, which began in the 1930's and reached its peak in the 1950's, that involved the intensive study of particular industries ("case studies") for the purpose of gaining additional insight into their operation. . . .

Another important defect exists in the Chicago School's attempts to cling to simple price theory as offering the best insights for the new law and economics of antitrust. Theoretical advances in microeconomics during the 1970's and 1980's have greatly surpassed the simple price theory formulated in the 1890's to provide an understanding of industrial practices. Much of this work . . . emphasizes the need for dynamic rather than static analysis, as well as the need to factor in the free rider problem when assessing strategic behavior. These recent advances also recognize the necessity of considering the implications of a variety of market imperfections that, while known for some time, have only recently been analyzed in sufficient depth to permit a greater understanding of their implications.

There have indeed been substantial changes in the methodology employed by economists studying industrial organization in the past decades, and the new learning of economists has substantial bearing on the appropriate content of antitrust doctrine. Some of this understanding favors the results advocated by the Chicago School, some is in opposition, and much is too tentative to permit confident conclusions at present. It is clearly not the case, however, that the methods and conclusions of the "new economics of antitrust," as embodied in the writings of the Chicago School, simply reflect what is new in economic analysis that has a bearing on antitrust.

. . .

B. Changes in Views of Antitrust Reflected in the New Law and Economics

The Chicago School of antitrust has advanced the position that belief in rigorous economic analysis is associated with their particular views toward antitrust. They offer opinions concerning the general operation of markets and the effects of particular restrictive practices. In addition, the new law and economics of antitrust is associated with certain preferences concerning procedural rules and presumptions, most notably the general preference for the rule of reason. The following two subsections consider whether the advocated positions on antitrust doctrine can best be understood simply as following from the application of economic analysis or instead as deriving from particular inclinations of those associated with the Chicago School.

1. ANALYSIS OF MARKETS AND PRACTICES

The Chicago School of antitrust generally believes that markets are largely self-correcting. Restrictive practices thus can be presumed to produce efficiencies rather than anticompetitive effects. . . . But if this were the fundamental premise, there would be no antitrust law. Antitrust law is necessarily based on the contrary assumption that courts at times can punish detrimental practices better than markets will. As a result, the tendency of the Chicago School to assume perfect markets when this may not be the case suggests that their economic analysis—even though rigorous and accurate in itself—is not always that most appropriate to the task. One of the most widely-noted shortcomings of Chicago School antitrust analysis is that it uses static models even when examining effects that are intrinsically dynamic—as in the case of all exclusionary practices that are alleged to affect market power over time.

Problems with the Chicago School analysis can be illustrated by its heavy reliance on the survivorship concept—the idea that only efficient practices will survive in competitive markets. . . . First, and most fundamentally, because it assumes that only efficient practices would survive, the approach largely begs the question for antitrust purposes. This problem relates rather directly to the previously noted tendency of the Chicago School to assume perfect markets. Simply, one must ask *why* truly anticompetitive practices never can survive. Strategic considerations combined with well-recognized market imperfections make this query important.

Second, the Chicago School's use of the survivorship concept often ignores or gives little weight to the question of how long the evolutionary process takes. If one had sufficient faith in self-correcting tendencies of the market, even a ban on cartels would be unnecessary, although most Chicago School analysts have stopped short of such a position. Similar reasoning also implies that market forces would tend to eliminate various forms of discrimination rather quickly in many contexts. A substantial history, however, as well as some current events, demonstrate that long time periods may be necessary for the process to work. That the problem may be largely one of substantial delay rather than a permanent lack of competition hardly renders antitrust unimportant.

A third problem involves the precision of the selection process as industry evolves. When there are many practices and outsiders have difficulty determining which are efficient, as the Chicago School would argue is often the case, the process of imitation in the market will not function as quickly or as effectively as it otherwise would. When the firm expects practices to have much of their payoff in the future, and when there are numerous random factors affecting the level of the payoff, self-correcting tendencies will operate more slowly. Furthermore, with conglomerates, market discipline may have less effect on the practices of particular divisions.

It would be a mistake to conclude from the limitations of the survivorship process that market evolution has little or no tendency to produce efficiency. What is required, and what much of the economic analysis responding to the shortcomings of simple price theory attempts, is a more subtle and intricate analysis of particular practices in particular contexts. Such examination would permit one to determine whether the market's corrective forces are sufficient to produce desirable consequences and, if not, whether there exist legal remedies that offer potential for improvement. This view is far less satisfying than the simple prescriptions of either the Chicago School or those who earlier took opposite positions, because it suggests that the most appropriate antitrust doctrine may have to be complex and it may not be possible to have great confidence in most conclusions reached concerning antitrust. In this state of affairs, even modest predilections about the outcome can produce substantial biases in the analysis, so extreme caution is necessary on the part of the analysts as well as the consumers of their product.

2. FORMULATION OF LEGAL RULES

Much of the argument of the new law and economics of antitrust as well as many of the recent doctrinal developments, both in the

Supreme Court and appellate courts, has been directed toward the formulation of legal rules and presumptions. For example, in areas such as vertical (intrabrand) restraints and tying, there has been advocacy and doctrinal movement from a per se prohibition to a rule of reason. Similarly, there has been increasing support for requiring proof of market power in an increasing range of contexts. In addition, the requirement that a plaintiff alleging predatory pricing prove that the defendant's prices were below cost, appropriately defined, has generally been well received by the courts in the past decade, although not without qualification. More generally, analysts advocating an economic approach have been hostile to considering evidence of a defendant's intent when evaluating conduct.

In each case, the suggestion is that these results follow from economic analysis. This subsection demonstrates how none of these results is the necessary implication of an economic approach; in each instance, economic analysis could be used to support contrary positions. The discussion here will not, however, consider which positions on each question are most convincing; rather it will be confined to the issue of whether particular results inhere in economic logic.

The rule of reason might appear to have a natural affinity with economic analysis because the rule requires consideration of all the economically relevant factors, whereas the per se rule cuts analysis short. Yet the distinction between per se rules and the rule of reason is much like the more general distinction between rules and standards. With respect to that general distinction, it has been long recognized that the choice often has less to do with the goals of the particular system of rules than with the degree to which more rigid rules will produce error and more open-ended rules will produce uncertainty and impose additional cost in their application. It is precisely such trade-offs that economic analysis of legal procedure demands be made. That a per se prohibition against horizontal price fixing is generally supported by those favoring an economic approach illustrates this point.

Complicating the choice between a per se rule and the rule of reason is the ambiguity that surrounds their meaning, especially in the case of the latter. . . . [C]alls for the rule of reason (which are now heard in connection with every doctrine, except simple horizontal price fixing) should be understood as either intentionally or unconsciously disguised attempts to remove the area from antitrust scrutiny. . . . In principle the approach of trying to design such presumptions, where possible, is sound. . . . Finally, it should be noted that the rule of reason, as currently formulated, does not permit the open-ended inquiry contemplated by statements equating it with a complete economic analysis in that it will not consider economic benefits of abandoning competition in particular instances.

The preference for a market power proof requirement also appears to involve the application of an economic approach, because economic analysis indicates that, absent any such power, there can be no anticompetitive effect from restrictive practices. Yet, as with the rule of reason, it does not immediately follow that economic analysis necessarily supports the rule that most directly reflects its application. Consider the context of horizontal price fixing. . . . If a naked horizontal price-fixing scheme has been detected, and one is virtually certain that such schemes are undesirable, what sense does it make to require proof of market power when such an inquiry is inevitably difficult and costly? In addition, even if market power must be established, one must decide how much market power must be demonstrated, by what evidence, and with what degree of confidence. Such requirements further suggest the complexity of the link between an economic approach and particular antitrust rules.[13]

The emergence of a marginal cost pricing test for predatory pricing could also be seen as an outgrowth of the application of an economic analysis, although much of the criticism of the Areeda-Turner test has come from the most prominent economists who study antitrust. A substantial portion of the dispute concerns the appropriate role to be given complex dynamic considerations that are central to predatory phenomena. Some of the more recent court decisions on predatory pricing have veered from the Areeda-Turner approach on precisely these grounds. . . . Discussion of the marginal cost pricing test compliments that of the rule of reason in that, although both have been associated with the economic approach, they represent opposite choices in analytically similar situations. This juxtaposition does not indicate that either rule is mistaken; rather, it reinforces the argument that there is no automatic connection between the use of economic analysis and particular methods of formulating antitrust rules.

As a final example, consider the hostility often associated with the economic approach to antitrust and expressed with growing frequency toward inquiries into defendants' intent in order to resolve antitrust disputes. The basic problem is that the arguments rejecting altogether the relevance of intent are often based primarily on mistakes commonly made in particular inquiries into intent. More specifically, if intent is interpreted to encompass the simple desire to operate so effectively as to surpass one's competitors, it does not indicate any basis for antitrust liability. It hardly follows, however, that intent is irrelevant to an economic inquiry. For example, clear evidence that firms' intent in entering a complex joint venture arrangement was to use their integrated activities as a cover for price fixing is relevant in determining the likely effect of such an agreement. In determining the effects of allegedly predatory behavior, one might be aided by evidence that a firm reduced its prices to a lower level than was profit maximizing in the short run precisely because it anticipated that this would bankrupt a new entrant, keep away future entrants, and thus permit higher, monopolistic prices in the future.

It may reasonably be objected that such evidence will often be hard to come by, and may necessitate costly discovery if deemed admissible. Yet it is hardly obvious that direct proof of the effects of various complex business arrangements and practices—itself involving extensive discovery and heavy reliance on expert witnesses—will be easier to come by, less costly, or more reliable. Just as intent is often inferred from effects, it is also reasonable in many circumstances to infer effects from intent. After all, if one assumes, as many Chicago School analysts are inclined to do, that firms in the market are a better judge of the effects of practices than are courts, then it follows that such evidence of intent should be given great weight indeed. This evidence would necessarily be deemed superior to any attempt to reconstruct firms' decisionmaking processes using expert witnesses in the course of litigation.

An economic approach does, however, have much relevance to

an intent inquiry in that it will help determine which courses of action, if successful, are likely to be detrimental. Economic analysis and inquiries into intent are not inherently at odds. The question of how much weight one should place on various evidence of a firm's intent is a difficult one, and the only substantial insight economic theory is likely to offer is the general natural selection argument that firms more able to fulfill their intentions are more likely to survive than those that are not.

4. Has There Been Significant Change in the Role of Economic Issues in Deciding Antitrust Cases? Economics as *A* Goal Versus the *Only* Goal

The first two parts of this article suggest that there has not been any significant increase in the degree to which the Supreme Court uses economic analysis in addressing economic questions, and that changes in the content of economic analysis over the past few decades have no necessary connection to most developments in antitrust doctrine and even less of a link to many of the positions advocated by the Chicago School of antitrust. This part examines a third possible explanation: that the politics and ideology of the Court and various antitrust analysts provide the best interpretation for much of the shift that has been noted.

One commonly offered observation is that economic efficiency—regardless of the particular content or method of economic analysis—has moved from being merely one of many dimensions of antitrust inquiry to the sole, or at least the heavily dominant, objective of antitrust in the mind of the Supreme Court. Of course, even if a radical transformation along these lines has taken place, [there is] some doubt on whether such a shift necessarily explains the changes in the content of doctrine usually associated with the Chicago School. Nonetheless, such a departure from past practice is unlikely to be without effect and would itself reflect changes in the Court's approach that might have broader ramifications. As the introduction to this article suggested, in the light of changes in Supreme Court jurisprudence in many areas over the past decades, one should expect to see parallel movements in antitrust.

. . .

A. *Assessing the Change in Antitrust Opinions*

1. THE EARLY CASES

Although some have taken the view that, from the beginning, the sole objective of the antitrust laws was to be economic efficiency, there has never been any dispute over the fact that leading antitrust opinions from the beginning have made explicit references to broader purposes, such as the protection of small business, entrepreneurial freedom, buyer freedom of choice, the maintenance of deconcentration both as a way of life and to avert undue influence on the political process, and the preservation or promotion of a fair distribution of income, particularly between large economic enterprises and consumers. One of the first well-known instances is Justice Peckham's reference in *Trans-Missouri* to "small dealers and worthy men whose lives had been spent" in business.[14] In *Alcoa*, Learned Hand stated that "[t]hroughout the history of these statutes it has been constantly assumed that one of their purposes was to perpetuate and preserve, for its own sake and in spite of possible cost, an organization of industry in small units which can effectively compete with each other."[15]

Interestingly, both statements refer explicitly to the Sherman Act, which has been the focus of the strongest claims to the effect that the antitrust laws contemplated only economic efficiency. . . . Moreover, these statements precede the Warren Court era, thus indicating a long-standing pattern rather than a temporary shift during that time. . . . Antitrust court decisions up through the time of the Warren Court thus clearly reflect the view that objectives other than economic efficiency, narrowly construed, are part of the purposes of antitrust litigation.

2. SUPREME COURT DECISIONS OF THE PAST DECADE

In light of the history briefly recounted . . . it would indeed represent an important shift if the Burger Court's recent decisions explicitly rejected earlier statements and adopted the view that economic efficiency was the sole objective of the antitrust laws. Most of the support for this frequently advanced description is confined to a handful of passages in some of the Court's recent opinions. As an initial observation, given that none of the referenced language spans more than a sentence or two and none represents a direct attempt to address this issue, it is impossible to make a persuasive claim beyond the argument that such language constitutes hints of things to come. One rather obvious source of support for this characterization of the evidence of a shift as modest at best is the simple fact that the Court neither cites nor otherwise addresses any of the well-known discussions of the multiple objectives position it has supposedly rejected in recent cases.

It is best to begin the inquiry with the most widely cited Supreme Court statement on the subject, that found in *Reiter v. Sonotone*: "On the contrary, [the floor debates] suggest that Congress designed the Sherman Act as a 'consumer welfare prescription.' ... "[16] Believe it or not, that single sentence and citation has been the major source of much of the argument. Not only is the evidence exceedingly thin in quantity, it also falls far short of supporting the position that the goal of economic efficiency, to the exclusion of all else, was therein adopted.

First, the phrase "consumer welfare prescription" admits substantial ambiguity. Although [some] may have economic efficiency in mind, it would hardly be surprising if the Court intended a meaning more literal and in accord with common usage—the welfare of consumers. That interpretation, of course, often conflicts with economic efficiency. It excludes, for example, economies that accrue to a firm but are not passed on to consumers. In fact, this straightforward reading is more in accord with the distributional interpretation of the Sherman Act's objectives.[17] One would be hard-pressed to support either position based on this brief passage.

A second major defect is that even if the statement in *Reiter v. Sonotone* is interpreted as expressing the antitrust laws' concern with economic efficiency, it does not on its face purport to exclude other objectives. Thus, the statement is irrelevant to the question at hand because those who advocate a multiple-goal interpretation and approach generally embrace efficiency as one of the important goals. In fact, the context of the quotation clearly suggests that the statement of the consumer welfare goal is being used in an inclusive, rather than exclusive, fashion. The issue in *Reiter v. Sonotone*, after all, was whether consumers who purchase products for their own use have standing under section 4 of the Clayton Act. The context thus stands the exclusive interpretation on its head, for it was conceded by all parties and apparently agreed by the Court that various other potential plaintiffs—businesses in particular—did have standing. Thus, to interpret the Court's remark as referring only to consumers would be odd indeed. The only question was whether consumers were to be included among those allowed to bring private suits. It is hardly surprising that the Court provided a unanimous affirmative response. The paragraph containing the "consumer welfare" reference exists to support the proposition that "[n]othing in the legislative history of § 4 conflicts with" the holding that injured consumers could bring private suits. The sentence preceding the reference to the floor debates refers to the respondent's assertion that the language of section 4 "was clearly intended to *exclude* pecuniary injuries" to consumers.

The only remaining argument that could be offered to support the claim concerning the historic significance of *Reiter v. Sonotone* is that the mere fact of the reference to the first part of Bork's book reflects a wholesale adoption of a new philosophy of antitrust. Gordon Spivak's assessment . . . provided a cogent reply: "Imagine that: the Supreme Court overruled decades of antitrust precedents simply by quoting three words from Judge Bork's book."[18]

Nor do the rest of the Supreme Court's recent pronouncements amount to a wholesale revolution on this front. One of the strongest statements in support of the Chicago School position is that found in *BMI*, indicating that the Court's per se inquiry is to determine "whether the practice facially appears to be one that would always or almost always tend to restrict competition and decrease output, . . . or instead one designed to 'increase economic efficiency and render markets more, rather than less competitive.' "[19] Yet statements to this effect are hardly new, as evidenced by the Court's citation of *Northern Pacific* in support of this proposition.[20] In addition, . . . the focus on competition in *Engineers* is not at all necessarily an endorsement of the efficiency approach, as either an exclusive objective or otherwise.[21] Surely additional passages could be cited, but, given the extremely limited support offered by the language most frequently employed in discussions of whether the efficiency objective has fully triumphed, one cannot reasonably expect that even lesser clues would substantially tip the balance.

Not only is the affirmative support weak, but some modest language cuts against the notion that efficiency now reigns alone. *Maricopa*[22] is probably the decision most embarrassing to the Chicago School position in that it failed to accept a more lenient approach toward maximum price fixing. . . . The Court placed "horizontal agreements to fix maximum prices on the same legal— *even if not economic*—footing as agreements to fix minimum or uniform prices."[23] Both *Maricopa* and *Associated General Contractors* quoted language from *Kiefer-Stewart* concerning the tendency of condemned practices to "cripple the freedom of traders and thereby restrain their ability to sell in accordance with their own judgment."[24] The existence of these opinions and the statements within them cast further doubt on the claim that the Supreme Court has fully reversed itself on the question of the goals of the antitrust laws.

Concerning both the objectives of antitrust, discussed in this part, and the content of economic analysis, . . . there is the danger of drawing stronger inferences than warranted from the fact that a larger portion of major antitrust decisions by the Burger Court had been in favor of antitrust defendants, in cases where the Chicago School would support such results, than was true of prior Courts. As a matter of logic, much of the optimistic reading by Chicago School proponents might be attributed to the following invalid syllogism: (1) The Court has produced a given set of results; (2) this set of results has been advocated by proponents of the new law and economics of antitrust (the Chicago School); (3) therefore, the Supreme Court has been convinced by and therefore has adopted the Chicago School's economic interpretation of and approach to antitrust law. The hidden premise necessary to make this argument valid is that it is impossible to reach the Court's results without adopting the Chicago School position, lock, stock, and barrel. In rebutting this argument, one obvious point is simply that many of the more recent statements and decisions have been approved by a wide array of commentators, including those hostile to the Chicago School. More generally, recalling the argument in the introduction to this article concerning general movements in

Supreme Court decisionmaking as well as the role of particular
rationalizations for decisions, it would be a difficult task indeed to
establish that positions of any particular group of commentators
have been adopted by the Court.

B. Political Meaning of the Change:
Judicial Activism

1. THE ANTITRUST STATUTES AND THEIR HISTORY

The very existence of continued debate over whether the antitrust
statutes and their legislative history contemplate economic efficiency as the sole objective of antitrust doctrine is striking. The
position of some Chicago School advocates in this area represents
an instance in which their arguments are so farfetched that it is
hard to take them seriously; yet the continued advocacy of this
position by some makes at least a limited discussion necessary.
Moreover, even for those advocates who make little use of the
statutes and their legislative history, the fact that they cut strongly
against the view of efficiency as the sole objective of the antitrust
laws is relevant for interpreting the advocates' implicit views concerning the role of the judiciary.

The claim that the antitrust laws contemplate economic efficiency as their sole objective has a number of deficiencies, many
of which are independently sufficient to rule out the possibility.
First, those enacting the laws—particularly in the case of the Sherman Act—could not have understood the concept as we are now
asked to believe they did. Second, if one accepts the Chicago
School's analysis of restrictive practices, the language of many of
the enactments is virtually impossible to reconcile with the idea of
efficiency being the sole objective. Third, the legislative history
and political context of all the enactments render the efficiency-
only interpretation implausible.

Regardless of any ambiguity in the statute itself or in its legislative history, it is virtually impossible that the Sherman Act could
have been crafted with only economic efficiency in mind. At this
time in history, legislators gave little attention to what economists
had to say on such issues.[25] If economists had been consulted, the
legislature would have known that the profession at that time was
generally hostile to the very idea of antitrust law.[26] Perhaps most

decisive, economists of the day did not yet understand economic efficiency in its current form. In particular, the most straightforward efficiency argument against cartels and monopoly—the one the Chicago School has in mind—refers not to efficiency in production but rather to allocative efficiency, which designates the welfare loss due to the misallocation of resources resulting from purchase decisions that are based upon super-competitive prices. Yet, at the time of the Sherman Act's passage, this aspect of efficiency was making only its first appearance in economics literature, and it was not until decades later that economists generally came to understand and apply the concept. It is thus inconceivable that members of Congress were motivated at all by such an argument—much less solely motivated by it. This is not to suggest that efficiency was irrelevant. To the extent industrial combinations might be the most efficient means of production, efficiency considerations constituted an argument against antitrust law, or at least against excessive application. Although such concerns can be found in the legislative debates, they can hardly be read as constituting the sole basis *favoring* enactment of the legislation.

The statutory language of antitrust legislation itself poses additional problems for the Chicago School positions. If one accepts the arguments advanced by some—that cartelization largely subsumes antitrust concerns from an efficiency perspective—then the rest of the antitrust laws, including section 2 of the Sherman Act, which are seen as conflicting with efficiency, must necessarily be explained by resort to other objectives. . . .

One particular question of interpretation of the statutory language—the meaning of "competition" in many of the antitrust provisions—arises in numerous contexts and has been the focus of substantial attention. The Chicago School position is that competition should be taken to mean economic efficiency, rather than some notion of business rivalry that would include the preservation of large numbers of competitors or entrepreneurial freedom as part of the objective. A commonly advanced corollary to this position is that competitors should not be permitted to bring antitrust suits. This interpretation, of course, is directly opposed to the sort offered in *Brown Shoe*. . . .

. . . Although hardly decisive, standard dictionary definitions of "competition" offer as a synonym "rivalry," the Chicago School's excluded meaning and all the definitions offered refer to the rivalry concept, none admitting the Chicago School's meanings. Not only does the Chicago School economics interpretation directly contradict common usage, it also is inconsistent with the usage of the term by economists, who do mean rivalry rather than economic efficiency when they refer to "competition." The standard definitions of perfect competition and monopolistic competition, both of which stress rivalry, make this fact apparent. Moreover, economists have no reason to define "competition" as "efficiency" because they have explicitly adopted separate terms for the two concepts. Economic theorists go about proving that competition produces efficiency in some circumstances and inefficiency in others; the language by which they describe their efforts clearly reveals that they use "competition" to describe the process of interaction (existence of rivalry, specified in various ways) and "efficiency" to characterize the properties of the result of many processes, of which competition is only one. It is clear that "competition" means economic efficiency in the minds of a few antitrust advocates and no one else.

. . . For the courts to proclaim efficiency as the sole objective of antitrust, however, would constitute a substantial political act indeed, and precisely the sort that would be condemned by those who generally counsel judicial restraint and defend the judicial role as being distinct from that of the legislature.

2. EFFICIENCY OF THE COMMON LAW VERSUS INEFFICIENCY OF ANTITRUST LAW

Until now, most of the discussion of the new law and economics of antitrust has been presented without consideration of the more recent and wider movement in law and economics, significant elements of which are particularly associated with a "Chicago School." Juxtaposing developments in both areas is illuminating, especially since the central tenets of the two Chicago Schools are in conflict. This conflict arises from the major proposition of the Chicago School of law and economics that the common law *is* efficient[27]—in contrast to claims that it should be efficient or that economic analysis is useful in predicting the effects of common law rules.

Antitrust law may not appear to fit within this framework, but the conflict appears once one recognizes that antitrust has long been viewed in many respects as a common law subject—in light of its common law origins in the law of restraint of trade and its development for nearly a century by courts faced with the task of interpreting many rather open-ended enactments. In fact, Congress apparently contemplated a common law type of development when it enacted the Sherman Act. . . . [28]

. . . One could argue that antitrust is not really a common law subject after all because the statutes, . . . simply give too much of a directive to take an approach other than one focused exclusively on economic efficiency. . . . Once this out is taken, however, the argument comes full circle: If the resolution of the apparent contradiction requires the claim that the antitrust laws preclude the efficiency approach, then the activism that would be involved in interpreting them as advocated by the Chicago School of antitrust becomes all the more clear.

5. Conclusion

Important changes in antitrust law have occurred over the past fifteen years. The thesis of this article is that this shift has been misunderstood—not as to the content of the newly evolved doctrine, but rather as to the explanation for the change. . . . [T]hese developments are more plausibly understood in the context of broader, and in many respects parallel, shifts in all the Supreme Court's decisions. . . . [I]t simply is not the case that economic analysis is used substantially more frequently in examining economic issues . . . . [A]lthough economic analysis has changed substantially in the past five decades, the Chicago School of antitrust and many of the doctrinal shifts by the Supreme Court are hardly necessary outcomes of such a change. Finally, . . . changes in the purported objectives of antitrust in the direction of considering only economic efficiency have been overstated. Moreover, to the extent these changes have occurred or will occur in the future, they are best understood as an activist recreation of antitrust rather than as any attempt to return to the statutes or their original meaning.

Overall, recent changes in antitrust—actual or advocated—are in large respect a function of politics, even though the position advocated is defined in terms of economics. In this respect, antitrust resembles constitutional law. Of course, when shifts in Supreme Court doctrine arise, one should not be surprised to observe the Court referring to academic literature supporting the results in order to lend further credibility to its opinions, just as the Warren Court used economics and cited relevant literature in support of its opinions.

. . .

The Modernization of Antitrust: A New Equilibrium

ELEANOR M. FOX

Antitrust law is in search of a new equilibrium. It is torn between claims that it should limit the power of large corporations and claims that it should increase the efficiency of American business. Regard for efficiency is in the ascendancy.

. . .

2. The Forging of the Link Between Antitrust and Efficiency

Antitrust emerged from the 1960s as a philosophy and body of law reflecting American political democracy. It favored dispersion of economic power and easing of access to markets. Faced with the choice between promoting cost-savings of firms with economic power and protecting freedom and opportunity of firms without economic power, the Supreme Court declared that the law favored the latter. By attempting to preserve the competition system as a process, it sought to protect both business opportunity and the consumer.

In general, neither Congress nor the Supreme Court envisioned sacrificing any one goal of antitrust for fuller realization of any

Reprinted from 66 Cornell L. Rev. 1140 (1986).

other. The members of Congress and the members of the Court who spoke on the point generally assumed that the goals of antitrust were complementary. In several decisions, however, the Supreme Court announced that it must honor the Congressional preference for decentralization of economic power, even if the law so applied occasionally would impose higher costs.

If there ever existed an antitrust policy to protect a society of small business units in spite of possible costs to the consumer, that policy has changed. A new mood emerged in the nation in the late 1970s. Influenced by rapidly accelerating inflation, lower productivity, an increasingly negative balance of payments, and dramatic advances by Japanese and German producers in world markets, the current national mood reflects a growing concern for productive efficiency.

Meanwhile, antitrust has become both target and scapegoat. Critics condemn decisions as frustrating the achievement of efficiency. They denounce the antitrust philosophy of the 1960s as populist and protective of inefficient business. They have been urging upon the courts an efficiency-based antitrust and have won some favor.[1] Proponents of one currently popular formula for the solution of all antitrust problems would examine challenged behavior to determine whether it is primarily output-restricting and therefore inconsistent with short-run aggregate consumer welfare as deduced from neo-classical price theory. If so, the business activity would be condemned. If not, it would be encouraged. This conception of antitrust would prohibit almost nothing at all. "Carried to its full logical rigor, as it has been by the Chicago School of economics, economic analysis keyed solely to 'efficiency' and 'consumer welfare' has revealed with stark simplicity that there will be very little remaining of antitrust."[2]

3. The Goals of Antitrust

Proponents of the view that efficiency is the purpose of antitrust law claim support in the legislative history and in judicial interpretations of the antitrust statutes. They imply that the efficiency goal is discovered and not chosen. However, the selection of efficiency as the only appropriate touchstone of antitrust policy is not indicated by either the statutory language, which is ambiguous, or the legislative history, which is multivalued. Moreover, the case law that has developed over time does not, as Judge Wyzanski discerned, fit together as do pieces of a jigsaw puzzle.[3] The isolation of efficiency as the sole goal of antitrust requires a conscious rejection of equally dominant values that underlie the antitrust statutes.

. . .

The Sherman Act, which is the oldest federal antitrust law, was adopted in 1890 during an age of revolutionary industrialization. Sprouting transportation networks brought into competition hundreds of firms that had enjoyed local monopolies. Prospects of expanding markets led to over-investment in productive facilities. Fierce and disabling competition ensued. Competitors responded by truce. They joined forces, usually in the form of trusts. They swallowed up hundreds of small proprietors and stamped out others. Farmers, shippers, and other suppliers and customers were, or so they believed, over-charged and underpaid. The legislative history of the Sherman Act illuminates the congeries of concerns that gave birth to that statute, perhaps none so strong as the distrust of the perceived power of the giant trusts. Urging enactment of a law against the trusts, Senator Sherman spoke of the problems that agitate "the popular mind":[4] "[A]mong them all none is more threatening than the inequality of condition, of wealth, and opportunity that has grown within a single generation out of the concentration of capital into vast combinations."[5] Senator Sherman posited the case in which "combinations reduce prices . . . by better methods of production." Even such a combination would not be justified, Senator Sherman said, because "[the] saving of cost goes to the pockets of the producers."[6]

While Senator Sherman denounced the trusts as tyrants,[7] Senator Pugh observed that the trusts had the power to limit production and thereby increase price "oppressive[ly] and merciless[ly]."[8] Senator Vest observed that if you "create competition you then secure lower prices to the consumer."[9] Representative Mason addressed yet a different concern, "Even if the price of oil is reduced

to one cent a barrel, it would not right the wrong done to the
people by the trusts which have destroyed legitimate competition
and driven honest men from legitimate business."[10]

. . .

In the early years, the Supreme Court applied the Sherman Act
to loose combinations (understandings among independent competitors) and abusive acts by single firms with market power in a
manner that reflected the multivalued legislative history and the
desire to protect competition for the benefit of all—consumers,
entrepreneurs, and "the public good."[11] However, the Court ignored the anticompetitive effects of tight combinations effected by
mergers and acquisitions.[12] Moreover, it announced principles
of law in amorphous terms ("unreasonable" restraints were
banned[13]), giving business little information as to what activities
were prohibited. Consequently supporters of big and little business
alike became disenchanted with the Sherman Act.

. . .

[In the 1960s and 1970s the Court] declared that the law prohibited contract restraints that "clogged" the channels of competition and deprived firms of an equal chance to compete on the
merits in free and open markets.[14] It protected the freedom of the
independent trader to sell where and to whom the seller pleased.[15]
The Court sometimes invoked consumers' interests, but only when
consumers' interests were consistent with competition as process
and the rights of free traders.[16] In applying the antitrust laws from
the 1950s to the early 1970s, the Court emphasized freedom of
traders and competition among many players, not efficiency.

Beginning in 1974, the first year on the Burger Court's antitrust
majority, antitrust law shifted course.[17] In a 1977 opinion, the
Supreme Court said that market impact must control antitrust
decisions.[18] Market impact was assessed in terms of efficiency. In
addition, majority opinions by some members of the Court began
to reveal a strong undercurrent that business should be left presumptively free to do what it wishes, apparently on the theory that
business freedom tends to maximize efficiency or on the theory
that greater private business freedom is crucial to a free society.
Whereas the word "power" dominates Warren Court antitrust
opinions, the words "efficiency" and "market impact" have prominence in Burger Court antitrust opinions. The Burger Court has

not given "efficiency" specific content. Moreover, recent opinions of the Court have triggered the claim that antitrust is valid only as a means to promote efficiency.

As history teaches, "efficiency" is not the reason for antitrust. Indeed, those who valued efficiency more than competition opposed antitrust bills on grounds that they would constrain some activity that might save costs for a producer and forbid some activity that does not interfere with optimal allocation of resources. Rather than standing for efficiency, the American antitrust laws stand against private power. Distrust of power is the one central and common ground that over time has unified support for antitrust statutes.[19] Interests of consumers have been a recurrent concern because consumers have been perceived as victims of the abuse of too much power. Interests of entrepreneurs and small business have been a recurrent concern because independent entrepreneurs have been seen as the heart and lifeblood of American free enterprise, and freedom of economic activity and opportunity has been thought central to the preservation of the American free enterprise system.

One overarching idea has unified these three concerns (distrust of power, concern for consumers, and commitment to opportunity for entrepreneurs): competition as process. The competition process is the preferred governor of markets. If the impersonal forces of competition, rather than public or private power, determine market behavior and outcomes, power is by definition dispersed, opportunities and incentives for firms without market power are increased, and the results are acceptable and fair. Some measure of productive and allocative efficiency is a by-product, because competition tends to stimulate lowest-cost production and allocate resources more responsively than a visible public or private hand.

In sum, the claim that efficiency has been *the* goal and *the* fulcrum of antitrust is weak at best. The values other than efficiency that underlie the commitment to power dispersion, economic opportunity, and competition as market governor demand equal attention. The basis upon which some scholars affirmatively have rejected these historic objectives as goals of antitrust is not apparent. The reasons offered do not withstand scrutiny.

The elevation of efficiency to the antitrust pedestal reflects something other than deference to stare decisis and something more than a choice of the only feasible route to reasonably clear antitrust principles. It, like all other choices for antitrust policy, reflects a normative judgment about what antitrust should do.

4. Microeconomics, Political Theory, and Personal Stake

. . .

. . . Economics teaches that markets work to maximize the material well-being of people. Business behavior that maximizes aggregate material well-being is deemed "efficient." Economics as a discipline values competition only as a process for the production of "efficient" outcomes. . . . [20]

Yet another basis for choosing efficiency as the fulcrum of antitrust is political philosophy. Certain political philosophies correspond with certain conceptions of what antitrust should do. The conservative and libertarian world-views lean towards less government intervention, in order to protect the established order and stability, or to maximize (a view of) individual freedom. Individuals having these perspectives question the existence of corporate power. The power that resides in one central government is far more worrisome to them than power that may reside in a number of private businesses. They see market entry barriers as almost always low and surmountable by skill and energy, and they view consumers as sovereign—that is, the controllers of producer behavior. They believe that all people of equal abilities have equality of economic opportunity, that those business people who serve consumers best will succeed, and that any attempt to equalize opportunity in the marketplace (like affirmative action) frustrates meritocracy. If the job of antitrust is, and is only, to prohibit transactions that impair efficiency, then government interference with private business transactions is minimized and the values of a free society (as they define it) are preserved. Therefore, the conservative and libertarian philosophies tend to correspond with the view that antitrust should be limited to a narrow role in monitoring efficiency.

By contrast, the liberal[21] tends to distrust large aggregations of wealth and power. The liberal world-view sees private corporate power as a reality and a danger. The liberal view tends to regard entry barriers to markets as high and often insurmountable and producers as sovereign and manipulative of consumer wants. Liberals tend to perceive great inequalities of economic opportunity caused by, among other things, power wielded and barriers strategically placed by large, established firms. The liberal view is compatible with government intervention to prevent concentrations of power and wealth and promote greater equality of economic opportunity. The liberal philosophy, therefore, tends to correspond with the multivalued view of antitrust. Indeed, at the extreme, the liberal might prefer dispersion of power and greater economic opportunity for business without power to efficiency.

. . .

5. The Concepts of Efficiency Claimed for Antitrust

. . . Virtually all contemporary scholars and jurists agree that antitrust law and enforcement should tend to increase the responsiveness of producers to consumers' wants, and many maintain that it should tend to optimize the use of scarce resources. There is, however, vigorous disagreement about the appropriate conceptual mode for attempting to attain the desired end. Approaches vary from reliance on interaction among numerous, rivalrous competitors to reliance on business judgment.

Thus, the notion that efficiency should be the guide to antitrust analysis on the theory that it provides a clear and certain path and eliminates the need for difficult choices among conflicting policy values is false. The very selection of one or another approach to efficiency involves confrontation of the same, difficult questions of policy.

As two distinguished scholars have discerned:

> The proposal [for using solely economic concepts in appraising all acts supposed to violate the antitrust laws] offers not the prospect of greater certainty and shorter litigation . . . but utter confusion. Economists are no more likely to agree than lawyers; only a disillusioned lawyer or a brash economist could believe otherwise.[22]

This section analyzes three approaches to assessing efficiency for purposes of antitrust. The first approach calls for microeconomic calculations to determine whether challenged activity is likely to lead to restriction of output. Using this approach, individuals applying welfare economics measure "producer and consumer welfare," the sum of which is "social welfare." Proponents urge that antitrust should reach only acts that artificially lower and thereby impair social welfare.

A second approach relies on business autonomy, limited only by the clearest evidence that private action wastes resources. This conception assumes that business behavior is efficient. By this approach, antitrust would have a yet narrower role. The third concept is preservation of competition as a process. This conception focuses upon rivalrous interaction among numerous firms in "free and open" markets and protects access and opportunity of firms without market power. This approach assumes that the process protected is likely to produce the best result for consumers.

. . .

A. Restriction of Output

Proponents of the output-restriction approach assert that antitrust lawsuits should be brought only to challenge inefficient transactions or conduct, and that inefficiency should be measured by the power of producers to restrict output. Even if artificial output-restriction is threatened, proponents may require the antitrust enforcer or jurist to examine whether enforcement would frustrate achievement of scale economies. Enforcement would proceed only if resource loss from failure to achieve scale economies does not outweigh resource loss from artificial output restriction.

Proponents assert that the only goal of antitrust is to improve allocative efficiency. The output-restriction theory is applied as the means to that end. Therefore, understanding of output limitation theory requires understanding of allocative efficiency.

Allocative efficiency is an ideal state. It contemplates that all resources across all markets in the economy are allocated to their best use in view of consumer wants and willingness to pay the price it costs society to make and distribute the goods. In a state of perfect allocative efficiency, the fewest possible resources are consumed to satisfy consumer wants. In such a state, the aggregate wealth of the nation is maximized, and individuals as consumers are assumed to be better off.

Because of the multitude of imperfections in markets in our economy, allocative efficiency cannot be achieved; the necessary conditions cannot be met.[23] Further, alteration of some conditions within one or another market to improve output therein does not necessarily even tend towards allocative efficiency. If, for example, resources are drawn into an oligopoly market from a monopoly market in an attempt to improve output in the former, the allocation of resources may be further distorted rather than improved.

Tendencies toward optimal output in a market will, however, improve the position of consumers as buyers of the targeted product, because more units of that product will be available. In addition, the greater output will have a distributive effect, because all units generally will be available at a lower price. The lower price to the buyer of the targeted product may be a worthy objective, but it is not an efficiency concern. The efficiency loss is, rather, "the loss associated with substituting an alternative good for the monopolized good."[24] Thus, society loses not because producers extract surplus from consumers, but because demand is deflected from goods in the monopolized market to other goods that cost society more resources to make.

1. OUTPUT RESTRICTION AND THE MEASUREMENT OF SOCIAL
WELFARE LOSS

In view of the absence of tools to measure resource misallocation caused by private acts, a number of economic theorists have adopted as a proxy the measurement of artificial output restraints within given markets. They frequently identify their goal as maximization of consumer welfare. As a consequence, the goal of preventing artificial output restraint and the goal of maximizing consumer welfare have become synonymous to many students, practitioners, and policy makers.

The terminology "social welfare" and "consumer welfare" may create confusion. The layperson may be led to believe that the words encompass all consumer interests, or that the well-being of the individual who buys the product in the market of the restricted output is the object of the economist's concern. This is not the case. The economic theory described is concerned with maximization of "social welfare." The social welfare loss is a resource loss—that is, the use of unnecessary resources to satisfy the diverted demand of individuals who would have been satisfied with a product in the market of the restricted output if that product were sold at cost.

In short, welfare economics uses "welfare" and "consumer welfare" in a technical sense that does not necessarily correspond with general notions of consumer interests. "Consumer welfare" does not reflect the interest of consumers in preventing monopolists from extracting monopoly profits. It ignores various other consumer interests that may be expected to flow from a competitive economy, including diversity of source, variety of product, and innovation. To avoid perpetuating the confusion caused by use of the technical phrase "consumer welfare," this Article calls the welfare approach "output-limitation theory."

. . .

The microeconomic concern is not that some consumers pay the monopoly price and are thereby successfully exploited by the monopolist. This phenomenon represents "merely" a transfer of wealth from willing consumers to the monopolist. . . . Output in the market is too low in light of consumer demand for the product at a competitive price. Too few of society's resources are allocated to this market, and the resources that should be so allocated are diverted to more costly production.

2. THE GOALS AND LIMITS OF POLICY BASED ON OUTPUT RESTRICTION

Power to control output, or to increase control over output, may result from monopoly, oligopoly, or conspiracy. . . . In the case of mere monopoly power or oligopoly power, many economic theorists would require inquiry to determine whether resource loss from output limitation is offset by resource gain from increased productive efficiency (that is, lower costs of inputs); and in all events, further inquiry is necessary to determine whether producers performed an act that the law reprehends.

The economist's prime example of power to limit output is a monopoly in a well-defined market, wherein the consumer has no good substitute and barriers are too high for a potential entrant to surmount. In the absence of any of the foregoing conditions, the producer does not have power to limit output or, at the least, the existence of alternatives seriously limits power.

United States v. Aluminum Company of America (Alcoa)[25] is a prominent example of alleged and adjudicated monopoly. Yet *Alcoa* would fail the power test of the output theorists. Alcoa was the only domestic producer of virgin aluminum. Foreign producers accounted for ten percent of all virgin aluminum sold in the United States. Alcoa did not extract monopoly profits, but realized only a reasonable rate of return. If Alcoa had restricted its output and had tried to extract monopoly profits, the rise in price probably would have brought into the United States a stream of imports to satisfy the residual demand, or else new entry by American producers probably would have closed the gap. If such were the facts, Alcoa did not have the power to control output. Proponents of the output-control theory of antitrust would conclude therefrom that Alcoa did not have monopoly status.

Oligopoly provides a second potential target for enforcement. Oligopoly behavior is characterized by lack of competitiveness. That condition is most likely to occur when only a few competitors occupy the market, they have similar technology, similar costs, and general commonality of interests, and barriers to entry are high. In such a situation, theory predicts that the producers will act interdependently and will price in lock-step to maximize their joint profits. At worst, they may reduce output to a point that approaches the monopoly condition. If any one of the conditions conducive to oligopoly behavior is absent, however, as is usually the case, the producers generally have little or no power to limit output.

Cartel agreements are a third means by which output limitation can be achieved. Cartels are agreements among competitors to control the market by fixing price, dividing customers or territories, or apportioning production quotas. Such agreements are likely to achieve market control only where there are relatively few producers in the market, the producers have similar costs, they all are parties to the agreement, and entry into the market is difficult. In the absence of these conditions, the higher cartel price is likely to attract entry by outsiders and induce cheating by insiders, and the cartel will self-destruct.

In sum, output theory provides a basis for challenging monopoly of a sort that virtually never exists, for challenging transactions such as mergers that produce increments in the power to cut back production (a condition that seldom can be proved), and for challenging cartel agreements that have a chance of success.

. . .

B. Business Autonomy

With increasing frequency, efficiency is defined in terms of business freedom: maximizing, with only limited constraints, the freedom or autonomy of firms to engage in private transactions of their choice.

The linkage between efficiency and autonomy may reflect one of two quite different ideas or goals. First, proponents claim that autonomy conduces to productive efficiency; efficiency is the desired outcome and autonomy is the means to that end. Second, advocacy of business autonomy may serve social, political, or personal objectives by minimizing government interference with business decisionmaking. A pragmatic way to minimize the role of government in antitrust is to confine antitrust to the role of increasing efficiency and, in turn, to define efficiency in terms of business autonomy.

The claim that autonomy conduces to efficiency may be stated as follows: Business firms are profit-maximizing. Private decisionmaking tends to maximize productive efficiency, because the firm itself knows best how to reduce costs and satisfy consumers. Competition among productively efficient firms tends to maximize allocative efficiency, because the competitive pressure exerted by such firms is the best spur to improved performance and to investment decisions that are responsive to consumer wants.

Antitrust law historically has valued freedom and autonomy of firms without market power.[26] In contemporary debates, however, proponents seek increased autonomy for firms with leading and dominant positions in concentrated markets. Increased autonomy could mean preference for freedom of firms with power at the expense of competitive opportunity for firms without power, and possibly at the expense of lower price or greater choice for the consumer.

The second approach—to minimize government intervention by confining antitrust to narrow efficiency goals—is a strategy rather than a theory. Commitment to the autonomy principle may reflect the political philosophy of the libertarian, or a less sweeping political preference for allocating more discretionary power to private business and less to government or private enforcers. It may reflect political disagreement with the socio-political goals of antitrust, or a preference for limiting judicial discretion. It may stem from a judgment that a need to muster American economic and political strength in the world overshadows the economic or political contributions of antitrust. Or it may signify merely the private interest of the business person in freer rein or greater profits.

The autonomy approach to antitrust cannot be carried to the extreme or it would trump the law. Therefore, even those who favor autonomy must make a concession to antitrust. A minimal concession is recognition of the output theory, limited by assumptions that reflect a faith in the free market to reward efficiency, to remove inefficiency, and to punish exploitation.[27]

C. Preserving Competition as Process

The third and final conception of efficiency is the traditional notion of competition as process. This conception does not presume to define desired, efficient outcomes. It does not focus on consumer surplus, marginal cost, or welfare loss. It centers, rather, on an environment that is conducive to vigorous rivalry and in turn (it is assumed), to efficiency and progressiveness.

Proponents of output-limitation theory and of autonomy theory share the value of an environment conducive to rivalry. All seek a dynamic market of efficient and flexible producers responsive to changing conditions of scarcity and consumers' changing wants. Those who stress competition process, however, reject the autonomy principle as the means to the desired end, and they reject the output-limitation formula as the exclusive or the central guide.

Thus far, this third conception describes an approach adopted by diverse thinkers who may not share assumptions about the existence or vulnerability of corporate power. As this Article further defines the approach, however, proponents of the refined conception do share a series of assumptions and values that distinguish their frame of reference. Proponents place value on diversity and pluralism. They focus on preserving lower barriers to

entry and greater opportunity for entry and success of unesta-
blished firms, more than on promoting productive efficiency of
established firms. They perceive that markets are inherently imperfect; producers garner and keep market power for reasons other
than excellence in performance; consumers are often, within
bounds, at the mercy of producers; barriers to entry and expansion
in numerous markets are high and may be so maintained by threats
of discipline by dominant firms; the market is often slow to discipline exploitative or marginally unresponsive established producers; and the unknown new entrant, unhoned and untraditional,
is a vital source of new spirit and new progressiveness. Finally,
unless antitrust law and enforcement preserves an environment
that keeps markets open and fluid, private power will grow and
will invite intrusive and inefficient government regulation and
control.

6. The Choice Among Efficiency Approaches

The three perspectives on efficiency are representative rather than
inclusive.[28] They represent a range of choices for a perspective on
an efficient economy. . . .

One of two prevailing contentions is that business, including business with market power, should be free to do virtually all
that it wishes on the theory that business knows best how to
please consumers and has the incentives to do so. This contention
is based on the assumption that business firms are rational profit-
maximizers—that their acts are always or virtually always efficient.
The assumption is vulnerable. Business managers frequently act
in order to realize personal goals, including political power or
personal security within their firms, as well as to build empires.
Moreover, even as would-be profit-maximizers, managers are limited by the absence of full information; they make decisions on
the basis of partial knowledge and intuition rather than full rationality. Finally, pursuit of profit-maximizing goals by a firm with
market power is inconsistent with consumers' interest in optimal
output and price near costs—interests that concerned the legislators far more than producers' profits and productive efficiency. A

view of efficiency defined by business autonomy is, accordingly, inappropriate for antitrust.

The second correlation between efficiency and autonomy is based upon political or personal desires to maximize autonomy rather than efficiency. This political strategy obviously is not an appropriate basis for antitrust economics, particularly because the political philosophy of antitrust (distrust of power) is at war with the philosophy that accords free rein to business.

Advocates of autonomy theory combine political and economic concerns in their protest against government intervention in the context of international competition. They charge that antitrust handicaps American competitors in their quest for both efficiency and power, and suggest, as an antidote, autonomy. In fact, antitrust law interferes very little with courses of action that an American firm may wish to take in attempts to produce or distribute its products abroad more efficiently. Antitrust does constrain the growth of domestic power by means other than competition on the merits. If the claim is that American antitrust stands in the way of productive enterprise, it is contrary to fact. If the claim is that American antitrust stands in the way of market power that may be useful in the competitive race abroad, then the concern could support proposals for revision or partial repeal of the antitrust laws. It could not, however, fairly inform a definition of efficiency.

Second, should output limitation theory be the antitrust measure of efficiency? The measurement of a firm's ability and incentives to limit output does have a relationship to the consumer concerns of the antitrust laws, although more because of the distributive effect of raising price to consumers and the political effect of limiting freedom of choice than the allocative effect of wasting resources.

Where economic analysis indicates that identified behavior, such as a merger or distribution system, will lead to output restrictions by the producers in the market, the behavior is likely to restrain trade and harm the consumer interests identified above, and to be illegal under traditional antitrust principles.[29] Therefore, the economists' yardstick that measures output limitation is a helpful tool.

The theory of output limitation assumes that if producers are induced to offer the quantity of output that consumers are willing to buy at a price compensatory to the producers, consumer interests in a competitive marketplace are exhausted. That assumption is not compatible with the antitrust laws. Output theory is narrow and static. It fails to reflect producers' potential to achieve lower costs or to deliver the new, the imaginative, and the yet unconceived. It fails to consider opportunities for reversing an anticompetitive trend or for inviting untested competition at the margins. It fails to capture individuality of producers and consumers or to grasp the dynamic qualities of an open enterprise system.

The point is not that welfare economics ignores strategic behavior and long-run effects. Some economists do, and some do not. The point is that all welfare analysis is narrowly confined to one question: Will producers limit output and thereby "waste" society's resources? This is not the central question of antitrust.

Finally, should efficiency as a goal of antitrust be conceived in terms of protection of the competition process? . . . [P]rotecting the process of competition among a significant number of rivals in free and open markets, with special regard for long-run consumer interests, is the most appropriate focus for antitrust economics.

I do not claim that protection of the process is the only means or the obviously superior route to greatest efficiency or happiest consumers. None of the perspectives on antitrust and efficiency can fairly present itself as the one right answer, in terms of greatest efficiency alone. All of the perspectives rely on assumptions and even articles of faith. I make, rather, a limited claim: The traditional antitrust focus on process, revised to eliminate any tilt towards small size for its own sake, should be retained for historical, social, and pragmatic reasons. First, this perspective has worked reasonably well in keeping markets open to competition on the merits and thus to creating an environment conducive to efficient performance; no other system promises to work better. Second, it is rooted in tradition, which produces continuity and thus relative certainty in enforcement of and compliance with the antitrust rule of law. Third, it is the one accepted economic perspective that harmonizes with the dominant non-efficiency values of antitrust. Finally, although reaffirmation of the traditional focus does involve some selection among economic modes of thinking, this focus has been deeply ingrained in antitrust for nearly a century, and it provides an open and flexible framework that does not lock the law into a closed, theoretical, economic construct.

Critics would abandon tradition and embrace either theoretical welfare economics or producer autonomy on grounds that the system fails to take sufficient account of the interests of American consumers in lower prices and better products, the interests of American producers in excelling in world markets, and a national political interest in reestablishing America as the major economic power in the world.

The critics' argument rests on the view that antitrust protects inefficiencies and aborts transactions that capture cost-savings and thereby harms the consumer, impedes the producer, and weakens the economic performance of American firms. The criticism has a genesis in rigidities in the law implanted by Supreme Court opinions of the 1960s and early 1970s. These opinions glorified small size and they created inflexible per se rules, which may have diverted efficient activity. The criticism, however, does not lead inexorably to a proposal to discard traditional focus on process. Rather, it supports a plan for the modernization of antitrust through change at the margins. It supports a design to build into the system a proper regard for long-run consumer interests and a proper respect for producer autonomy. Such change is in progress.

· · ·

8. The Place of Efficiency in the Law of Antitrust

· · ·

B. An Approach

The framework for the new equilibrium requires a synthesis of four concepts: (1) the centrality of the competition process; (2) the use of economics to promote the competition process; (3) the harmonious integration of converging efficiency and nonefficiency goals; and (4) use of consumers' interests as a trump over goals that conflict.

The central component of this synthesizing view is the competition process. The process presupposes dynamic interaction among firms that are both flexible and adaptable to changing desires and needs. It presupposes an environment conducive to entry, survival, and success. Of more importance, this conception rejects the assumption that, absent government interference, competition is virtually always robust and the best will win. It operates on the assumption that established firms tend to garner the power to place roadblocks before their competitors and to perpetuate success for reasons other than merits. For this reason, the concept focuses on preserving opportunities at the margin for firms without market power, more than promoting opportunities for cost-savings for firms with market power, but it facilitates both.

Given this context, we must define the linkage between efficiency, economics, and antitrust policy. "Efficiency" is not an ultimate goal. It is an intermediate goal pursued in order to facilitate freedom of choice, to serve other interests of consumers, and to make the best use of society's resources. Economics provides useful tools to achieve solutions that promote or harmonize with efficiency.

Efficiency frequently corresponds directly with promotion of the competition process and with developed antitrust case law. The correlation is particularly clear in the law directed against the growth, use, and effects of market power. The tools of economics can be employed most usefully in such cases. For example, economic analysis can appropriately be used as a guide and as supporting authority in cases challenging monopolization and attempts to monopolize, oligopolists' collusion, mergers that threaten to create power over price and output, and manufacturers' restraints on resellers' customers and territories.

In other areas, rights and principles that have a less obvious connection with consumer benefit are deeply embedded in antitrust law and heritage. This category includes many mergers prohibited by the merger law. It includes applications of the per se rule against tying arrangements, horizontal price-fixing in fragmented markets, and market divisions among small firms. The category prominently includes the access cases, which give firms a limited right of access to scarce but vital facilities and sources of supply and a right not to be fenced out of any substantial market by the leverage of a better situated competitor.

The bases of these rights are varied. They reflect concerns for fairness, opportunity, and autonomy for sellers without power. They reflect also the concern that individuals in a democratic society should be relatively free from great aggregations of power, lest those centers of power, however benign and progressive today, exploit them economically or control them politically tomorrow. Moreover, every one of these rights has a connection with an interest of consumers, even though that connection would be disputed by those who believe that the market always rewards merit. Each one of the principles fits into a vision of a free and open market, wherein opportunity for producers without power correlates with interests of consumers in diversity, choice, and the new invention by the maverick who may revolutionize the industry.

. . . Antitrust should serve consumers' interests and should also serve other, established, non-conflicting objectives. There are four major historical goals of antitrust, and all should continue to be respected. These are: (1) dispersion of economic power, (2) freedom and opportunity to compete on the merits, (3) satisfaction of consumers, and (4) protection of the competition process as market governor. A fifth possible goal of antitrust is the preservation of small size for its own sake. Because of the unusual potential for conflict between this objective and consumers' interests, I do not propose incorporation of this goal into antitrust policy. A sixth possible goal, justice, is vague in conception and is in fact a by-product of several more specific goals. I therefore do not treat this value separately.

. . . [W]hen developed principles of antitrust serve one of the four basic historical goals of antitrust and do not threaten increased costs to consumers over the long run, stare decisis should be respected by the courts. However, long-run consumer interests should be a limiting principle. Antitrust should not be applied in ways likely to harm consumers over the long run.

In cases of hard-core violations, such as horizontal price-fixing and market divisions, the limiting principle would not come into play. Freedom to decide what and how much to produce, and where, to whom, and at what price to sell, is central to the nervous system of markets and therefore to long-run consumers' interests. No defense of efficiency would be allowed. So, too, there would be no change in the established per se rule against classic group boycotts, which protects economic opportunity and freedom to compete on the merits, because enforcement of the rule causes no harm to consumers.

Other per se principles could be candidates for challenge as inconsistent with consumer interests. These include the rules of law that prohibit maximum vertical price-fixing, minimum vertical price-fixing, especially in fragmented markets by producers without market power, and tying arrangements in which the tie does not endanger price or quality of the goods in the market for the tied product. A successful challenger would be required to demonstrate that application of the per se rule harms long-run consumer interests viewed from a perspective harmonious with the proposed conception of competition process. . . .

Moreover, virtually all of the per se rules reflect a perceived need for a prophylactic effect. Even consumer-based per se rules are more inclusive than necessary to protect consumers against clearly anticompetitive conduct. The breadth of the rules is commonly justifiable by their deterrent force, their contribution to the efficiency of enforcement, and their contribution to the efficiency of business decisionmaking geared toward compliance. Accordingly, my proposal would retain a per se rule against behavior in clearly defined categories where (1) it is difficult to distinguish between restraints in the category that are anticompetitive and threaten harm to consumers, and those that are neutral or potentially beneficial; (2) it is important to prohibit and effectively deter the harmful restraints; and (3) there is little likelihood of loss to buyers of the product in question from overdeterrence. The flat prohibition against all cartel activities, even those such as specialization agreements that could save resources, falls within this characterization.

In the case of activity not per se illegal under existing law, evidence of efficiency currently comes into the litigation, usually to support a defendant's claims that the challenged activity does or will improve its performance, render the market more competitive, and benefit consumers. The limiting principle concerns the weight and respect to be given to the evidence of efficiency. Courts do and should take seriously credible evidence that particular antitrust enforcement is likely to lead to the long-run detriment of users of the product in question. If enforcement would deprive consumers of the benefits of competition, such as the benefit of an important consumer option, the defendant should prevail.

Within a broad area, consumer and non-consumer values are compatible and mutually reinforcing, and I conceive of the limiting principle not as a harbinger of a rewritten law but as a safety valve to guarantee sufficient flexibility to protect consumers from unnecessarily increased costs or decreased options. In the following paragraphs, to demonstrate the high degree of harmony of values, I describe and suggest appropriate integration of the non-efficiency aspects of power dispersion and opportunity.

1. POWER DISPERSION AND CONSUMER INTERESTS
Power dispersion has particular relevance in monopoly cases under section 2 of the Sherman Act. . . . For purposes of the monopoly law, power dispersion as a socio-political goal coincides with efficiency and other consumer concerns. Consumer interests, like the nonconsumer social concerns, lie against monopoly prices and favor greater output and diversity of products and sources. The non-economic concern is not a conflicting political value to be reckoned with. It neither requires nor contemplates atomization of a monopolist into units too small to achieve economies of scale. It does not mandate break-ups where the forces of competition can be introduced through less drastic means. Like the consumer concern, the socio-political values tend to favor dissipation of substantial, persistent monopoly, but not in ways that harm the consumer.

The dilemma in monopoly law comes not from a conflict between the economic and non-economic goals of antitrust, but from very different tensions. A tension exists between equity for the good monopolist and efficiency for the consumer. There is tension between consumer interest against dead weight loss in a particular market and general consumer interest in preservation of incentives to business to strive to be the best. In addition, there is hesitancy to interfere with a system that works, for a predicted but not certain consumer gain. Given these tensions and uncertainties, the monopoly law has been molded more by notions of fairness (to the good monopolist) than by either economics or populism. The culpable monopolist is subject to break-up without necessary inquiry into possible loss of efficiencies. The monopolist that has not been culpable is legitimized.

How courts interpreting the monopoly law should account for the potentially conflicting interests in low price, diversity of product and source, and progressiveness is not free from doubt. Current law respects freedom of a firm to grow to monopoly proportions and to retain monopoly power achieved through competitive merits, in view of the desire to preserve incentives to be the best and in spite of possible monopoly pricing. The battleground centers on characterization of behavior of a monopoly-sized firm as abusive or competitive. The development of law in this area can and should be informed by compatible notions of efficiency and diversity: a tilt at the margin toward protecting opportunities for efficient challengers of the dominant firm.

. . .

2. ENTREPRENEURIAL OPPORTUNITY AND CONSUMER INTERESTS

Like power dispersion, entrepreneurial opportunity informs interpretations of the Sherman Act . . . , and would continue to do so under my proposal. The Sherman Act prohibition against concerted boycotts of single victims and the prohibition against certain tie-ins are illustrative.

In *Klor's, Inc. v. Broadway-Hale Stores, Inc.*,[30] Klor's, the operator of a retail store, was a victim of a concerted refusal to sell electrical appliances. Hundreds of other retail stores in the vicinity offered the merchandise of the boycotting manufacturers. Thus, the elimination of Klor's as a retailer of those goods did not perceptibly affect consumer choice or the vigor of competition in electrical appliances. The district court dismissed the case, and the court of appeals affirmed on the ground that the boycott had caused no public injury. The Supreme Court reversed, holding that the injury to Klor's alone was sufficient to sustain the violation. The boycott deprived Klor's of a fair opportunity to compete on the merits. The principle protecting Klor's opportunity to compete coincides with the principle of keeping markets free and open, and does not threaten harm to consumers. Therefore, it would be preserved under the proposal.

The tie-in case law also protects fair opportunity to compete on the merits, and much of the law is not based upon harm to consumers' interests. *International Salt Co., Inc. v. United States*[31] is an example. International Salt made patented salt machines and required that its lessees buy from it the salt to be used in the machines. If, however, a competitor offered salt at lower than the contract price, International Salt's customer had the right to buy the salt from the competitor or to pay the lower price to International Salt. The tied salt represented a substantial dollar volume of business, although apparently not a significant percentage of the salt market. On these facts, the tie was held illegal. The Court protected the right of competing salt sellers to an equal chance to compete on the merits. "[I]t is unreasonable, *per se*," said the Court, "to foreclose competitors from any substantial market [by use of leverage]."

In *International Salt*, unlike *Klor's*, possible efficiency claims may be asserted. Some economists argue that tying may be conducive to efficiency in the market of the tying product and should be allowed unless it provably harms competition (e.g., by restricting output) in the market for the tied product. When a firm with market power over a tying product forces a tie, however, the efficiency claims in support of tying are not obviously more weighty than the efficiency claims against tying. Although economics provide no clear answer, traditional antitrust values that protect access to markets on the basis of merits, not leverage, are exceedingly strong. Therefore, the proposal would preserve the prohibition against unjustified tying by firms with market power over the tying product, unless the case is made that applications of the rule deprive consumers of a lower price, better quality, or a new alternative.

Conclusion

Antitrust law and policy is at the heart of a storm of criticism leveled against government regulation. Detractors' major claim is that antitrust impairs efficiency and harms consumers. Critics would drastically curtail the scope of the law by eliminating the non-efficiency values and by limiting the efficiency goals of antitrust.

... [T]here are many ways of conceiving of efficiency and of an antitrust system most likely to produce it, that the central non-efficiency values of the Sherman and Clayton Antitrust Acts are compatible with their efficiency goals, and that the Sherman and Clayton Acts can and should be modernized to meet the major criticism by changes at the margin to assure protection of the interests of consumers.

· · ·

... [T]he following principles should apply: (1) Antitrust law and policy should, as its central mission, seek to preserve and promote the competition process. (2) Within the constraints of the antitrust statutes and stare decisis, where consumer interests and other antitrust goals coincide, economics should be used as a tool to protect the functioning of markets and to advance consumers' interests, and efficiency so conceived should be a major guide to antitrust policy. (3) Where established antitrust principles and rights exist apart from consumer interests, the courts should respect stare decisis, except, (4) efficiency should serve as a limiting principle, in the sense that antitrust law should never be applied in a manner that threatens to hurt consumers over the long run.

Finally, the consumer/efficiency goals of antitrust should be refined. In theory, dominant weight might be accorded to all cost savings, including those claimed to be forthcoming by leading firms in concentrated markets; credence might be given to the view that business is profit-maximizing and will make cost-saving decisions if left free from government interference; and focus might be placed on output-restriction as the central or only economic concern. On the other hand, special value might be given to the pressures from the forces of competition, and to dynamic efficiencies likely to be gained from open markets with lower barriers to entry and greater economic incentives for firms without market power.

The first preference corresponds generally with resistance to antitrust and is used in defense of concentration and market power. The second preference corresponds generally with the historical goals of antitrust and is used in defense of the competition process. Proponents of both perspectives claim to protect the consumer interest. Where the choice must be made, the second conception should be preferred because it is harmonious with, rather than hostile to, the fabric of antitrust.

In sum, antitrust should be modernized. The law should be responsive to societal needs for enhanced efficiency, in the interest of consumers. At the same time, antitrust should and can retain compatibility with its multivalued, flexible charter, tested by more than ninety years of history, and still the richest framework for progressive, pluralistic free enterprise.

Notes

Hofstadter Notes

1. G.W. STOCKING & M.W. WATKINS, MONOPOLY AND FREE EN-
TERPRISE (1951).
2. 21 CONG. REC. 2460 (1890). "Although this body is always conservative,"
Sherman said hopefully, "yet, whatever may be said of it, it has always been ready
to preserve not only popular rights in their broad sense, but the rights of individuals
as against associated and corporate wealth and power."
3. H. THORELLI, THE FEDERAL ANTITRUST POLICY 198 (1955).
There is a mass of information about the antimonopoly aspects of the American
tradition in Arthur P. Dudden's unpublished doctoral dissertation, Antimonopo-
lism, 1865–1890, UNIVERSITY OF MICHIGAN (1950).
4. 21 CONG. REC. 3146 (1890).
5. Hans B. Thorelli, after examining carefully the congressional debates on the
Sherman Act, concludes that "the Sherman Act is not to be viewed exclusively as
an expression of economic policy," and that in safeguarding the rights of the
common man in business it "embodies what is to be characterized as an eminently
'social' purpose." H.B. Thorelli, *supra* note 3, at 227. Thorelli believes that Sherman and many of his contemporaries in Congress saw the legislation as "an important means of achieving freedom from corruption and maintaining freedom of
independent thinking in political life."
6. *Id*. at 112 n.316.
7. *Id*. at 314–15.
8. W. LETWIN, LAW AND ECONOMIC POLICY IN AMERICA: THE
EVOLUTION OF THE SHERMAN ANTITRUST ACT (1965).
9. 21 CONG. REC. 2460 (1890). Sherman was here conceding the difficulty of
defining in law the precise difference between legal and illegal combinations, and
expressing a preference for leaving such decisions to the courts in particular cases.
10. W. WILSON, THE NEW FREEDOM 163–222 (1913); W. DIAMOND,
THE ECONOMIC THOUGHT OF WOODROW WILSON (1943). Wilson had
been committed to the evolutionist acceptance of size but became more devoted

to the competitive principle as he came before the public eye and as he accepted the advice of Brandeis. By 1913 he seems to have been persuaded that dissolution was an essential tactic. "Real dissolution in the case of the trusts is the only thing we can be satisfied with," he wrote privately, and he indicated that this was part of a program necessary "to satisfy the conscience of the country." *Id.* at 112.

11. C.W. ELIOT, THE WORKING OF THE AMERICAN DEMOCRACY, AMERICAN CONTRIBUTIONS TO CIVILIZATION 85–6 (1907); D. LYNCH, THE CONCENTRATION OF ECONOMIC POWER 112–13 (1946).

12. H.B. Thorelli, *supra* note 5, at 336.

13. K.H. PORTER & D.B. JOHNSON, NATIONAL PARTY PLATFORMS 114 (1956).

14. W. Wilson, *supra* note 10, at 57–8.

15. *Id.* at 118, 207, 286.

16. J.H. BUNZEL, THE AMERICAN SMALL BUSINESSMAN 84 (1962).

17. R.L. WEISSMAN, SMALL BUSINESS AND VENTURE CAPITAL 164 (1945).

Stigler Notes

1. H. THORELLI, THE FEDERAL ANTITRUST POLICY: ORIGINATION OF AN AMERICAN TRADITION 58–60 (1955).

2. *Id.* at 155–56.

3. *Id.* at 143.

4. STATISTICAL ABSTRACT OF THE U.S. 1888 (1889), at 183 (based on Poor's Manual).

5. The rate for grain from St. Louis to New York fell 40 percent from 1879–81 to 1898–1900. Average railroad freight charges per ton per mile had fallen by 1887 to 54 percent of the 1873 level, with all lines in both the eastern and western regions showing similar declines. *See* STATISTICAL ABSTRACT OF THE U.S. 1888 (1889), at 188.

6. W.M. ACWORTH, THE RAILWAYS AND THE TRADERS 206 (1891), sets the average American rate at half the English rate.

7. The railroads helped to bring the Midwestern farm area into the world market. . . .

8. In U.S. v. E.C. Knight Company, 156 U.S. 1 (1895), the court ruled that manufacture of refined sugar was not in interstate commerce.

9. The primary sources for identifying states with antitrust legislation are H.R. SEAGAR & C.A. GULICK, JR., TRUST AND CORPORATION PROBLEMS ch. 17 (1929); and H. THORELLI, THE FEDERAL ANTITRUST POLICY 79–84, 155–56 (1955). Information from the following is also of use: W. Shaw, *Social and Economic Legislation of the States*, Q.J. ECON., annual issues, vols. 5–11, April 1891-January 1897; W.S. STEVENS, INDUSTRIAL COMBINATIONS AND TRUSTS (1914); J. Jenks, *Recent Legislation and Adjudication on Trusts*, 12 Q.J. ECON. 461 (1898); and L.H. HANEY, BUSINESS ORGANIZATION AND COMBINATION (1913).

10. Britain had a vigorous amalgamation movement at the end of the nineteenth century, and vast mergers then and later led to high concentration in industries

such as cement. *See* L. HANNAH, THE RISE OF THE CORPORATE ECON-
OMY ch. 2 (1976).

11. *See* L.J. REYNOLDS, THE CONTROL OF COMPETITION IN CAN-
ADA 134–35 (1940), J.A. BALL, JR., CANADIAN ANTI-TRUST LEGISLA-
TION 10–13 (1934).

12. A moderately favorable sketch is given in my essay, *The Economic Effects
of the Antitrust Laws*, 9 J. LAW & ECON. 225 (1966), but it does not study the
adverse effects of the laws.

Bork Notes

1. United States v. Aluminum Co. of America, 148 F.2d 416, 428 (2d Cir.
1945).

2. 148 F.2d at 429.

3. United States v. Associated Press, 52 F. Supp. 362, 370 (1943).

4. 21 CONG. REC. 2457 (1890).

5. *Ibid.*

6. *Id.* at 2569.

7. 21 CONG. REC. 2462 (1890).

8. 21 CONG. REC. 2570 (1890).

9. *Id.* at 2466.

10. *Id.*

11. *Id.* at 2558.

12. *Id.* at 2571.

13. 21 CONG. REC. 4101 (1890).

14. 21 CONG. REC. 2729 (1890).

15. *Id.* at 4099.

16. 21 CONG. REC. 2457 (1890).

17. *Id.*

18. *E.g.*, "If their [the individuals'] business is lawful they can combine in any
way and enjoy the advantage of their united skill and capital, provided they do
not combine to prevent competition." *Id.*

19. *Id.*

20. "When corporations unite merely to extend their business, as connecting
lines of a railway without interfering with competing lines, they are proper and
lawful. Corporations tend to cheapen transportation, lessen the cost of production,
and bring within the reach of millions comforts and luxuries formerly enjoyed by
thousands." 21 CONG. REC. 2457 (1890).

21. *Id.* at 2460.

22. 21 CONG. REC. 2654–2655 (1890).

23. H. THORELLI, THE FEDERAL ANTITRUST POLICY 195 (1954).

24. Champion v. Ames, 188 U.S. 321 (1903).

25. 21 CONG. REC. 2462 (1890).

26. *Id.* at 2727.

27. *Id.* at 2456. Later in the same speech, his main presentation of the topic to
the Senate, Sherman stated: "I admit that it is difficult to define in legal language
the precise line between lawful and unlawful combinations. This must be left for

the courts to determine in each particular case. All that we, as lawmakers, can do is to declare general principles, and we can be assured that the courts will apply them so as to carry out the meaning of the law, as the courts of England and the United States have done for centuries. This bill is only an honest effort to declare a rule of action.... " *Id.* at 2460. The declaration of a "rule of action" is hardly equivalent to the bestowal of unconfined discretion. The reference in this passage to the common law also defines the range of the courts' discretion, as will be shown in the text.

28. *Id.* at 2456.
29. *Id.* at 2459.
30. *Id.*
31. *Id.* at 2457.
32. *Id.* at 2457.
33. *Id.* at 2460.
34. *Id.* at 2598. George was here recording his sentiments preparatory to announcing his inability to find any constitutional power in the Senate to deal with the problem. And, in fact, George thought that because of Congress' limited power the bill finally passed did not cover many cases.... Thus, even if one thought that George did wish in the abstract to serve values that might conflict with consumer welfare, it would seem probable that he did not believe the Sherman Act would bear any such construction.
35. *Id.* at 1767–1768.
36. W. Hamilton and I. Till, Antitrust in Action II (1940).
37. 21 CONG. REC. 3152 (1890).

Lande Notes

1. Consumers' surplus is the difference between the maximum amount that a consumer would pay and the price that he or she actually pays. Suppose that widgets are priced at $2.00, the competitive price. Marginal consumers of widgets would be willing to pay only this amount. Some consumers, however, would particularly desire widgets and willingly pay more—as much as $3.00. These consumers receive $1.00 in consumers' surplus when they purchase competitively priced widgets. If a monopolist gained control of the widget market and raised the price of widgets to $3.00, marginal consumers would no longer purchase widgets, and nonmarginal consumers would lose their surplus. The widget monopoly would acquire $1.00 of monopoly profits at the expense of widget consumers. For a more detailed definition, see E. MANSFIELD, MICROECONOMICS: THEORY AND APPLICATIONS 15 (4th ed. 1982); G. STIGLER, THE THEORY OF PRICE 78–81 (1966).

2. Thus, although Congress was strongly interested in increasing the size of the economic "pie" when it passed the antitrust laws, it was even more interested in ensuring its "fair" ownership. It should also be observed that all purchasers were to be protected, whether they were resellers, farmers or ultimate consumers.

3. *See* W. LETWIN, LAW AND ECONOMIC POLICY IN AMERICA ch. 2 (1965).

4. A. SMITH, AN INQUIRY INTO THE NATURE AND CAUSES OF THE WEALTH OF NATIONS 61 (Modern Library Ed. 1978) (1st ed. 1776).

5. Williamson, *Economies as an Antitrust Defense Revisited*, 125 U. PA. L. REV. 699, 711 (1977).

6. Limbaugh, *Historic Origins of Anti-Trust Legislation*, 18 MO. L. REV. 215, 217 (1953).

7. Standard Oil Co. v. Federal Trade Comm'n, 340 U.S. 231, 248–49 (1951) (quoting A.E. Staley Mfg. Co. v. Federal Trade Comm'n, 135 F.2d 453, 455 (7th Cir. 1943)).

8. Alfred Marshall, for example, devoted seventeen pages of the 1890 edition of *Principles of Economics* to a chapter entitled "The Theory of Monopolies" in which only one footnote discussed either allocative inefficiency or any incipient version of this concept. A. MARSHALL, PRINCIPLES OF ECONOMICS 466 n.1 (1890). Modern understanding of allocative efficiency is based, inter alia, on the assumption of Pareto optimality, first proposed in 1909. V. PARETO, *supra* note 5. Some of the precursors of this concept can arguably be found in Pareto's first major work, *Cours D'Economie Politique*, which was published in 1896–1897. Not until 1938 did the first modern and rigorous discussion of allocative efficiency appear. Hotelling, *The General Welfare in Relation to Problems of Taxation and of Railway and Utility Rates*, 6 ECONOMETRICA 242 (1938). Even this path-breaking and influential discussion, concerned with allocative inefficiency resulting from improper taxation and incorrect railroad and public utility rate-setting, did not discuss the antitrust implications of allocative inefficiency. . . .

9. "A careful student of the history of economics would have searched long and hard, on July 2 of 1890, the day the Sherman Act was signed by President Harrison, for any economist who had ever recommended the policy of actively combatting collusion or monopolization in the economy at large." Stigler, *The Economists and the Problem of Monopoly*, 72 AM. ECON. REV. 1, 3 (1982).

10. *See, e.g.*, McGee, *Predatory Price Cutting: The Standard Oil (N.J.) Case*, 1 J.L. & ECON. 137 (1958).

11. 21 CONG. REC. 2457 (1890).

12. 21 CONG. REC. 2460 (1890) (emphasis added). Senator Sherman and others expressed similar views elsewhere. The Senator, for example, commented that "[the courts] will distinguish between lawful combinations in aid of production and unlawful combinations to prevent competition and in restraint of trade. . . ." *Id.* at 2456. He also said, "If they [the Standard Oil trust] conducted their business lawfully, without any attempt by these combinations to raise the price of an article consumed by the people of the United States, I would say let them pursue that business." *Id.* at 2469. . . .

13. *See* 21 CONG. REC. 2461 (1890).

14. 21 CONG. REC. 2462 (1890). Sherman also stated: "The sole object of such a combination is to make competition impossible. It can control the market, raise or lower prices, as will best promote to selfish interests. . . . Its governing motive is to increase the profits of the parties composing it. The law of selfishness, un-controlled by competition, compels it to disregard the interest of the consumer. It dictates terms to transportation companies, it commands the price of labor without fear of strikes, for in its field it allows no competitors. Such a combination is far

more dangerous than any heretofore invented, and, when it embraces the great body of all the corporations engaged in a particular industry in all of the States of the Union, it tends to advance the price to the consumer of any article produced." *Id.* at 2457.

15. 21 CONG. REC. 2461 (1890).

16. *Id.* at 2614.

17. *Id.* at 4101 (emphasis added).

18. *Id.* at 4098.

19. *Id.* at 4103. (Fithian was reading, with apparent approval, a letter from a constituent.)

20. 21 CONG. REC. 2728 (1890).

21. 21 CONG. REC. 1768.

Millon Notes

1. 21 CONG. REC. 2561 (1890) (Statement of Senator Teller during floor debate of the Sherman Antitrust Act.)

2. *See* Standard Oil Co. v. United States, 221 U.S. 1, 56, 64, 77 (1911).

3. *See* Posner, *The Chicago School of Antitrust Analysis*, 127 U. PA. L. REV. 925 (1979).

4. *See, e.g.*, R. BORK, THE ANTITRUST PARADOX: A POLICY AT WAR WITH ITSELF (1978); R. POSNER, ANTITRUST LAW: AN ECONOMIC PERSPECTIVE (1976).

5. This Article makes no claims about "legislative intent," which is, of course, a fictitious construct. It is fictitious in at least two senses. It is implausible to assert that legislators as a group possess a definite, agreed upon, collective intention even as to a statute's general purposes—that is, a concrete set of normative principles or guiding policies. In any event, the intent question is interesting only with respect to particular controversies that arise after the statute's enactment. It is pure pretense to assert that the legislators intended that a statute be applied in a certain way to a situation they never imagined, let alone discussed and agreed upon. *See* Radin, *Statutory Interpretation*, 43 HARV. L. REV. 863, 869–71 (1930). Even if it were discernible, one could also question the relevance of original intent. *See id.* at 871–72.

[This Article] . . . attempts to describe the Sherman Act's meaning within its contemporary intellectual context, rather than to hypothesize about how Congress as a group thought it should be applied in the future.

6. R. HOFSTADTER, THE AGE OF REFORM 137 (1955). *See generally id.* 131–72 (describing "status revolution").

7. *Id.* at 218–23.

8. R. WIEBE, THE SEARCH FOR ORDER, 1877–1920, 45–46 (1967).

9. *See generally* L. GOODWYN, THE POPULIST MOMENT: A SHORT HISTORY OF THE AGRARIAN REVOLT IN AMERICA (1978) (historical survey); R. HOFSTADTER, *supra* note 6, 60–93 (discussing Populist resistance to industrialization).

10. *See* M. KELLER, AFFAIRS OF STATE: PUBLIC LIFE IN LATE NINETEENTH CENTURY AMERICA 394–404 (1977).

11. W. LETWIN, LAW AND ECONOMIC POLICY IN AMERICA 59 (1965).
12. Mickey, *Trusts*, 22 AM. L. REV. 538, 549 (1888).
13. Hudson, *Modern Feudalism*, 144 NO. AM. REV. 277, 290 (1887).
14. A. SMITH, THE WEALTH OF NATIONS 423 (E. Cannan ed. 1937); *see also* R. NISBET, SOCIAL CHANGE AND HISTORY 150–54 (1969).
15. T. JEFFERSON, NOTES ON THE STATE OF VIRGINIA 216–17 (M. Peterson ed. 1975).
16. 1 A. MARSHALL, PRINCIPLES OF ECONOMICS 346 (1890).
17. 21 CONG. REC. 2457 (1890).
18. *Id.* at 2460.
19. *Id.*
20. *Id.* at 3146.

Peritz Notes

1. S. 3445, 50th Cong., 2d Sess., 20 CONG. REC. 1120 (1889) (as amended); S. 3440, 50th Cong., 2d Sess., 19 CONG. REC. 7512 (1888) (as amended).
2. S. 1, 51st Cong., 1st Sess., 21 CONG. REC. 2901 (1890); *see* S. 3445, 50th Cong., 2d Sess., 20 CONG. REC. 1120 (1889); *see also* S. 3440, 50th Cong., 1st Sess., 19 CONG. REC. 7512 (1888) (predecessor bill).
3. 21 CONG. REC. 2457 (1890) (statement of Sen. Sherman).
4. *Id.*
5. *Id.*; 21 CONG. REC. 1768 (1890) (Sen. George: extorted wealth); 21 CONG. REC. 2572 (1890) (Sen. Teller: predatory pricing).

The term "combination" was used to represent a wide range of agreements, trusts, corporate holding companies, and secret understandings. There were "loose" combinations, such as agreements to agree on price, and "tight" combinations, such as the Standard Oil Trust. Although today we tend to use the term less inclusively, this Article's use of the term will follow the more relaxed usage of the congressional debates. "Combination" will mean any private agreement producing a cartel, pooling arrangement, trust, or merger. In contrast, "cartel," "pooling arrangement," "trust," "merger" are used in their narrow senses.

6. S. 3445, 50th Cong., 1st Sess., 19 CONG. REC. 8483 (1888) (Sen. Sherman's original bill).
7. 21 CONG. REC. 137 (1889) (statement of Sen. Turpie); *cf.* Kennedy, *The Role of Law in Economic Thought*, 34 AM. U.L. REV. 944 (1985) (describing the relationship between classical economic and legal thought).
8. 21 CONG. REC. 2458 (1890) (remarks of Sen. Sherman, quoting from Craft v. McConoughy, 79 Ill. 346, 350 (1875); *see also* 20 CONG. REC. 1458 (1889) (statement of Sen. Jones) (these combinations of capital could "plunder the public").
9. 20 CONG. REC. 1457 (1889) (statement of Sen. Teller); 21 CONG. REC. 2726 (1890) (statement of Sen. Edmunds) (the "great monopolies . . . command everybody, laborer, consumer, producer, and everybody else.").
10. 21 CONG. REC. 2561 (1890) (statement of Sen. Teller).
11. 21 CONG. REC. 4100 (1890) (statement of Rep. Mason).
12. S. 3440, 50th Cong., 1st Sess., 19 CONG. REC. 7512 (1888).

13. 21 CONG. REC. 3146 (1890).

14. 21 CONG. REC. 2729 (1890) (statement of Sen. Platt).

15. *Id.* at 5956 (statement of Rep. Stewart).

16. 21 CONG. REC. 2457 (1890); *see, e.g.*, R. ELY, PROBLEMS OF TODAY: A DISCUSSION OF PROTECTIVE TARIFFS, TAXATION, AND MONOPOLIES 126 (2d ed. 1890) (asserting that honest government and monopoly were not compatible).

17. 21 CONG. REC. 1457 (1890); *cf.* F. HAYEK, THE ROAD TO SERFDOM 25 (1944) (arguing that political freedom is dependent upon economic freedom); Stigler, *Wealth, and Possibly Liberty*, 7 J. LEGAL STUD. 213, 214–15 (1978) (analyzing personal liberty in terms of economic endowment).

18. 21 CONG. REC. 2460 (1899) (remarks of Sen. Sherman).

19. Indeed, markets were seen as uniformly uncompetitive. *See* 21 CONG. REC. 2726–27 (1890).

20. A modern analogue of "industrial liberty" and its impulse toward equality is the notion of "workable competition," described as a pragmatic tool for judging whether a market is competitive. *See, e.g.*, Clark, *Toward a Concept of Workable Competition*, 30 AM. ECON. REV. 241, 253–56 (1940); Stocking, *The Rule of Reason, Workable Competition, and Monopoly*, 64 YALE L.J. 1107, 1108–12 (1955). Whereas the ideals of perfect competition and perfect monopoly are purely analytic tools rather than desirable and attainable market conditions, "workable competition" rather than "workable monopoly" is the appropriate antitrust goal.

21. 21 CONG. REC. 1768 (1899) (statement of Sen. George).

22. 20 CONG. REC. 1457 (1889) (statement of Sen. Jones).

23. 21 CONG. REC. 137 (1889) (statement of Sen. Turpie).

24. *Id.* at 2720–30 (1890) (statement of Sen. Platt).

25. *Id.* at 5957 (statement of Rep. Stewart).

26. *Id.* at 5954 (statement of Rep. Morse).

27. *Id.* at 2901 (1890) (Chief Clerk reading substitute bill reported by the Committee on the Judiciary); *id.* at 3146, 3148, 3152 (monopoly "a technical term known to the common law").

28. *Id.* at 3153 (Senate passage, April 8, 1890); *id.* at 6314 (House passage June 20, 1890). The delay in House action was due to an eleventh-hour attempt to include a specific reference in section one to transportation, in order to assure the Bill's priority over the Interstate Commerce Act. *Id.* at 4088–104, 5950–61, 6312–14.

29. *See id.* at 3152 (statement of Sen. Hoar) ("I do not mean to say that [the committee] stated what the signification was, but I become satisfied that they were right and that the word 'monopoly' is a merely technical term which has a clear and legal signification.").

30. *Id.* at 3146, 3152.

31. *Id.* at 3148.

32. *Id.* at 3151 (statement of Sen. Edmunds).

33. 21 CONG. REC. 3152 (1890). The example given of unfair means is merger—"the buying up of all other persons engaged in the same business." *Id.*

34. *See, e.g.*, Central Shade-Roller Co. v. Cushman, 143 Mass. 353, 364, 9 N.E. 629, 631 (1887).

35. *Id.*, 9 N.E. at 630.

36. 23 Q.B.D. 598, 612 (1889), *aff'd*, 1892 A.C. 25.

37. *Id.* at 614–19. Taking a middle ground of sorts, the opinion later confided that a party to the agreement could challenge it. *Id.* at 620. The court deemed the agreement not void, but rather unenforceable. *Id.* at 632.

38. The classical economists were the strongest supporters of the view that the tendency to compete was natural and that competitive markets were inevitable. *See, e.g.*, A. WALKER, THE SCIENCE OF WEALTH: A MANUAL OF PO-LITICAL ECONOMY EMBRACING THE LAWS OF TRADE, CURRENCY, AND FINANCE (1875); F. WAYLAND, THE ELEMENTS OF POLITICAL ECONOMY (1837); *cf.*, 3 J. DORFMAN, THE ECONOMIC MIND IN AMER-ICAN CIVILIZATION 1865–1918 359–89 (1949) (demonstrating that there was a substantial relationship between the classical economists' work and the public per-ceptions of the times); R. HOFSTADTER, SOCIAL DARWINISM IN AMER-ICAN THOUGHT, 1860–1915, at 145 (1949) (observing that Francis Wayland's book was the most popular college textbook in political economy during the period).

The neoclassicists asserted that, although markets were not competitive, there was always potential competition lurking in the wings. Andrew Carnegie articulated this view most sublimely. *See* Carnegie, *The Bugaboo of Trusts*, 148 N. AM. REV. 141, 150 (1889). Scholarly renditions of the neoclassical position include J.B. CLARK, ESSENTIALS OF ECONOMIC THEORY viii (1907); Giddings, *The Persistence of Competition*, 2 POL. SCI. Q. 62, 65 (1887); Gunton, *The Economic and Social Aspects of Trusts*, 3 POL. SCI. Q. 385–408 (1888). For a direct critique of this view, see Bullock, *The Trusts and Public Policy*, 87 ATLANTIC MONTHLY 737, 742 (1901) ("There can be no *potential* competition when *actual* competition is hopeless.").

The New School of Economics was an American response to the foregoing views of markets as inevitably competitive. Although the adherents to this school had differing solutions, they all agreed that the problem was the inevitability of com-bination. *See, e.g.*, A. HADLEY, RAILROAD TRANSPORTATION—ITS HIS-TORY AND ITS LAWS 124 (1885); Andrews, *Trusts According to Official Investigations*, 3 Q.J. ECON. 117 (1889); Clark, *The Limits of Competition*, 2 POL. SCI. Q. 45 (1887). Ultimately, the most influential New Schoolers asserted that competition and combination were both possible and that some industries tended toward combination, based on their characteristic of high fixed costs and low mar-ginal costs. Adams, *The Relationship of the State to Industrial Action*, in 1 PUB-LICATIONS OF THE AMERICAN ECONOMIC ASSOCIATION 471 (1887); *cf.* R. ELY, PROBLEMS OF TODAY, *supra* note 44.

39. 21 CONG. REC. 5956 (1890). For examples of contemporaneous views of concentration as the result of a natural evolutionary process, see Andrews, *The Economic Law of Monopoly*, 26 J. SOC. SCI. 1, 11–12 (1890); Jenks, *Capitalistic Monopolies and Their Relation to the State*, 9 POL. SCI. Q. 486, 503–09 (1894).

40. 94 U.S. 113, 126 (1877).

41. Adams, *Publicity and Corporate Abuses*, in 1 PUBLICATIONS OF THE MICH. POL. SCI. ASS'N 109, 116 (1894), *reprinted in* H. THORELLI, THE FEDERAL ANTITRUST POLICY: ORIGINATION OF AN AMERICAN TRADITION 320 (1955).

42. *Id.*

43. Pound, *The Theory of Judicial Decision*, 36 HARV. L. REV. 641, 653 (1923).

44. *See, e.g.*, D. WELLS, RECENT ECONOMIC CHANGES AND THEIR EFFECT ON THE PRODUCTION AND DISTRIBUTION OF WEALTH AND THE WELL-BEING OF SOCIETY 73–75 (1896); Carnegie, *Popular Illusions About Trusts*, in THE GOSPEL OF WEALTH, AND OTHER TIMELY ESSAYS 81–82 (2d ed. 1933).

45. Pound, *supra* note 59, at 654.

46. 2 J. BRYCE, THE AMERICAN COMMONWEALTH 407–08 (1889).

47. *See, e.g.*, Kaysen, *The Corporation: How Much Power? What Scope?*, in THE CORPORATION IN MODERN SOCIETY 85–105 (E. Mason ed. 1959).

Hovenkamp Notes

1. R. BORK, THE ANTITRUST PARADOX: A POLICY AT WAR WITH ITSELF 20 (1978).

2. *See* Hovenkamp, *The Political Economy of Substantive Due Process*, 40 STAN. L. REV. 379, 408–09, 437–38 (1988).

3. For arguments that antitrust policy has only recently become "economic," *see* Gerhart, *The Supreme Court and Antitrust Analysis: The (Near) Triumph of the Chicago School*, 1982 Sup. Ct. Rev. 319; and Posner, *The Rule of Reason and the Economic Approach: Reflections on the Sylvania Decision*, 45 U. CHI. L. REV. 1, 5, 12–13 (1977).

4. *E.g.*, Arthur, *Farewell to the Sea of Doubt: Jettisoning the Constitutional Sherman Act*, 74 CALIF. L. REV. 266 (1986).

5. T. SEDGWICK, PUBLIC AND PRIVATE ECONOMY 31 (1836).

6. A. and M.P. MARSHALL, THE ECONOMICS OF INDUSTRY 2 (2d ed. 1881).

7. A. MARSHALL, PRINCIPLES OF ECONOMICS (1890).

8. M. HORWITZ, THE TRANSFORMATION OF AMERICAN LAW: 1780–1860 (1978).

9. For recognition of the unique expression of public policy concerns in the English law of contracts in restraint of trade, *see* 8 W. HOLDSWORTH, A HISTORY OF ENGLISH LAW 56 (2d ed. 1937); *see also* Foulke, *Restraints on Trade* 12 COL. L. REV. 97, 105 (1912) (same).

10. C.F. BEACH, SR., A TREATISE ON THE LAW OF MONOPOLIES AND INDUSTRIAL TRUSTS 107 (1898).

11. For the meaning of "competition" in the classical tradition, *see* Stigler, *Perfect Competition, Historically Contemplated*, 65 J. POL. ECON. 1 (1957). Stigler traces the modern illustration of perfect competition—the horizontal demand curve—to A. COURNOT, MATHEMATICAL PRINCIPLES OF THE THEORY OF WEALTH (1838; English ed., New York, 1929), 90; and to the third edition of A. MARSHALL'S PRINCIPLES OF ECONOMICS, 517, 849–850 (1895).

12. F.A. WALKER, POLITICAL ECONOMY 91–92 (3d ed. 1888).

13. A.T. HADLEY, ECONOMICS: AN ACCOUNT OF THE RELATIONS BETWEEN PRIVATE PROPERTY AND PUBLIC WELFARE (1896).

14. *See* E. SREISSLER, "To What Extent Was the Austrian School Marginalist?," in THE MARGINAL REVOLUTION IN ECONOMICS (R.D.C. Black, A.W. Coats, C.D.W. Goodwin eds. 1973) at 160. The Austrian economist whom Hadley relied on most was Friedrich von Wieser, particularly his NATURAL VALUE (Malloch trans.) (London, 1893).

15. J.B. CLARK, THE DISTRIBUTION OF WEALTH 58-78, 390–93 (New York, 1899).

16. *See* Kales, *Contracts to Refrain from Doing Business or from Entering or Carrying on an Occupation*, 31 HARV. L. REV. 193, 198 (1917).

17. *See* Pierce v. Fuller, 8 Mass. 223 (1811) (upholding a naked covenant not to compete given for recited consideration of $1.00).

18. *See* Gompers v. Rochester, 56 PA. ST. 194 (1867) (sale of store and its goods adequate consideration for accompanying covenant not to compete, but court requires consideration to be recited "on the face of the agreement").

19. *E.g.*, McCurry v. Gibson, 108 ALA. 451, 18 S. 806, 808 (1895), discussed *supra*. See also Hubbard v. Miller, 27 MICH. 15, 25 (1873) (even in restraint case the law "allows the parties to judge for themselves of the sufficiency in value of such consideration for their contracts"); Duffy v. Shockey, 22 IND. 70, 73 (1853) (question of consideration in restraint case is the same as that involving "any other contract made by parties capable of contracting. They should, in the absence of fraud, be presumed to have determined that point for themselves.... ").

20. *See* Peppin, *Price-Fixing Agreements under the Sherman Antitrust Law*, 28 CALIF. L. REV. 297 (1940).

21. Although mergers were frequently challenged in court during the period 1850–1890, most challenges attacked them as ultra vires, not as anticompetitive. *See generally* W.C. NOYES, A TREATISE ON THE LAW OF INTERCORPORATE RELATIONS (1909).

22. Northern Securities Co. v. United States, 193 U.S. 197, 403 (1904) (Holmes, J., dissenting).

23. Northern Securities, 193 U.S. at 405. Given this definition of combinations or conspiracies, all that Section Two of the Sherman Act added to Section One "is that like penalties are imposed upon every single person, who, without combination, monopolizes, or attempts to monopolize...." Section Two "is more important as an aid to the construction of 1 than it is on its own account."

24. A. EDDY, THE LAW OF COMBINATIONS 657 at 673 (1901).

25. *Id.* at 674.

26. F.H. COOKE, THE LAW OF COMBINATIONS, MONOPOLIES AND LABOR UNIONS (1898; 2d ed. 1909).

27. *See, e.g.*, Prugnell v. Gosse, Aleyn 67, 82 ENG. REP. 919 (K.B. 1648).

28. Union Strawboard Co. v. Bonfield, 193 ILL. 421, 427, 61 N.E. 1038, 1040 (1901).

29. 1 P. Wms. 181, 24 ENG. REP. 347 (K.B. 1711).

30. Nordenfelt v. Maxim-Nordenfelt Guns & Ammunition Co., (1894) A.C. 535 (upholding covenant unlimited as to space and lasting for the life of the promisor).

31. *E.g.*, Nester v. Continental Brewing Co., 161 PA. 473, 29 A. 102 (1894); People v. Sheldon, 139 N.Y. 251, 264–65 (1893); Judd v. Harrington, 139 N.Y. 105, 34 N.E. 790 (1893); More v. Bennett, 140 ILL. 69 (1892).

32. *E.g.*, Connolly v. Union Sewer Pipe Co., 184 U.S. 540 (1902), which held that the Illinois antitrust statute violated the federal Equal Protection clause because it exempted agricultural products and livestock; *In re* Grice, 79 F. 627 (N.D. Tex. 1897), which declared unconstitutional a state antitrust statute that applied to transactions outside the state and exempted agricultural products. *See* May, *Antitrust Practice and Procedure in the Formative Era: The Constitutional and Conceptual Reach of State Antitrust Law*, 1880–1918, 135 U. PA. L. REV. 495 (1987).

33. Gibbs v. Consolidated Gas Co. of Baltimore, 130 U.S. 396, 408–09 (1889). The court relied on: Transportation Co. v. Pipe Line Co., 22 W. VA. 600 (1883); Chicago Gas Co. v. People's Gas Co., 121 ILL. 530 (1887); Telegraph Co. v. Telegraph Co., 65 GA. 161 (1880).

34. United States v. Trans-Missouri Freight Assn., 166 U.S. 290 (1897).

35. Peckham was the author of the Supreme Court's decision in Lochner v. New York, 198 U.S. 45 (1905).

36. 75 U.S. 211, at 228–29 (1899).

37. Appalachian Coals, Inc. v. United States, 288 U.S. 344, 359–60 (1933).

Part II

1. United States v. General Dynamics, 415 U.S. 486 (1874).

2. F.M. SCHERER, INDUSTRIAL MARKET STRUCTURE AND ECONOMIC PERFORMANCE (2d ed. 1980); J. BAIN, INSTRUCTIONAL ORGANIZATION (1959); Mason, *Price and Production Policies of Large Scale Enterprise*, 28 Am. Econ. Rev. 61 (1939).

3. *See generally* K. LEVIN, BEYOND MODERNISM (1988).

4. *Id.* at xii.

5. *See e.g.*, Hovenkamp, *Antitrust Policy After Chicago*, 84 Mich. L. Rev. 213 (1985).

6. DiLorenzo and High, *Antitrust and Competition, Historically Considered*, 26 Econ. Inquiry 423 (1988).

7. *Id.* at 425.

8. H.C. ADAMS, DESCRIPTION OF INDUSTRY 27 (1918), *cited* in DiLorenzo and High, *supra* note 6, at 429.

9. *Id.*

10. Young, *The Sherman Act and the New Antitrust Legislation*, 23 J. Pol. Econ. 201, 213 (1915), *cited* in DiLorenzo and High, *supra* note 6, at 429. *See also* A. WALKER, HISTORY OF THE SHERMAN ACT 58 (1910): "[I]t follows that where a particular monopolizer does or does not possess or use superior skill and superior facilities for doing the work monopolized, but does attain a monopoly of that work by the aid of impediments placed by him in the paths of his competitors that the monopolizer violates Section 2 of the Sherman Act." *See also* Krattenmaker and Salop, *Anticompetitive Exclusion: Raising Rivals' Costs To Achieve Power Over Price*, 96 Yale L.J. 209 (1986).

11. Stigler, *Perfect Competition, Historically Contemplated*, 65 J. Pol. Econ. 1 (1957).

12. *See generally* Hovenkamp, *The Sherman Act and the Classical Theory of Competition*, 74 Iowa L. Rev. 1019 (1989).

13. *Id.*
14. *Id.*
15. Northern Securities Co. v. United States, 193 U.S. 197, 405 (Holmes, J. dissenting) *cited* in Hovenkamp, *supra* note 12.
16. *See, e.g.*, Krattenmaker and Salop, *Anticompetitive Exclusion: Raising Rivals' Costs to Achieve Power Over Price*, 96 Yale L.J. 209 (1986).
17. Hovenkamp, *supra* note 12.
18. Sullivan, *The Economic Jurisprudence of the Burger Court's Antitrust Policy: The First Thirteen Years*, 58 Notre Dame L. Rev. 1 (1982).
19. As one economist who favors repeal of the Sherman Act has said, "Even though modern economics embodies an 'efficiency' rationale for the Sherman Act, that rationale was never used to make a case for the original enactment of the law. Rather, it was constructed, *ex post*, as a rationalization for a law that already existed." DiLorenzo, *The Origins of Antitrust: An Interest-Group Perspective*, 5 Intern. Rev. L. Econ. 73, 87 (1985).
20. *But cf.* Bork, *Contrasts in Antitrust Theory*, 65 Colum. L. Rev. 400, 415 (1965).
21. C. KAYSEN AND D. TURNER, ANTITRUST POLICY: AN ECONOMIC AND LEGAL ANALYSIS 45 (1959).
22. *Id.* at 14.
23. *Id.*
24. *Id.* at 15.
25. *Id.*
26. Kaplow, *Antitrust, Law and Economics, and the Courts*, 50 Law and Contemp. Probs. 181, 215–16 (1987).

Kaysen and Turner Notes

1. Standard Oil Co. v. FTC, 340 U.S. 231, 249 (1951).
2. United States v. Aluminum Co. of America, 148 F.2d 416 (2d Cir. 1945).
3. 21 Cong. Rec. 3146-52, *cited* in United States v. United Shoe Machinery Co., 110 F. Supp. 295, 341 (D. Mass. 1953).
4. American Tobacco Co. v. United States, 328 United States 781 (1946); United States v. Aluminum Co. of America, 148 F.2d 416 (C.A. 2, 1945); United States v. United Shoe Machinery Co., 110 F. Supp. 295 (D. Mass. 1953); United States v. E.I. du Pont de Nemours & Co., 351 United States 377 (1956), *affirming* 118 F. Supp. 41 (D. Del. 1953); United States v. Paramount Pictures, Inc., 334 United States 131 (1948); United States v. National Lead Co., 332 United States 319 (1947).

Posner Notes

1. Director formulated his ideas mainly orally. *But see*, Director & Levi, *Law and the Future: Trade Regulation*, 51 NW. U.L. REV. 281 (1958).
2. *See, e.g.*, Bork, *Vertical Integration and the Sherman Act: The Legal History of an Economic Misconception*, 22 U. CHI. L. REV. 157 (1954); Bowman, *Tying Arrangements and the Leverage Problem*, 67 YALE L.J. 19 (1957); McGee, *Predatory Price Cutting: The Standard Oil (N.J.) Case*, 1 J.L. & ECON. 137 (1958); Telser, *Why Should Manufacturers Want Fair Trade?*, 3 J.L. & ECON. 86 (1960).

For the most complete and most orthodox statement of the Chicago position see R. BORK, THE ANTITRUST PARADOX (1978); for an anthology in which Chicago writings are heavily represented see THE COMPETITIVE ECONOMY: SELECTED READINGS (Y. Brozen ed. 1974). *See also* R. POSNER, ANTI-TRUST LAW (1976).

3. A "free rider" in this context would be a dealer who undersold competing dealers by selling the product itself at a lower price while relying on them to provide the necessary presale services to the customer.

4. Rather than suffer financial loss as a result of a price war, the rational would-be monopolist would buy out the competing company.

5. This is the same reason why manufacturers would not want their dealers to catalyze distribution and why, therefore, Director sought an alternative explanation for resale price maintenance.

6. By this I mean action that does not involve agreement with a competitor. It may, of course, involve agreement with a customer or supplier, and generally does: even a sale below cost involves at least an implicit contract between seller and purchaser.

7. *See, e.g.,* United States v. American Tobacco Co., 221 U.S. 106 (1911); Standard Oil Co. v. United States, 221 U.S. 1 (1911).

8. *See, e.g.,* E. MASON, ECONOMIC CONCENTRATION AND THE MO-NOPOLY PROBLEM (1957); C. KAYSEN, *United States v. United Shoe Machinery Corporation:* AN ECONOMIC ANALYSIS OF AN ANTI-TRUST CASE (1956).

9. *See* Turner, *The Validity of Tying Agreements Under the Antitrust Laws*, 72 HARV. L. REV. 50, 60–62, 63 n.42 (1958).

10. *See* C. KAYSEN & D. TURNER, ANTITRUST POLICY 73 & n.33 (1959).

11. *See* G. STIGLER, THE ORGANIZATION OF INDUSTRY (1968).

12. *See* Harberger, *Monopoly and Resource Allocation*, 44 AM. ECON. REV. PAPERS & PROC. 77 (1954).

13. C. KAYSEN & D. TURNER, *supra* note 10, at 157.

14. J. ROBINSON, THE ECONOMICS OF IMPERFECT COMPETITION 190–94 (1933). *See also* P. SAMUELSON, FOUNDATIONS OF ECONOMIC ANALYSIS 42–45 (1947).

15. *See* C. KAYSEN & D. TURNER *supra* note 10, at 120–21. Kaysen and Turner also espoused a leverage theory of vertical integration. *Id.* 121–22.

16. *See* Peltzman, *Issues in Vertical Integration Policy*, in PUBLIC POLICY TOWARD MERGERS 167 (1969).

17. This assumes equal access to capital markets and equal cost of obtaining capital. These assumptions have been criticized by Professor Williamson, Williamson Book Review, 83 YALE L.J. 647 (1974), among others.

18. *See* Vernon & Graham, *Profitability of Monopolization by Vertical Integration* 79 J. POLITICAL ECON. 924 (1971), *discussed in* McGee & Bassett, *Vertical Integration Revisited*, 19 J.L. & ECON. 17 (1976). *See also* Blair & Kaserman, *Vertical Integration, Tying, and Antitrust Policy*, 68 AM. ECON REV. 397 (1978), and references cited therein. Blair and Kaserman note that the same result can be obtained by the input monopolist's tying potentially substitutable inputs to the sale

of the input he controls. They offer no example showing that this has ever been done.

19. C. KAYSEN & D. TURNER, *supra* note 10, at 133.

20. *See* Comanor, *Vertical Territorial and Customer Restrictions: White Motor and Its Aftermath*, 81 HARV. L. REV. 1419, 1425–33 (1968).

21. 433 U.S. 36 (1977).

22. Areeda & Turner, *Predatory Pricing and Related Practices Under Section 2 of the Sherman Act*, 88 HARV. L. REV. 697 (1975); 3 P. AREEDA & D. TURNER, ANTITRUST LAW, 711 (1978).

23. Scherer, *Predatory Pricing and the Sherman Act: A Comment*, 89 HARV. L. REV. 869 (1976); *see* Areeda & Turner, *Scherer on Predatory Pricing: A Reply*, 89 HARV. L. REV. 891 (1976); Scherer, *Some Last Words on Predatory Pricing*, 89 HARV. L. REV. 901 (1976).

24. *See* Williamson, *Predatory Pricing: A Strategic and Welfare Analysis*, 87 YALE L.J. 284 (1977).

25. *See* Spence, *Entry, Capacity, and Oligopolistic Pricing*, 8 BELL J. ECON. 534 (1977).

26. *See* Williamson, *supra* note 17, at 656–59.

27. *See* Williamson, *Dominant Firms and the Monopoly Problem: Market Failure Considerations*, 85 HARV. L. REV. 1512, 1518–19 (1972).

28. A further aspect of the Chicago-Harvard difference on deconcentration arises from the difference between the deep distrust of government intervention that is associated with the Chicago School of Economics (in the broader, Milton Friedman sense) and the (rapidly diminishing) complacency toward such intervention associated with traditional Harvard-M.I.T. economic thinking. Deconcentration is a more ambitious form of public control than is usually involved in antitrust enforcement, so one's attitudes toward the capabilities of regulatory-type governmental interventions naturally come into play. That is why adherents of the Chicago school believe it unsound to base a policy of deconcentration on the assumption that a deconcentration proceeding is a swifter method than entry itself of deconcentrating markets in which there are no barriers to entry in the technical sense but in which entry at minimum cost requires substantial time.

Rule and Meyer Notes

1. *See* Waldman & Cuneo, *The Court Is Winking at "Price Fixing,"* N.Y. Times, May 15, 1988, at F-1.

2. *See* Williamson, *Economies as an Antitrust Defense: The Welfare Tradeoffs*, 58 AM. ECON. REV. 18 (1968).

3. *See, e.g.,* R. POSNER, ANTITRUST LAW: AN ECONOMIC PERSPECTIVE 11-12 (1976); Posner, *The Social Costs of Monopoly and Regulation*, 83 J. POL. ECON. 807 (1975).

4. *See* Posner, *The Social Costs of Monopoly and Regulation*, 83 J. POL. ECON. 807, at 811 (1975).

5. Marbury v. Madison, 5 U.S. (1 Cranch) 137, 171 (1803).

6. *See, e.g.,* United States v. Socony-Vacuum Oil Co., 310 U.S. 150, 221-22,

225-27 (1940). *But see* Appalachian Coals v. United States, 288 U.S. 344 (1933) (possible exception "all but overruled" by *Socony-Vacuum*. P. AREEDA & D. TURNER, *supra* note 21, at ¶ 104, n.1.).

7. *See, e.g.*, United States v. United States Steel Corp., 251 U.S. 417, 451 (1920).

8. *See* Northern Pacific Railway Co. v. United States, 356 U.S. 1, 4 (1958) (Sherman Act rests on premise "that the unrestrained interaction of competitive forces will yield the best allocation of our economic resources, the lowest prices, the highest quality and the greatest material progress, while at the same time providing an environment conducive to the preservation of our democratic political and social institutions").

9. United States v. General Dynamics Corp., 415 U.S. 486 (1974).

10. Continental T.V., Inc. v. GTE Sylvania, Inc., 433 U.S. 36 (1977).

11. Monsanto Co. v. Spray-Rite Service Co., 465 U.S. 752 (1984).

12. Matsushita Elec. Indus. Corp. v. Zenith Radio Corp., 475 U.S. 574 (1986).

13. Business Electronics Corp. v. Sharp Electronics Corp., 108 S. Ct. 1515 (1988).

14. 433 U.S. at 59; *see also* Sharp, 108 S. Ct. at 1519.

15. Reiter v. Sonotone Corp., 442 U.S. 330, 343 (1979) (quoting R. BORK, THE ANTITRUST PARADOX 66 (1978)).

16. United States v. Trans-Missouri Freight Ass'n., 166 U.S. 290, 323-24 (1897).

17. United States v. Aluminum Co. of America, 148 F.2d 416 (2d Cir. 1945).

18. *See* Northern Pacific Railway Co. v. United States, 356 U.S. 1, 5 (1958).

19. *See* P. AREEDA & D. TURNER, ANTITRUST LAW ¶ 112 (1978).

20. *See, e.g.*, Matsushita, 475 U.S. at 594 (in predatory pricing area, courts "must be concerned lest a rule or precedent that authorizes a search for a particular type of undesirable pricing behavior end up by discouraging legitimate price competition") [quoting Barry Wright Corp. v. ITT Grinnell Corp., 724 F.2d 227, 234 (1st Cir. 1983)].

21. *See* Landes, *Optimal Sanctions for Antitrust Violations*, 50 U. CHI. L. REV. 652 (1983).

22. *See* Werden & Simon, *Why Price Fixers Should Go to Prison*, 32 ANTI-TRUST BULL. 917 (1987).

23. United States v. Topco Associates, Inc., 405 U.S. 596 (1972).

24. Continental T.V., Inc. v. GTE Sylvania, Inc., 433 U.S. 36 (1977).

25. *Id.*

26. Business Electronics Corp. v. Sharp Electronics Corp., 108 S. Ct. 1515 (1988).

Flynn Notes

1. A similar movement in political science, based on the advocacy of Leo Strauss, has been made the basis of the conservative political appeal to "original intent." It is premised on the belief that there are eternal and unchanging "truths" that can be discovered from the careful reading of selected original documents by great thinkers divorced from the history and circumstances in which they wrote. As in the fundamentalist religious movement, behaviorism and relativism are rejected in the name of pursuing eternal truths from original texts and divorced from their

historical, economic, psychological or sociological background. Despite modern insights in language theory, words and the concepts they generate are treated as fixed and immutable. It is "a philosophical conservatism of a special kind," a philosophy based on faith that is no longer philosophy. See Wood, *The Fundamentalists and the Constitution*, N.Y. REVIEW OF BOOKS 33 (Feb. 18, 1988).

2. *See* M. Friedman, *The Methodology of Positive Economics*, in ESSAYS IN POSITIVE ECONOMICS 3 (1966); R. BORK, THE ANTITRUST PARADOX 120 (1978). *But cf.* Mason, *Some Negative Thoughts on Friedman's Positive Economics*, 3 J. POST-KEYNESIAN ECON. 235, 244 (1980-81).

Thus, if the only concern of antitrust policy is with allocative efficiency, only that reality concerning price and output will be "facts" for purpose of the analysis. In addition, those "facts" permitted to be "facts" will be interpreted in light of the assumptions of the model.

3. It has been observed: "No small part of the attraction of an excessive reliance upon economic theorizing is the assertion by some that economics is a *science* capable of producing "truth" like the supposed truths of physics, chemistry or astronomy. There is the paradox that just as science was coming to the realization that its models did not necessarily produce eternal and unchanging truths, and indeed were incapable of doing so, the discipline of economics was becoming captured by an outmoded concept of the nature of scientific knowledge. For descriptions of the evolution in the nature of scientific reasoning, see J. CONANT, MODERN SCIENCE AND MODERN MAN (1953); T. KUHN, THE STRUCTURE OF SCIENTIFIC REVOLUTIONS (2d ed. 1970); A. WHITEHEAD, THE MODES OF THOUGHT (1958); A. WHITEHEAD, THE FUNCTION OF REASON (1957). For a critical analysis of the claim that economics is a "science," see Rosenberg, *If Economics Isn't Science, What Is It?*, 14 PHIL. FORUM 296, 311 (1983): "[W]e should view it as a branch of mathematics, one devoted to examining the formal properties of a set of assumptions about the transitivity of abstract relations: axioms that implicitly define a technical notion of "rationality," just as geometry examines the formal properties of abstract points and lines."....

4. Hovenkamp, *Antitrust Policy After Chicago*, 84 MICH. L. REV. 213, 249 (1985): "The legislative histories of the various antitrust laws fail to exhibit anything resembling a dominant concern for economic efficiency." See also W. LETWIN, LAW AND ECONOMIC POLICY: THE EVOLUTION OF THE SHERMAN ANTITRUST ACT (1966); H. THORELLI, THE FEDERAL ANTITRUST POLICY: ORGANIZATION OF AN AMERICAN TRADITION (1954).

5. Fox, *The Modernization of Antitrust: A New Equilibrium*, 66 CORNELL L. REV. 1140 (1982).

6. The claim is often made that the neoclassical model is morally neutral and can be mechanically applied without invoking the decision maker's own moral values. By its assumptions, of course, the model is making a choice of what facts and what values ought to be deemed relevant to the analysis. For a classic criticism of such a rigid form of logical positivism, see Cohen, *Transcendental Nonsense and the Functional Approach*, 35 COLUM. L. REV. 809 (1935).

7. Elsewhere, I have suggested: "Little attention is paid today to a profound lesson the legal realists gave us—the significance of the difficult process by which it is determined what "facts" are relevant to a dispute, what those "facts" mean

and how those "facts" operate in the application of the rules to the dispute. Legal realists were fact skeptics as well as rule skeptics, noting the close interrelationship between determining the relevance, meaning and application of the rules to the determination of the relevance, meaning and application of the facts. See J. FRANK, COURTS ON TRIAL 316-25 (1950); Cook, *"Facts" and "Statements of Fact"*, 4 U. CHI. L. REV. 233 (1936); Cohen, *Field Theory and Judicial Logic*, 59 YALE L.J. 238 (1950); Oliphant, *Facts, Opinions, and Value-Judgments*, 10 TEXAS L. REV. 127 (1932). Cf., Leff. *Some Realism About Nominalism*, 60 VA. L. REV. 451 (1974).

8. Posner defines "efficiency" as "exploiting economic resources in such a way that human satisfaction as measured by aggregate consumer willingness to pay for goods and services is maximized." R. POSNER, ECONOMIC ANALYSIS OF LAW 4 (1972). The concept is further broken into various types of "efficiency." Bork maintains there are two types of efficiency of concern—allocative efficiency and productive efficiency: "Allocative efficiency, as used here, refers to the placement of resources in the economy, the question of whether resources are employed in tasks where consumers value their output most. Productive efficiency refers to the effective use of resources by a particular firm. The idea of effective use, as we shall see, encompasses much more than mere technical or plant-level efficiency," R. BORK, *supra* note 2 at 91.

9. A leading Keynesian, the late Joan Robinson, observed: "It is not legitimate to say: Let us first assume perfect competition, and bring in the complications later; for an economy in which textbook-perfect competition was possible would be different from our own in important respects; we do not know what contradictions we may be letting ourselves in for by assuming it. Indeed, it usually has to be buttressed by a range of further assumptions, such as: the plant is perfectly durable, there is no interest on working capital, and so forth. Very drastic assumptions are useful to hack out a new path, but it hardly seems worthwhile making them in order to stroll up a well-trodden blind alley." J. ROBINSON, 4 COLLECTED ECONOMIC PAPERS 134 (1973).

This process of simplifying rules for deductive application to facts in the name of a scientific approach was called "mechanical jurisprudence" by Pound: "I have referred to mechanical jurisprudence as scientific because those who administer it believe it such. But in truth it is not science at all. We no longer hold anything scientific merely because it exhibits a rigid scheme of deduction from *a priori* conceptions. In the philosophy of today, theories are instruments, not answers to enigmas, in which we can rest." Pound, *Mechanical Jurisprudence*, 8 COLUM. L. REV. 605, 608 (1908).

10. R. POSNER, *supra* note 8. *See generally Symposium on Efficiency as a Legal Concern*, 8 HOFSTRA L. REV. 485 (1980) for an examination of some of the complexities of the concept.

11. R. BORK, *supra* 2, at 91.

12. *Id.*

13. Flynn and Ponsoldt, *Legal Reasoning and the Jurisprudence of Vertical Restraints: The Limitations of Neoclassical Economic Analysis in the Resolution of Antitrust Disputes*, 62 N.Y.U. L. REV. 1125, 1135 (1987).

14. *Id.* Judge Bork is perhaps the clearest and most sophisticated exponent of

the necessity (value) of courts following a positivistic approach in antitrust analysis, although he does not address the troubling jurisprudential question of whether it is possible. R. BORK, *supra* note 2, at 72, 89, 117.

15. See Posner, *Some Uses and Abuses of Economics in Law*, 46 U. CHI. L. REV. 281, 285 (1979) (describing his form of economic analysis of law as a methodology for describing what "is" as opposed to a normative approach attempting to define what law "ought" to be). In legal analysis, the "is" cannot be divorced from the "ought."

16. *See generally* Flynn, *Rethinking Sherman Act Section 1 Analysis: Three Proposals for Reducing the Chaos*, 49 ANTITRUST L.J. 1593 (1980); Flynn, *Monopolization Under the Sherman Act: The Third Wave and Beyond*, 26 ANTITRUST BULL. 1 (1981).

Kaplow Notes

1. *See, e.g.*, J. DIRLAM & A. KAHN, FAIR COMPETITION: THE LAW AND ECONOMICS OF ANTITRUST POLICY (1954); C. KAYSEN & D. TURNER, ANTITRUST POLICY (1959).

2. *See, e.g.*, Bowman, *Tying Arrangements and the Leverage Problem*, 67 YALE L.J. 19 (1957); Director & Levi, *Law and the Future: Trade Regulation*, 51 NW. U.L. REV. 281 (1956).

3. Rowe, *The Decline of Antitrust and the Delusions of Models: The Faustian Pact of Law and Economics*, 72 GEO. L.J. 1511, 1520–22 (1984).

4. United States v. Aluminum Co. of Am., 148 F.2d 416 (2d Cir. 1945).

5. *See* 148 F.2d at 424–27. The claim here is not that Hand's analysis is beyond criticism based on the economic analysis of the time or that developed since, but rather that his opinion reflects a serious and substantial attempt to apply economics to antitrust.

6. United States v. United Shoe Mach. Corp., 110 F. Supp. 295 (D. Mass. 1953), *aff'd per curiam*, 347 U.S. 521 (1954).

7. United States v. E.I. Du Pont De Nemours & Co., 351 U.S. 377 (1956).

8. Brown Shoe Co. v. United States, 370 U.S. 294 (1962).

9. 15 U.S.C. 18 (1982 & Supp. III 1985).

10. United States v. General Dynamics Corp., 415 U.S. 486 (1974).

11. Continental T.V., Inc. v. GTE Sylvania, Inc., 433 U.S. 36 (1977).

12. United States v. Arnold, Schwinn & Co., 388 U.S. 365 (1967). *Schwinn* itself had reversed the earlier Warren Court decision adopting a rule of reason approach. White Motor Co. v. United States, 372 U.S. 253 (1963).

13. The Supreme Court has recently and clearly reaffirmed its rejection of a market power requirement in cases involving naked restraints. *See* NCAA v. Board of Regents of the Univ. of Okla., 468 U.S. 85, 109 (1984).

14. United States v. Trans-Missouri Freight Ass'n, 166 U.S. 290, 323–24 (1897). Interestingly, although Klor's, Inc. v. Broadway-Hale Stores, Inc., 359 U.S. 207 (1959), an early Warren Court decision, is perhaps most strongly associated with this view of antitrust laws, it contains no reference to this statement in *Trans-Missouri* or similar statements, and devotes only passing attention to the objectives

of the antitrust laws, concluding its brief discussion by referring to the potential for monopoly, as traditionally understood.

15. United States v. Aluminum Co. of Am., 148 F.2d 416, 429 (2d Cir. 1945).
16. 442 U.S. 330, 343 (1979) *citing* R. BORK, THE ANTITRUST PARADE 66 (1978).
17. *See, e.g.*, Lande, *Wealth Transfers as the Original and Primary Concern of Antitrust: The Efficiency Interpretation Challenged*, 34 HASTINGS L.J. 65 (1982).
18. Spivak, *The Chicago School Approach to Single Firm Exercises of Monopoly Power: A Response* 52 ANTITRUST L.J. 651, 673.
19. Broadcast Music, Inc. v. CBS, 441 U.S. 1, 19–20 (1979) [quoting United States v. United States Gypsum Co., 438 U.S. 422, 441 n.16 (1978)].
20. Northern Pac. Ry. v. United States, 356 U.S. 1, 4 (1958).
21. *See supra* at 196 & note 89.
22. Arizona v. Maricopa Co. Med. Soc'y, 457 U.S. 332 (1982).
23. 457 U.S. at 348 (emphasis added).
24. Kiefer-Stewart Co. v. Joseph E. Seagram & Sons, Inc., 340 U.S. 211, 213 (1951), *cited in* Arizona v. Maricopa Co. Med. Soc'y, 457 U.S. 332, 346 (1982), and Associated Gen'l Contractors v. California State Council of Carpenters, 459 U.S. 519, 528–29 & n.18 (1983). *Associated General Contractors* also indicated that adverse effects on "free choices between market alternatives is inherently destructive of competitive conditions and may be condemned even without proof of its actual market effect." *Id.* at 528 (citing Klor's, Inc. v. Broadway-Hale Stores, Inc., 459 U.S. 207, 210-14 (1959)).
25. *See, e.g.*, R. HOFSTADTER, THE PARANOID STYLE IN AMERICAN POLITICS AND OTHER ESSAYS 200 (1965).
26. *See, e.g., id.* at 200–02; W. LETWIN, LAW AND ECONOMIC POLICY IN AMERICA 71–77 (1965); Blake, *Conglomerate Mergers and the Antitrust Laws*, 73 COLUM. L. REV. 555, 577 (1973); Stigler, *The Economists and the Problem of Monopoly*, 72 AM. ECON. REV. 1, 3 (1982) (one "would have searched long and hard" in 1890 to find "any economist who had ever recommended" such a policy).
27. Posner, *Some Uses and Abuses of Economics in Law*, 46 U. CHI. L. REV. 281, 287–97 (1979).
28. *See, e.g.*, United States v. Associated Press, 52 F. Supp. 362, 370 (S.D.N.Y. 1943) (Hand, J.) ("Congress has incorporated into the Anti-Trust Acts the changing standards of the common law"), *aff'd*, 326 U.S. 1 (1945).

Fox Notes

1. *See, e.g.*, Continental T.V., Inc. v. GTE Sylvania Inc., 433 U.S. 36 (1977).
2. Rowe, *New Directions in Competition and Industrial Organization Law in the United States*, in ENTERPRISE LAW OF THE 80's, at 177, 201 (Rowe, Jacobs & Joelson eds. 1980).
3. United States v. United Shoe Mach. Corp., 110 F. Supp. 295, 342 (D. Mass. 1953), *aff'd per curiam*, 347 U.S. 521 (1954).
4. 21 CONG. REC. 2460 (1890).
5. *Id.*

6. *Id.*

7. *Id.* at 2457. Representative Taylor spoke of "this monster, [the trust, which] robs the farmer on the one hand and the consumer on the other." *Id.* at 4098. Senator Heard referred to the beef trust as "this giant robber combination." *Id.* at 4101.

8. *Id.* at 2558.

9. *Id.* at 2466.

10. *Id.* at 4100.

11. Standard Oil Co. v. United Sates, 221 U.S. 1 (1911) (abusive acts by single firm); United States v. Trans-Missouri Freight Ass'n, 166 U.S. 290 (1896) (self-regulation by agreement among competitors).

12. *See* United States v. United States Steel Corp., 251 U.S. 417 (1920). *But see* Northern Sec. Co. v. United States, 193 U.S. 197, 329 (1904).

13. Standard Oil Co. v. United States, 221 U.S. 1, 58 (1911) (dictum).

14. *E.g.*, United States v. Topco Assocs., Inc., 405 U.S. 596 (1972); Zenith Radio Corp. v. Hazeltine Research, Inc., 395 U.S. 100 (1969); Fortner Enterprises, Inc. v. United States Steel Corp., 394 U.S. 495 (1968); Albrecht v. Herald Co., 390 U.S. 145 (1968); Simpson v. Union Oil Co., 377 U.S. 12 (1964); United States v. Lowe's Inc., 371 U.S. 38 (1962); United States v. Parke, Davis & Co., 362 U.S. 29 (1960); Northern Pac. Ry. v. United States, 356 U.S. 1 (1958); United States v. United Shoe Mach. Corp., 347 U.S. 521 (1954), *aff'ing per curiam* 110 F. Supp. 295 (D. Mass. 1953), *further divestiture ordered*, 391 U.S. 244 (1968).

In Standard Oil Co. v. United States, 337 U.S. 293,312 (1949), Justice Frankfurter said for the Court: "[T]he choice between greater efficiency and freer competition . . . has not been submitted to our decision." Congress had decided in favor of freer competition.

15. United States v. Arnold, Schwinn & Co., 388 U.S. 365 (1967), *overruled by* Continental T.V., Inc. v. GTE Sylvania Inc., 433 U.S. 36 (1977).

16. *E.g.*, Northern Pac. Ry. v. United States, 356 U.S. 1 (1958).

17. *See, e.g.*, Broadcast Music, Inc. v. Columbia Broadcasting Sys., Inc., 411 U.S. 1 (1979); United States v. United States Gypsum Co., 438 U.S. 422 (1978); National Soc'y of Professional Eng'rs v. United States, 435 U.S. 679 (1978); Continental T.V., Inc. v. GTE Sylvania Inc., 433 U.S. 36 (1977); United States v. Marine Bancorporation, Inc. 418 U.S. 602 (1974); United States v. General Dynamics Corp., 415 U.S. 486 (1974).

18. Continental T.V., Inc. v. GTE Sylvania Inc., 433 U.S. 36 (1977).

19. Dispersion of economic power serves economic and political goals. Politically, dispersion tends to prevent any one firm or combination of firms from having undue access to the political system. Pitofsky, *The Political Content of Antitrust*, 127 U. PA. L. REV. 1051, 1053–54 (1979). . . . Economically, dispersion tends to promote flexibility of firms to respond to new and changing consumer needs. Concentration may tend to calcify and rigidify.

20. *See* P. SAMUELSON, ECONOMICS 508–09 (11th ed. 1980). Consumer surplus is one measure of consumer satisfaction. Consumer surplus represents the difference between what consumers would be willing to pay for a given quantity of goods and what they actually pay. *Id.* at 412–14.

21. "Liberal" here refers to its twentieth century political meaning. The word does not refer to the eighteenth century laissez-faire liberal.

22. J. DIRLAM & A. KAHN, FAIR COMPETITION: THE LAW AND ECONOMICS OF ANTITRUST POLICY 269–70 (1954).

23. Allocative efficiency in a free enterprise economy can be achieved only if all firms are of sufficient size to realize all significant economies of scale, and all markets are either competitively structured (that is, they comprise a significant number of producers with no one or few having market dominance) or entry barriers are low. In such cases, all producers are price takers; the market, not the producers, sets the price. The market forces cause resources to move to the production of goods that consumers want, given the distribution of wealth. Prices move down to marginal cost, and output is optimal to serve consumer wants at that cost.

Optimal allocation of resources is frustrated by externalities, market imperfections, and the problem of the second best. Externalities are costs that are imposed by a business firm that are not borne by that firm, such as certain costs of pollution. Thus, externalities are social costs not accounted for in private costs. Because the price of the good does not reflect its full cost, consumers get the "wrong" signal and will buy too much of that product. Therefore, output will be inefficiently high.

Market imperfections are defects in the functioning of markets. Malfunction may be caused by monopoly, the absence of information, and government regulation. Market imperfections that increase the price of a product give the wrong signal to consumers. Consumers will buy too little of the product, and output will be inefficiently low.

The problem of the second best connotes the circumstance that an apparently second best solution may be no solution at all. Corrective action in one market does not necessarily improve resource allocation. For example, conversion of pricing in one market from monopoly pricing to competitive pricing does not improve resource allocation if resources are drawn from a market in which output is already too low, causing output in the market of deflected demand to be even lower.

24. Schwartz, *An Overview of the Economics of Antitrust Enforcement*, 68 GEO. L.J. 1075, 1084 (1980).

25. 148 F.2d 416 (2d Cir. 1945).

26. *See, e.g.*, United States v. Topco Assocs., Inc., 405 U.S. 596, 610 (1972): "Antitrust laws in general, and the Sherman Act in particular, are the Magna Carta of free enterprise. They are as important to the preservation of economic freedom and our free enterprise system as the Bill of Rights is to the protection of our fundamental personal freedoms. And the freedom guaranteed each and every business, no matter how small, is the freedom to compete—to assert with vigor, imagination, devotion, and ingenuity whatever economic muscle it can muster."

Topco was later approved in City of Lafayette v. Louisiana Power & Light Co., 435 U.S. 389 (1978) and California Retail Liquor Dealers Ass'n. v. Midcal Aluminum, Inc. 445 U.S. 97 (1980). *See also* Albrecht v. Herald Co., 390 U.S. 145 (1968); United States v. Von's Grocery Co., 384 U.S. 270 (1966).

27. The assumptions include: business is motivated to achieve lowest cost of imputs and thus to achieve greatest scale economies; resource loss from failure to achieve scale economies almost always exceeds resource loss caused by deviation from marginal-cost pricing; competition is presumptively dynamic and incentives

to innovate are great, even if few firms occupy a market; consumers are sovereign and firms must cater to their wishes to survive and achieve success; markets function well and will quickly punish an exploitative or unresponsive producer; resources move quickly to their highest and best use (what consumers want most); there are no barriers to entry other than technology or government imposed restraints, and any barriers that do exist are virtually always surmountable by the enterprising potential entrant; finally, private business decisions almost always improve resource allocation, and even in the exceptional case when behavior threatens a waste of resources, there is a thin line between conduct that impairs and conduct that improves resource allocation.

28. Other perspectives on efficiency include theory based on the experience curve, a perspective that views monopoly in a specialized niche as a means to greatest efficiency, and a perspective that is based on preserving the competition process but is not further defined by assumptions that credit the existence of corporate power. For the experience curve perspective, see B. HENDERSON, ON CORPORATE STRATEGY (1979); Shapiro, *Corporate Strategy and Antitrust Policy: The Experience Curve Model,* in SHIFTING BOUNDARIES BETWEEN REGULATION AND COMPETITION: CRITERIA FOR AN ENTERPRISE SYSTEM AND THE EXPERIENCE CURVE MODEL, THE CONFERENCE BOARD, Info Bull. No. 77, at 11 (1980). For a perspective on the competition process, see Bock, *Concentration: Issues, Convictions and Facts—Overview* in INDUSTRIAL CONCENTRATION AND THE MARKET SYSTEM.

29. On the other hand, a monopoly or oligopoly that can be shown to restrict output is not for that reason illegal. There is no law against oligopoly or monopoly; nor is there a law against unilateral output restriction or monopoly pricing. *See* Berkey Photo, Inc. v. Eastman Kodak Co., 603 F.2d 263 (2d Cir. 1979), *cert. denied,* 444 U.S. 1093 (1980). Nonetheless, evidence of power to restrict output is relevant to alleged use of power in a manner that the law reprehends.

30. 359 U.S. 207 (1959).

31. 332 U.S. 392 (1947).

Bibliography

Books

W. Acworth, *The Railways and the Traders*. London: J. Murray, 1891.

P. Areeda & D. Turner, *Antitrust Law*. (Vols. I-V). Boston: Little, Brown, 1978–80.

A. Alchian & W. Allen, *Exchange and Production*. Belmont, California: Wadsworth Publishing Co., (1983).

K. Arrow, *Essays in the Theory of Risk-Bearing*. Amsterdam: North-Holland Publishing Co., (1971).

P. Atiyah, *The Rise and Fall of Freedom of Contract*. Oxford: Clarendon Press, (1979).

J. Bain, *Barriers to New Competition*. Cambridge: Harvard University Press, (1956).

C. Beach, *A Treatise on the Law of Monopolies and Industrial Trusts*. St. Louis: Central Law Journal Co., (1898).

R. Black, A. Coats & C. Goodwin, eds. *The Marginal Revolution in Economics*. Durham, North Carolina: Duke University Press, (1973).

R. Bork, *The Antitrust Paradox: A Policy at War with Itself*. New York: Basic Books, (1978).

W. Bowman, *Patents and Antitrust Law: A Legal and Economic Appraisal*. Chicago: University of Chicago Press, (1973).

L. Brandeis, *The Curse of Bigness*. Port Washington, New York: Kennikat, (1934).

Y. Brozen, ed. *The Competitive Economy: Selected Readings*. Morristown, New Jersey: General Learning Press, (1974).

J. Bryce, *The American Commonwealth*. London & New York: Macmillan, (1889).

J. Buchanan, *Costs and Choice: An Inquiry in Economic Theory*. Chicago: University of Chicago Press, (1969).

J. Bunzel, *The American Small Businessman*. New York: Afred A. Knopf, (1962).

R. Caves, *American Industry: Structure, Conduct, Performance*. 2d ed. Englewood Cliffs, New Jersey: Prentice-Hall, (1964).

E. Chamberlin, *The Theory of Monopolistic Competition*. Cambridge: Harvard Unversity Press, (1933).

A. Chandler, *The Visible Hand: The Managerial Revolution in American Business*. Cambridge: The Belknap Press of the Harvard University Press, (1977).

J. Clark, *The Distribution of Wealth*. New York: Macmillan, (1899).

J. Clark, *Essentials of Economic Theory*. New York: Macmillan, (1907).

J. Clark, *Competition As A Dynamic Process*. Washington: Brookings Institution, (1961).

W. Comanor, T. Wilson, *Advertising and Market Power*. Cambridge: Harvard University Press, (1974).

H. Commager, *The American Mind*. New Haven: Yale University Press, (1950).

F.H. Cooke, *The Law of Combinations: Monopolies and Labor Unions*. 2d ed. Chicago: Callaghan & Co., (1909).

A. Cournot, *Mathematical Principles of the Theory of Wealth*. (English ed. 1838, New York ed. 1929). New York: Macmillan.

D. Dewey, *Monopoly In Economics and Law*. Chicago: Rand, McNally & Co., (1959).

W. Diamond, *The Economic Thought of Woodrow Wilson*. Baltimore: The Johns Hopkins Press, (1943).

J. Dirlam & A. Kahn, *Fair Competition: The Law and Economics of Antitrust Policy*. Ithaca, New York: Cornell University Press, (1954).

J. Dorfman, *The Economic Mind in American Civilization 1865-1918*. New York: Viking Press, (1949).

A. Eddy, *The Law of Combinations*. Chicago: Callaghan & Co., (1901).

C. Eliot, *American Contributions to Civilization*. New York: The Century Co., (1907).

R. Ely, *Problems of Today: A Discussion of Protective Tariffs, Taxation, and Monopolies*. New York, Boston: T.Y. Crowell & Co., 2d ed. (1890).

E. Gellhorn, *Antitrust Law and Economics*. St. Paul: West Publishing Co., (1976).

E. Goffman, *Strategic Interaction*. Philadelphia: University of Pennsylvania Press, (1969).

L. Goodwyn, *The Populist Movement: A Short History of the Agrarian Revolt in America*. New York: The Oxford University Press, (1978).

E. Greenhood, *The Doctrine of Public Policy in the Law of Contracts, Reduced to Rules*. Chicago: Callaghan & Co., (1886).

E. Grether, *Price Control Under Fair Trade Legislation*. New York: Oxford University Press, (1939).

G.E. Hale & R.D. Hale, *Market Power Size and Shape Under the Sherman Act*. Boston: Little, Brown & Co., (1958).

A. Hadley, *Economics: An Account of the Relations Between Private Property and Public Welfare*. New York & London: G.P. Putnam's Sons, (1896).

A. Hadley, *Railroad Transportation—Its History and Its Laws*. New York & London: G.P. Putnam's Sons, (1885).

W. Hamilton & I. Till, *Antitrust in Action*. Washington: U.S. Government Printing Office, 1940.

M. Handler, *Antitrust in Perspective*. Ann Arbor, Michigan: University Microfilms, (1957).

M. Handler, *Reforming the Antitrust Law*. New York: Law Journal Seminars-Press, (1982).

L. Haney, *Business Organization and Combination*. New York: Macmillan, (1913).

L. Hannah, *The Rise of the Corporate Economy*. London: Methuen, (1976).

F. Hayek, *The Road to Serfdom*. Chicago: University of Chicago Press, (1944).

B. Henderson, *On Corporate Strategy*. Cambridge: Abt Books (1979).

J. Hirshleifer, *Price Theory and Applications*. Englewood Cliffs, New Jersey: Prentice-Hall, (1976).

R. Hofstadter, *The Age of Reform*. New York: Alfred A. Knopf, (1955).

R. Hofstadter, *The Paranoid Style in American Politics and Other Essays*. New York: Alfred A. Knopf, (1965).

R. Hofstadter, *Social Darwinism in American Thought, 1860-1915*. Philadelphia: University of Pennsylvania Press, (1949).

W. Holdsworth, *A History of English Law*. London: Methuen, 2d ed. (1937).

O. Holmes, *The Common Law*. Cambridge: Belknap Press of the Harvard University Press, (1881).

M. Horwitz, *The Transformation of American Law: 1780-1860*. Cambridge: Harvard University Press, (1978).

H. Hovenkamp, *Economics and Federal Antitrust Law*. St. Paul: West Publishing Co., (1985).

M.D. Howe, ed. *Holmes-Pollock Letters*. Cambridge: Harvard University Press, (1941).

C. Kaysen, *United States v. United Shoe Machinery Corporation: An Economic Analysis of an Anti-Trust Case*. Cambridge: Harvard University Press, (1956).

C. Kaysen & D. Turner, *Antitrust Policy*. Cambridge: Harvard University Press, (1959).

M. Keller, *Affairs of State: Public Life in Late Nineteenth Century America*. Cambridge: Belknap Press of the Harvard University Press, (1977).

W. Letwin, *Law and Economic Policy in America: The Evolution of the Sherman Antitrust Act*. New York: Random House, (1965).

C. Lindblom, *Politics and Markets*. New York: Basic Books, (1977).

C. Lynch, *The Concentration of Economic Power*. New York: Columbia University Press, (1946).

E. Mansfield, *Microeconomics: Theory and Applications*. 4th ed. New York: Norton, (1982).

A. Marshall, *Principles of Economics*. London & New York: Macmillan, (1890).

E. Mason, *Economic Concentration and the Monopoly Problem*. Cambridge: Harvard University Press, (1957).

T. McCraw, *Prophets of Regulation*. Cambridge: Belknap Press of the Harvard University Press, (1984).

J.E. Meade, *The Controlled Economy*. Albany: State University of New York Press, (1971).

A.D. Neale, *The Antitrust Laws of the United States of America*. Cambridge, England & New York: Cambridge University Press, (1966).

C. Murchison, *Resale Price Maintenance*. New York: Columbia University Press, (1919).

R. Nisbet, *Social Change and History*. London & New York: Oxford University Press, (1969).

W.C. Noyes, *A Treatise on the Law of Intercorporate Relations*. Boston: Little, Brown & Co., (1909).

A. Okun, *Equality and Efficiency: The Big Tradeoff*. Washington: The Brookings Institute, (1975).

V. Pareto, *Manual D'Economie Politique*. Paris: V. Girard & E. Brière, (1909).

A. Pigou, *The Economics of Welfare*. London: Macmillan, (1920).

Bibliography   313

K. Porter & D. Johnson, *National Party Platforms*. Urbana: University of Illinois Press, (1956).

R. Posner, *Antitrust Law: An Economic Perspective*. Chicago: University of Chicago Press, (1976).

C.F. Pratten, *Economies of Scale in Manufacturing Industry*. Cambridge, England: Cambridge University Press, (1971).

L. Robbins, *Essays on the Nature and Significance of Economic Science*. London: Macmillan, (1932).

J. Robinson, *Economics of Imperfect Competition*. 2d ed. London: Macmillan, (1969).

E. Rozwenc, *Roosevelt, Wilson and The Trusts*. Boston: Heath, (1950).

P. Samuelson, *Economics*. 11th ed. New York: McGraw-Hill, (1980).

F. Scherer, *Industrial Market Structure and Economic Performance*. 2d ed. Chicago: Rand, McNally & Co., (1980).

F. Scherer, A. Beckenstein, E. Kaufer, & R. Murphy, *The Economics of Multiplant Operation: An International Comparison Study*. Cambridge: Harvard University Press, (1975).

W. Schwartz, *Private Enforcement of the Antitrust Law*. Washington: American Enterprise Institue for Public Policy Research, (1981).

H. Seager & C.A. Gulick, Jr., *Trust and Corporation Problems*. New York: Harper & Brothers, (1929).

T. Sedgwick, *Public and Private Economy*. New York: Harper & Brothers, (1836).

E. Seligman & R. Love, *Price Cutting and Price Maintenance*. New York: Harper & Brothers, (1932).

W. Shepherd, *The Economics of Industrial Organization*. Englewood Cliffs, New Jersey: Prentice-Hall, (1979).

A. Smith, *An Inquiry into the Nature and Causes of the Wealth of Nations*. (1st ed. 1776). Modern Library ed., 1977.

W. Stevens, *Industrial Combinations and Trusts*. New York & London: Macmillan, (1914).

A. Stickney, *State Control of Trade and Commerce by National or State Authority*. N.p.: Boker, Voorhis, (1897).

G. Stigler, *The Organization of Industry*. Homewood, Illinois: R.D. Irwin, (1968).

G. Stigler, *The Theory of Price*. New York: Macmillan, (1966).

G. Stocking & M. Watkins, *Monopoly and Free Enterprise*. New York: Twentieth Century Fund, (1951).

E.T. Sullivan and H. Hovenkamp, *Antitrust Law, Policy and Procedure*. 2d ed. Charlottesville, Virginia: Michie, (1989).

E.T. Sullivan & J. Harrison, *Understanding Antitrust and Its Economic Implications*. New York: Matthew Bender, (1988).

L. Sullivan, *Handbook of the Law of Antitrust*. St. Paul: West Publishing Co., (1977).

D. Teece, *Vertical Integration and Vertical Divestiture in the U.S. Oil Industry*. Stanford, California: Graduate School of Business, Stanford University, (1976).

H. Thorelli, *The Federal Antitrust Policy: Origination of an American Tradition*. Baltimore: Johns Hopkins Press, (1955).

A. Walker, *History of the Sherman Law*. Westport, Connectictu: Greenwood Press, (1910).

A. Walker, *The Science of Wealth: A Manual of Political Economy Embracing the Laws of Trade, Currency, and Finance*. Philadelphia: J.B. Lippincott, (1875).

F. Walker, *Political Economy*. 3d ed. New York: Henry Holt & Co., (1888).

F. Wayland, *The Elements of Political Economy*. N.p.: Butler, (1837).

R. Weissman, *Small Business and Venture Capital*. New York: Harper & Brothers, (1945).

D. Wells, *Recent Economic Changes and Their Effect on the Production and Distribution of Wealth and the Well-Being of Society*. N.p.: Appleton, (1896).

M. White, *Social Thought in America: The Revolt Against Formalism*. London & New York: Oxford University Press, (1957).

S. Whitney, *Antitrust Policies*. New York: Twentieth Century Fund, (1958).

O. Williamson, *The Economic Institutions of Capitalism*. New York: Free Press; Collier Macmillan, (1985).

O. Williamson, *Markets and Hierarchies: Analysis and Antitrust Implications*. New York: Free Press, (1975).

W. Wilson, *The New Freedom*. New York: Doubleday, (1913).

D. Worcester, *Welfare Gains from Advertising: The Problem of Regulation*. Washington: American Enterprise Institute for Public Policy Research, (1978).

President's Task Force on Productivity and Competition. (1969).

Articles

E. B. Andrews, *The Economic Law of Monopoly* 26 J. Soc. Sci. 1 (1890).

E. B. Andrews, *Trusts According to Official Investigations* 3 Q. J. Econ. 117 (1889).

P. Areeda & D. Turner, *Predatory Pricing and Related Practices Under Section 2 of the Sherman Act* 88 Harv. L. Rev. 697 (1975).

P. Areeda & D. Turner, *Scherer on Predatory Pricing: A Reply* 89 Harv. L. Rev. 891 (1976).

T. Arthur, *Workable Antitrust Law: The Statutory Approach to Antitrust* 62 Tul. L. Rev. 1163 (1988).

T. Arthur, *Farewell to the Sea of Doubt: Jettisoning the Constitutional Sherman Act* 74 Calif. L. Rev. 266 (1986).

W. Baumol, *Informed Judgment, Rigorous Theory and Public Policy* 32 S. Econ. J. 137 (1965).

G. S. Becker, *A Theory of the Allocation of Time* 75 Econ. J. 493 (1965).

R. L. Bishop, *Elasticities, Cross-Elasticities, and Market Relationships* 42 Am. Econ. Rev. 779 (1952).

G. Bittlingmayer, *Did Antitrust Policy Cause the Great Merger Wave?* 38 J. L. Econ. 77 (1985).

R. Blair & D. Kaserman, *Vertical Integration, Tying, and Antitrust Policy* 68 Am. Econ. Rev. 397 (1978).

H. Blake, *Conglomerate Mergers and the Antitrust Laws* 73 Colum. L. Rev. 555 (1973).

H. Blake & W. Jones, *The Goals of Antitrust: A Dialogue on Policy* 65 Colum. L. Rev. 377 (1965).

M. Block, F. Nold & G. Sidak, *The Deterrent Effect of Antitrust Enforcement* 89 J. Pol. Econ. 429 (1981).

L. Boisot, *The Legality of Trust Combinations* 39 (n.s. 30) Am. L. Reg. 751 (1891).

D. Bok, *Section 7 of the Clayton Act and the Merging of Law and Economics* 74 Harv. L. Rev. 226 (1960).

R. Bork, *The Rule of Reason and the Per Se Concept: Price Fixing and Market Division* 74 Yale. L. J. 775 (1965).

R. Bork, *Vertical Integration and the Sherman Act: The Legal History of an Economic Misconception* 22 U. Chi. L. Rev. 157 (1954).

R. Bork, *Vertical Restraints: Schwinn Overruled* 1977 Sup. Ct. Rev. 171 (1978).

W. Bowman, *Tying Arrangements and the Leverage Problem* 67 Yale L. J. 19 (1957).

J. Brodley, *Potential Competition Mergers: A Structural Synthesis* 87 Yale L. J. 1 (1977).

C. Bullock, *The Trusts and Public Policy* 87 Atlantic Monthly 737 (1901).

R. Butters, *A Survey of Advertising and Market Structure* 66 Am. Econ. Rev. Papers & Proc. 392 (1976).

A. Carnegie, *The Bugaboo of Trusts* 148 N. Am. Rev. 141 (1889).

P. Carstensen, *Antitrust Law and the Paradigm of Industrial Organization* 16 U.C. Davis L. Rev. 487 (1983).

R. Caves & M. Porter, *From Entry Barriers to Mobility Barriers: Con-*

jectural Decisions and Contrived Deterrence to New Competition 91 Q. J. Econ. 241 (1977).

J. B. Clark, *The Limits of Competition* 2 Pol. Sci. Q. 45 (1887).

J. M. Clark, *Toward a Concept of Workable Competition* 30 Am. Econ. Rev. 241 (1940).

R. Coase, *The Nature of the Firm* 4 Economica 506 (1937).

W. Comanor, *Vertical Territorial and Customer Restrictions: White Motors and Its Aftermath* 81 Harv. L. Rev. 1419 (1968).

J. Commons, *Institutional Economics* 21 Am. Econ. Rev. 648 (1931).

R. Cooter & P. Rappaport, *Were the Ordinalists Wrong About Welfare Economics?* 22 J. Econ. Lit. 507 (1984).

H. Demsetz, *The Effect of Consumer Experience on Brand Loyalty and the Structure of Market Demand* 30 Econometrica 22 (1962).

T. DiLorenzo & J. High, *Antitrust and Competition, Historically Considered* 36 Econ. Inquiry 423 (1988).

A. Director & E. Levi, *Law and the Future: Trade Regulation* 51 Nw. U. L. Rev. 281 (1956).

A. Dixit & V. Norman, *Advertising and Welfare* 9 Bell J. Econ. 1 (1978).

A. Dixit & J. Stiglitz, *Monopolistic Competition and Optimum Product Diversity* 67 Am. Econ. Rev. 297 (1977).

G. Dodd, *The Present Legal Status of Trusts* 7 Harv. L. Rev. 157 (1893).

G. Dorsey, *Free Enterprise v. The Entrepreneur: Redefining the Entities Subject to the Antitrust Laws* 125 U. Pa. L. Rev. 1244 (1977).

F. Easterbrook, *The Limits of Antitrust* 63 Texas L. Rev. 1 (1984).

K. Elzinga, *The Goals of Antitrust: Other Than Competition and Efficiency, What Else Counts?* 125 U. Pa. L. Rev. 1191 (1977).

R. Foulke, *Restraints on Trade* 12 Col. L. Rev. 97 (1912).

E. Fox, *The Politics of Law and Economica in Judicial Decision Making: Antitrust as a Window* 61 N.Y.U. L. Rev. 554 (1986).

P. Gerhart, *The Supreme Court and Antitrust Analysis: The (Near) Triumph of the Chicago School* 1982 Sup. Ct. Rev. 319 (1982).

H. Gerla, *A Micro-Microeconomic Approach to Antitrust Law: Games Managers Play* 86 Mich. L. Rev. 892 (1988).

F. Giddings, *The Persistence of Competition* 2 Pol. Sci. Q. 62 (1887).

G. Gunton, *The Economic and Social Aspects of Trusts* 3 Pol. Sci. Q. 385 (1888).

M. Hall & L. Weiss, *Firm Size and Profitability* 49 Rev. Econ. & Statistics 319 (1967).

A. Harberger, *Monopoly and Resource Allocation* 44 Am. Econ. Rev. Papers & Proc. 77 (1954).

W. Herbruck, *Forestalling, Regrating & Engrossing* 27 Mich. L. Rev. 365 (1929).

J. Hirshleifer, *Economics From a Biological Standpoint* 20 J. L. & Econ. 1 (1977).

O. Holmes, *Privilege, Malice and Intent* 8 Harv. L. Rev. 1 (1894).

H. Hotelling, *The General Welfare in Relation to Problems of Taxation and of Railway and Utility Rates* 6 Econometrica 242 (1938).

H. Hovenkamp, *Antitrust Policy After Chicago* 84 Mich. L. Rev. 213 (1985).

H. Hovenkamp, *The Classical Corporation in American Legal Thought* 76 Geo. L. J. 1593 (1988).

H. Hovenkamp, *Labor Conspiracies in American Law, 1880-1930* 66 Tex. L. Rev. 919 (1988).

H. Hovenkamp, *The Political Economy of Substantive Due Process* 40 Stan. L. Rev. 379 (1988).

H. Hovenkamp, *Regulatory Conflict in the Gilded Age: Federalism and the Railroad Problem* 97 Yale L. J. 1017 (1988).

H. Hovenkamp, *Technology, Politics, and Regulated Monopoly: An American Historical Perspective* 62 Tex. L. Rev. 1263 (1984).

J. Hudson, *Modern Feudalism* 144 No. Am. Rev. 277 (1887).

J. Jenks, *Capitalistic Monopolies and Their Relation to the State* 9 Pol. Sci. Q. 486 (1894).

J. Jenks, *Recent Legislation and Adjudication on Trusts* 12 Q. J. Econ. 461 (1898).

A. Kales, *Coercive and Competitive Methods in Trade and Labor Disputes* 8 Cornell L. Q. 1 (1922).

A. Kales, *Contracts to Refrain from Doing Business or from Entering or Carrying on an Occupation* 31 Harv. L. Rev. 193 (1917).

D. Kennedy, *The Role of Law in Economic Thought* 34 Am. U. L. Rev. 944 (1985).

R. Kessel, *A Study of the Effect of Competition in the Tax-Exempt Bond Market* 79 J. Pol. Econ. 706 (1971).

J. Kwoka, *The Effect of Market Share Distribution on Industry Performance* 61 Rev. Econ. & Statistics 101 (1979).

T. Krattenmaker, R. Lande & S. Salop, *Monopoly Power and Market Power In Antitrust Law* 72 Geo. L. J. 241 (1987).

R. Lande, *Wealth Transfers as the Original and Primary Concern of Antitrust: The Efficiency Interpretation Challenged* 34 Hastings L. J. 65 (1982).

R. Lande, *The Rise and (Coming) Fall of Efficiency as the Ruler of Antitrust* 33 Antitrust Bull. 429 (1988).

A. Lerner, *The Concept of Monopoly and the Measurement of Monopoly Power* 1 Rev. Econ. Stud. 157 (1934).

R. Limbaugh, *Historic Origins of Anti-Trust Legislation* 18 Mo. L. Rev. 215 (1953).

J. May, *Antitrust in the Formative Era: Political and Economic Theory in Constitutional and Antitrust Analysis, 1880-1918* 50 Ohio State L. J. 257 (1989).

J. May, *Antitrust Practice and Procedure in the Formative Era: The Constitutional and Conceptual Reach of State Antitrust Law, 1880-1918* 135 U. Pa. L. Rev. 495 (1987).

H. Malmgren, *Information, Expectations and the Theory of the Firm* 75 Q. J. Econ. 399 (1961).

E. Mason, *Monopoly in Law and Economics* 47 Yale L. J. 34 (1937).

J. McGee, *Predatory Price Cutting: The Standard Oil (NJ) Case* 1 J. L. & Econ. 137 (1958).

J. McGee & L. Bassett, *Vertical Integration Revisited* 19 J. L. & Econ. 924 (1971).

D. Mickey, *Trusts* 22 Am. L. Rev. 538 (1888).

D. Millon, *The Sherman Act and the Balance of Power* 61 So. Cal. L. Rev. 1220 (1988).

V. Morawetz, *The Anti-Trust Act and the Merger Case* 17 Harv. L. Rev. 533 (1904).

P. Nelson, *Advertising as Information* 82 J. Pol. Econ. 729 (1974).

P. Nelson, *Information and Consumer Behavior* 78 J. Pol. Econ. 311 (1970).

R. Nelson & S. Winter, *Forces Generating and Limiting Concentration Under Schumpeterian Competition* 9 Bell J. Econ. 524 (1978).

Newman, *Strategic Groups and the Structure-Performance Relationship* 60 Per. Econ. & Statistics 417 (1978).

Note, *The Rule of Reason in Loose-Knit Combinations* 32 Colum. L. Rev. 291 (1932).

S. Peltzman, *The Gains and Losses from Industrial Concentration* 20 J. L. & Econ. 229 (1977).

J. Peppin, *Price-Fixing Agreements under the Sherman Antitrust Law* 28 Calif. L. Rev. 197 (1940).

A. Phillips, *Schwinn, Rules and the "New Economics" of Vertical Relations* 44 Antitrust L. J. 573 (1975).

R. Pitofsky, *The Political Content of Antitrust* 127 U. Pa. L. Rev. 1051 (1979).

H. Pope, *The Legal Aspect of Monopoly* 20 Harv. L. Rev. 167 (1907).

R. Posner, *The Chicago School of Antitrust Analysis* 127 U. Pa. L. Rev. 925 (1979).

R. Posner, *Oligopoly and the Antitrust Laws: A Suggested Approach* 21 Stan. L. Rev. 562 (1969).

R. Posner, *The Rule of Reason and the Economic Approach: Reflections on the Sylvania Decision* 45 U. Chi. L. Rev. 1 (1977).

R. Posner, *The Social Costs of Monopoly and Regulation* 83 J. Pol. Econ. 807 (1975).

R. Posner, *Some Uses and Abuses of Economics in Law* 46 U. Chi. L. Rev. 281 (1979).

R. Pound, *The Theory of Judicial Decision* 36 Harv. L. Rev. 641 (1923).

L. Preston, *Restrictive Distribution Arrangements: Economic Analysis and Public Policy Standards* 30 L. & Contemp. Prob. 506 (1965).

G. Priest, *The Common Law Process and the Selection of Efficient Rules* 6 J. Legal Stud. 65 (1977).

M. Radin, *Statutory Interpretation* 42 Harv. L. Rev. 863 (1930).

F. Rowe, *The Decline of Antitrust and the Delusions of Models: The Faustian Pact of Law and Economics* 72 Geo. L. J. 1511 (1984).

W. Royall, *The "Pool" and the "Trust"* 6 Va. L. Reg. 163 (1897).

P. Rubin, *Why Is the Common Law Efficient?* 6 J. Legal Stud. 51 (1977).

S. Salop, *Strategic Entry Deterrence* 69 Am. Econ. Rev. 335 (1979).

P. Samuelson, *The Pure Theory of Public Expenditure* 36 Rev. Econ. & Stat. 387 (1954).

F. M. Scherer, *Predatory Pricing and the Sherman Act: A Comment* 89 Harv. L. Rev. 869 (1976).

F. M. Scherer, *Some Last Words on Predatory Pricing* 89 Harv. L. Rev. 901 (1976).

R. Schmalensee, *Brand Loyalty and Barriers to Entry* 40 S. Econ. J. 579 (1974).

R. Schmalensee, *Entry Deterrence in the Ready-to-Eat Breakfast Cereal Industry* 9 Bell J. Econ. 305 (1978).

R. Schmalensee, *On the Use of Economic Models in Antitrust: The ReaLemon Case* 127 U. Pa. L. Rev. 994 (1979).

W. Schwartz, *American Antitrust Laws and Free Enterprise* 2 Swiss Rev. of Inter. Antitrust L. 2 (Jan. 1978).

W. Schwartz, *An Overview of the Economics of Antitrust Enforcement* 68 Geo. L.J. 1075 (1980).

L.B. Schwartz, *Institutional Size and Individual Liberty: Authoritarian Aspects of Bigness* 55 Nw. U. L. Rev. 4 (1960).

W. Shroder, *Price Restriction on the Re-Sale of Chattels* 25 Harv. L. Rev. 59 (1911).

A. Spence, *Entry, Capacity, Investment and Oligopolistic Pricing* 8 Bell J. Econ. 534 (1977).

A. Spence, *Investment Strategy and Growth in a New Market* 10 Bell J. Econ. 1 (1979).

M. Spence, *Product Differentiation and Welfare* 66 Am. Econ. Rev. Papers & Proc. 407 (1976).

G. Spivak, *The Chicago School Approach to Single Firm Exercises of Monopoly Power: A Response* 52 Antitrust L. J. 651 (1983).

G. Stigler, *The Economic Effects of the Antitrust Laws* 9 J. Law & Econ. 225 (1966).

G. Stigler, *The Economics of Information* 69 J. Pol. Econ. 213 (1961).

G. Stigler, *The Economists and the Problem of Monopoly* 72 Am. Econ. Rev. 1 (1982).

G. Stigler, *Perfect Competition, Historically Contemplated* 65 J. Pol. Econ. 1 (1957).

G. Stigler, *Wealth, and Possibly Liberty* 7 J. Legal Stud. 213 (1978).

G. Stocking, *The Rule of Reason, Workable Competition, and Monopoly* 64 Yale L. J. 1107 (1955).

E. T. Sullivan, *The Economic Jurisprudence of the Berger Court's Antitrust Policy: The First Thirteen Years* 58 Notre Dame L. Rev. 1 (1982).

E. T. Sullivan, *On Nonprice Competition: An Economic and Marketing Analysis* 45 U. Pitt. L. Rev. 771 (1984).

Symposium, *The Goals of Antitrust: A Dialogue on Policy* 65 Colum. L. Rev. 363 (1965).

Symposium, *Antitrust Law and Economics* 127 U. Pa. L. Rev. 918 (1979).

Symposium, *Anticipating Antitrust's Centennial, Part I* 75 Calif. L. Rev. 787 (1987).

Symposium, *Anticipating Antitrust's Centennial, Part II* 9 Cardozo L. Rev. 1135 (1988).

Symposium, *The Antitrust Alternative: Airlie House Conference* 62 N.Y.U. L. Rev. 931 (1987); 76 Geo. L. J. 237 (1987).

Symposium, *Retrospective Examination, the Reagan Years* 33 Antitrust Bulletin 201-395 (1988).

Symposium, *The 100th Anniversary of the Sherman Act* 35 Antitrust Bulletin 1-295 (1990).

Symposium, *The Sherman Act's First Century: A Historical Perspective,* 74 Iowa L. Rev. 987 (1989).

Symposium, *On the 100th Anniversary of the Sherman Act and upon the 75th Anniversary of the Clayton Act,* 35 Antitrust Bulletin 1 (1990).

L. Telser, *Abusive Trade Practices: An Economic Analysis* 30 L. & Contemp.Prob. 488 (1965).

L. Telser, *Advertising and Competition* 72 J. Pol. Econ. 537 (1964).

L. Telser, *Why Should Manufacturers Want Fair Trade?* 3 J. L. & Econ. 86 (1960).

D. Turner, *Advertising and Competition* 26 Fed. B. J. 93 (1966).

D. Turner, *Conglomerate Mergers and Section 7 of the Clayton Act* 78 Harv. L. Rev. 1313 (1965).

D. Turner, *The Validity of Tying Arrangements Under the Antitrust Laws* 72 Harv. L. Rev. 50 (1958).

J. Vernon & D. Graham, *Profitability of Monopolization by Vertical Integration* 79 J. Pol. Econ. 924 (1971).

M. Wachter & O. Williamson, *Obligational Markets and the Mechanics of Inflation* 9 Bell J. Econ. 549 (1978).

L. Weiss, *Advertising, Profits, and Corporate Taxes* 51 Rev. Econ. & Statistics 423 (1969).

L. Weiss, *The Structure-Performance Paradigm and Antitrust* 127 U. Pa. L. Rev. 1104 (1979).

O. Williamson, *Dominant Firms and the Monopoly Problem: Market Failure Considerations* 85 Harv. L. Rev. 1512 (1972).

O. Williamson, *Economies as an Antitrust Defense Revisited* 125 U. Pa. L. Rev. 699 (1977).

O. Williamson, *The Economics of Antitrust: Transaction Cost Considerations* 122 U. Pa. L. Rev. 1439 (1974).

O. Williamson, *Predatory Pricing: A Strategic and Welfare Analysis* 87 Yale L. Rev. 284 (1977).

O. Williamson, *The Vertical Integration of Production: Market Failure Considerations* 61 Am. Econ. Rev. 112 (1971).

B. Wyman, *Competition and the Law* 15 Harv. L. Rev. 427 (1902).

B. Wyman, *The Law of the Public Callings as a Solution of the Trust Problem* 17 Harv. L. Rev. 156 (1903-1904).

B. Yamey, *Predatory Price Cutting: Notes and Comments* 15 J. L. & Econ. 129 (1972).

Index